"Learned and astute, this book on chance and probability demonstra~~~~
reliance on the authority of God's Word. This is the only way that nothing can be left
to chance."

> **Douglas Wilson**, Senior Fellow of Theology, New St. Andrews College; Pastor,
> Christ Church, Moscow, Idaho

"The prolific Dr. Poythress has gifted us with a unique and uniquely needed work that
is both mathematically adept and theologically deep. I know of no other work that so
thoroughly addresses the modern sense of chance in a deeply Reformed and philosophi-
cally oriented way."

> **Douglas Groothuis**, Professor of Philosophy and Director of the Apologetics and
> Ethics Master's Degree, Denver Seminary

"Is this the go-to book for a biblical theological perspective on chance, coincidence,
randomness, risk, probability, prediction, and gambling? You bet it is! Dr. Poythress has
hit another one out of the park. This book will transform the way you think about everything from quantum physics and weather forecasts to life insurance and card games."

> **James N. Anderson**, Associate Professor of Theology and Philosophy, Reformed
> Theological Seminary, Charlotte; author, *Paradox in Christian Theology*; *What's
> Your Worldview?*

"Back when I was a researcher in Systems Engineering and Operations Research, probability was my daily breath, so I was delighted to see this work. Not only was this a fun
read for me, but I find in Vern Poythress a firm grasp of the mathematical, philosophical,
theological, and apologetic issues necessary to guide those who want to think clearly
on this topic—a topic which, because of its technicality, many will be daunted by. And
Poythress always has an eye for the helpful illustration!"

> **C. John Collins**, Professor of Old Testament, Covenant Theological Seminary;
> author, *The God of Miracles, Science and Faith: Friends or Foes?*

"Many think Calvinists simply reject the idea of chance, random events, and probability. But that is not entirely true. My friend Vern Poythress shows in this book that the
God of the Bible—and of Calvin—is in fact the foundation, both of causation and of
randomness in the world. Poythress is well-suited to develop this argument, with doctor-
ates in both New Testament and mathematics, and as the author of important recent
books on logic and science. I do not fully understand the mathematics of this book, but
the theology is entirely biblical, and I can't imagine a better place to start for readers
interested in this subject matter."

> **John M. Frame**, J. D. Trimble Chair of Systematic Theology and Philosophy,
> Reformed Theological Seminary, Orlando

CHANCE AND THE SOVEREIGNTY OF GOD

CHANCE AND THE SOVEREIGNTY OF GOD

A GOD-CENTERED APPROACH TO
PROBABILITY AND RANDOM EVENTS

VERN S. POYTHRESS

WHEATON, ILLINOIS

Chance and the Sovereignty of God:
A God-Centered Approach to Probability and Random Events

Copyright © 2014 by Vern S. Poythress

Published by Crossway
   1300 Crescent Street
   Wheaton, Illinois 60187

Cover design: Matt Naylor

First printing 2014

Printed in the United States of America

Trade paperback ISBN: 978-1-4335-3695-3
ePub ISBN: 978-1-4335-3698-4
PDF ISBN: 978-1-4335-3698-4
Mobipocket ISBN: 978-1-4335-3697-7

Library of Congress Cataloging-in-Publication Data
Poythress, Vern S.
 Chance and the sovereignty of God : a God-centered approach to probability and random events / Vern Sheridan Poythress.
  pages cm
 Includes bibliographical references and index.
 ISBN 978-1-4335-3695-3 (tp)
 1. Providence and government of God--Christianity.
I. Title.
BT135.P69   2014
231'.5—dc23   2013036218

Crossway is a publishing ministry of Good News Publishers.

VP		24	23	22	21	20	19	18	17	16	15	14
15	14	13	12	11	10	9	8	7	6	5	4	3	2	1

CONTENTS

TABLES AND ILLUSTRATIONS

INTRODUCTION

EXPERIENCES WITH UNPREDICTABLE EVENTS

One time, when my family and I were on vacation, I drove around a curve to find, directly ahead of me, a line of cars stopped dead because of roadwork. I put the brakes on hard, relieved that I had time to stop. But what about cars coming behind me? The highway, consisting of one lane in each direction, curved to the right, with a mountain rising just to the right of the road, and a drop-off to the left. The drivers coming in my direction could not see me because their vision was blocked by the mountain. Would they be able to stop in time? Should I run back to warn them? Should I blow my horn to warn them? If I blew the horn, would the sound be blocked by the mountainside? Before I could decide, looking backward I saw a car coming round the curve, too fast to stop. To avoid hitting us, the driver swerved left into the lane of oncoming traffic. Fortunately, no car was coming in the other direction, and he was able to stop in the lane to our left.

At that point I started blowing the horn. Too late. Another car came round the curve, again too fast. I thought, "It can't stop. It is going to crash into us." The driver braked hard but lost control, and the car spun 180 degrees. It ended up facing backward on the berm, squeezed between us and the mountain. The driver was emotionally shaken but physically intact. Now we had a car to our left and a car to our right. There was no more room. A third car followed, coming right at us, as our children in the back seat watched helplessly. It managed to stop a couple of feet behind us. Finally, the roadwork opened and we proceeded forward. All the people had escaped an accident. My family and I had escaped what seemed to be certain injury and a wrecked vehicle.

THE ISSUE OF CHANCE

What do we say about this incident? Some people would say we were "lucky." We escaped "by chance." It just *happened* to be the case that the oncoming cars found room to our left and to our right. Or was it the hand of God's providence? We felt afterwards as if an angel had pushed the cars to this side and to that. God had sent an angel to protect us. But we did not actually *see* an angel. Nor did we see a hand reaching down from heaven to move the cars. Was it just our imagination? Was our escape a "miracle," or was it just an "accidental" result of driver reactions and physical processes?

We escaped. But not everyone does. For every story of a narrow escape, someone else can tell a distressing story of not escaping. Someone tells of being in a horrible auto accident, nearly dying from the injuries, losing an arm or a leg, and spending months recovering. And the accident could have been avoided, if only the oncoming car had swerved a little earlier or a little later. Was the accident "by chance"? Was God in control? If I am ready to acknowledge God's control when my family escapes an accident, should I also acknowledge that God is in control when someone else suffers from an unpredictable tragedy? Or do tragic cases involve pure chance, beyond God's control? And if God is in control, did he actually *plan* the events beforehand, or did he just react to the unfolding events at the last moment?

Big accidents and near accidents have drama to them. But what about the small things? Yesterday I could not find my checkbook. Today I found it in a pocket of my briefcase where it did not belong. *Accidentally*, it must have fallen into the wrong pocket when I dropped it into my partially opened briefcase. It got misplaced "by chance," someone might say.

What about totally unpredictable events, like the flip of a coin or the roll of dice? Every time we flip a coin, the result is unpredictable. It comes up heads or tails "by chance." What do we mean by the word *chance*? What is it?

INTEREST IN CHANCE

People are most interested in chance when a chance event makes a big difference in their lives. Why did my family escape the mountain highway accident? Why did another person suffer from a "chance" accident? We would like to know. Is God in charge of these "accidental" events or not? If he is in charge, why does he let bad things happen? Is God good or not? And if he is not in charge, what should we think? It seems that we are at the mercy of events that have no innate meaning. No one knows when we will have to suffer without purpose. That is not good news.

We see another dimension of human interest when people try to find out about the future. About some future events we can be relatively confident. We expect the sun to rise tomorrow. We expect to wake up in the same bed and the same room in which we went to sleep. Yet we also know that there are troubling uncertainties about the future. Will a violent storm or earthquake destroy our home? Will someone in the family get cancer? Will we be in a car accident? Some people consult fortune-tellers, palm readers, and astrological charts to try to get extra clues about events beyond their control. The astrologer may warn them not to make a big purchase today, because there is too much danger of making a disastrous decision. Or he advises them to stay at home because there is too much danger of an acci-dent. Or they should go out because they may begin a promising romance.

Compulsive gamblers have a fascination with chance—in particular, the chance of making a "killing" and winning a fortune on a hoped-for "lucky" day at the gambling tables. Some of them think they can see patterns in the events. If a roulette wheel has come up with an even number seven times in a row, they may feel that it is time for an odd number to come up, so they bet on odd. They are finding meaning in the chance alteration between odd and even.

On occasion a gambler does have a so-called "lucky" day. He leaves the casino $500 or even $50,000 richer. But if he goes back, his one-day win-nings will soon be gone. The casino would not be in business if it did not make a profit in the long run. So was the gambler deluded in his feeling that it was time for an odd number to come up, or time for a big win from a slot machine? Do the casino managers know something that the gambler does not know? And how do they know? What is the truth about chance?

CHANCE IN DARWINISM

Chance events play a role not only in ordinary life but also in some scien-tific theories. In particular, chance plays a key role in the Darwinian theory of evolution. According to the standard Darwinian account, all the forms of life that we can observe today originated through chance events in the distant past. Darwinism says that the first life originated by chance. Once the first life existed, chance mutations led gradually to other forms of life; chance matings between living things led to new combinations of genetic material; chance deaths and escapes from death that befell living creatures led gradually to increasing fitness among the survivors. Chance changes in the habitats sometimes led to separation of species and various pressures on "fitness." As a result of accumulating eons of such chance events, we enjoy the diversity of life that we see today.

What do we think of this Darwinist account? To evaluate Darwinism as a whole is beyond the scope of this book.[1] But it is appropriate to ask, what is this idea of "chance" on which Darwinism builds?

CHANCE IN SCIENCE

Chance and uncertainty also play an indispensable role in science as a whole. Some people might think that science is mostly about certainties rather than uncertainties, namely the certainties of scientific laws. They are thinking of laws like Newton's laws of motion that completely determine the outcome, once we know the initial conditions. But not all scientific laws are of this kind. The laws of quantum mechanics intrinsically involve uncertainties. So do the laws of statistical mechanics. In this kind of case, most individual outcomes cannot be predicted, but a scientist can predict the average outcome or the probability of a particular outcome.

Moreover, virtually all forms of scientific experiment involve chance and probability. When scientists are trying to find new laws or regularities, they may repeat an experiment several times, or even hundreds of times, and obtain a record that includes chance variations. Even in a simple measurement like the measurement of a distance or a weight, there are minute variations when a scientist performs the measurement a second or a third time. For example, a scientist weighs a chemical sample on a precision scale and finds that it has a mass of 3.27 grams. If he weighs it a second or a third time, he obtains the same result. But if he tries to obtain more accuracy, he may find variations. A first weighing gives the result 3.2703 grams. A second weigh-

---

[1] See Vern S. Poythress, *Redeeming Science: A God-Centered Approach* (Wheaton, IL: Crossway, 2006), chapters 18 and 19; C. John Collins, *Science and Faith: Friends or Foes?* (Wheaton, IL: Crossway, 2003), chapters 16–18.

ing 3.2695 grams. A third gives the result 3.2698 grams. The exact result is unpredictable.

After data have been collected from repeated measurements or repeated experiments, scientists analyze their data to see whether they reveal important regular patterns. The analysis uses mathematical methods that take into account the variations in experimental outcomes. These methods reckon with what might be called chance variations that occur in the midst of an experiment designed primarily to explore regularities rather than chance variation itself.

CHANCE IN SOCIAL SCIENCES

Chance also plays an important role in many areas in social sciences. Social sciences study human beings. And any one individual human being is not completely predictable. Social scientists know very well that in many cases they cannot hope to formulate an exact law of human behavior that will have no exceptions anywhere in the world. Rather, they work with averages and with probabilities. They reckon with chance variations that belong to each individual case, but they achieve interesting results by averaging over the variations among a sufficiently large number of individual cases.

Thus, chance plays an integral role in the processes of experimental science. Since scientific theories are validated by experiment, chance lies at the foundation that supports scientific theories. Virtually the whole edifice of science—both physical sciences and social sciences—depends on assumptions about chance variations. So we need to look at the nature of chance not only to address personal questions that we have about the meaning of everyday events in human life, but to address the issue of what confidence we should have in the sciences and their claims.

PART I

THE SOVEREIGNTY
OF GOD

CHAPTER 1

THE BIBLE AS A SOURCE FOR KNOWLEDGE

What is *chance*? Can we know? How can we find out the truth about accidental events?

THE BIBLE AS A SOURCE

The Bible indicates that God is the ultimate source for knowledge. God knows all things, including everything that there is to know about chance. God's "understanding is unsearchable" (Isa. 40:28). Whatever we know, we know because God has made it known to us: "He who *teaches man knowledge*—the LORD—knows the thoughts of man, that they are but a breath" (Ps. 94:10–11).

God is the source of knowledge even of an ordinary sort (Isa. 28:24–29). He is present when we read a book or a page on the Internet, and he has given to the writers of books and Internet articles whatever abilities and sources that they use. He is also present in giving us memories and preserving them. I know from my memory and from my own eyesight what happened when my family escaped the near accident on our vacation. According to the Bible, such knowledge is a gift from God.

But some knowledge is not so ordinary. Can I know *why* my family escaped an accident? Why does one gambler win $50,000 and another lose? Is there a reason? Or is it just "chance" or "luck"? Is there no further explanation? And what do we mean by "chance" or "luck"? What is it, at a fundamental level?

God knows the answer to such questions. But we do not—unless God says something to us to explain and to give answers. The Bible claims to be God's own word: "All Scripture is *breathed out by God* and profitable for teaching, for reproof, for correction, and for training in righteousness" (2 Tim. 3:16). I believe that the Bible's claim is true. It does indeed give us God's instruction. So we can study the Bible to find answers to these questions. And when we do, we find that the Bible does have teaching about so-called "chance" events.

IS THE BIBLE RELIABLE?

But we live in a time of widespread skepticism. People doubt whether God exists. Or if they think there is a God, they doubt whether the Bible is really God's word. Many books have argued the case.[1] We are not going to repeat all the arguments here, but we may briefly note two of them.

First, the Old Testament part of the Bible, written hundreds of years before the coming of Christ, contains prophecies about Christ's coming that were fulfilled in his earthly life. Christ was born in Bethlehem, just as it was prophesied 700 years beforehand in the prophecy of Micah (Mic. 5:2; compare Matt. 2:1–6). Jesus's crucifixion was prophesied 700 years beforehand in Isaiah 53. Jesus established God's reign of salvation during the time of the Roman Empire, just as Daniel had prophesied 600 years earlier (Dan. 2:44). Jesus's ministry was preceded by a forerunner, John the Baptist, just as the prophet Malachi had predicted 400 years earlier (Mal. 3:1; compare Mark 1:2–4).[2]

Second, Jesus himself testifies to the divine authority of the Old Testament when he says,

> Do not think that I have come to abolish the Law or the Prophets; I have not come to abolish them but to fulfill them. For truly, I say to you, until heaven and earth pass away, not an iota, not a dot, will pass from the Law until all is accomplished. (Matt. 5:17–18)

---

[1] For the question of God's existence, see, for example, Timothy Keller, *The Reason for God: Belief in an Age of Skepticism* (New York: Dutton, 2008). For the character of the Bible, see Archibald A. Hodge and Benjamin B. Warfield, *Inspiration* (Grand Rapids, MI: Baker, 1979); Benjamin B. Warfield, *The Inspiration and Authority of the Bible* (Philadelphia: Presbyterian & Reformed, 1967); Ned B. Stonehouse and Paul Woolley, eds., *The Infallible Word: A Symposium by Members of the Faculty of Westminster Theological Seminary*, 3rd rev. printing (Philadelphia: Presbyterian & Reformed, 1967); John M. Frame, *The Doctrine of the Word of God* (Phillipsburg, NJ: Presbyterian & Reformed, 2010).

[2] Readers may be aware that, because of the importance of the Bible, arguments back and forth about its authority have continued for centuries. Over the centuries, skeptics have tried to come up with replies and attempted refutations with respect to virtually any piece of evidence that has been used to confirm the authority of the Bible. I do not wish to sweep under the rug the fact that these matters are all debated. But the pursuit of such debates belongs to other books.

We leave to other books the detailed arguments about the authority of the Bible. Here we are going to rely on it to instruct us about issues involving chance and chance events. If you are not yet convinced about God or the Bible, I would still invite you to read, because God may still be pleased to use his wisdom in the Bible to teach you both about him and about chance.

CHAPTER 2

GOD'S SOVEREIGNTY

According to the Bible, God created the world[1] and everything in it:

> In the beginning, God *created the heavens and the earth*. (Gen. 1:1)

> The God who *made the world and everything in it*, being Lord of heaven and earth, does not live in temples made my man. (Acts 17:24)

> there is one God, the Father, *from whom are all things* and for whom we exist, and one Lord, Jesus Christ, through whom are all things and through whom we exist. (1 Cor. 8:6)

> My help comes from the LORD, who *made heaven and earth*. (Ps. 121:2)

God created heaven and earth long ago. What about his *present* involvement in the world? The philosophy called *deism* says that God created everything, but afterwards was uninvolved. He made the world as if he were winding a clock. After the clock is wound up, it runs "by itself," and the clockmaker—that is, God—does not need to attend to it.

But the Bible contradicts deism. It indicates that God continually sustains the world that he has made:

> He [God the Son] *upholds* the universe by the word of his power. (Heb. 1:3)

> In him [the Son] all things *hold together*. (Col. 1:17)

> In him we live and move and have our being. (Acts 17:28)

---

[1] For a fuller exposition of the nature of God, creation, and providence, see John M. Frame, *The Doctrine of God* (Phillipsburg, NJ: Presbyterian & Reformed, 2002). For discussion of the relation of creation to modern science, see Vern S. Poythress, *Redeeming Science: A God-Centered Approach* (Wheaton, IL: Crossway, 2006).

In addition, Psalm 121:2 talks about "help" from the Lord in the present: "My help comes from the LORD." God's past work in creating the world, far from being an excuse for him to walk away, confirms and undergirds God's availability in the present. (See fig. 2.1.) He is active with his power and his help. Psalm 121:2 adds the reminder "who made heaven and earth" partly to back up the conviction that, in the present time as in the beginning, "my help comes from the LORD."

Fig. 2.1: Deism and Theism

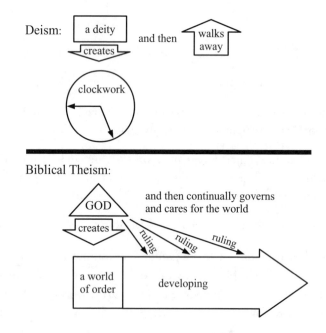

Other psalms make the same point:

> Our help is in the name of the LORD,
>   who *made heaven and earth*. (Ps. 124:8)

> May the LORD bless you from Zion,
>   he who *made heaven and earth*. (134:3)

> Blessed is he whose help is the God of Jacob,
>   whose hope is in the LORD his God,
> who *made heaven and earth*,

the sea, and all that is in them,
who keeps faith forever; (146:5–6)

We can see a similar point in Isaiah 51:12–13:

I, I am he who comforts you;
> who are you that you are afraid of man who dies,
> of the son of man who is made like grass,
and have forgotten the LORD, your *Maker*,
> *who stretched out the heavens*
> *and laid the foundations of the earth*,
and you fear continually all the day
> because of the wrath of the oppressor,
when he sets himself to destroy?
> And where is the wrath of the oppressor?

Isaiah 51:12–13 says that the LORD made the heavens and the earth. Before and after this key claim, the passage gives practical comfort. Its says, "I, I am he who *comforts you*"; and it counsels God's people not to fear the power of man or the power of "the oppressor." Why do they not need to fear? Because God is more powerful—in fact, supremely powerful. The power exhibited when God created the world is still available for the comfort and protection of God's people today. Thus, biblical teaching on creation supports faith in God in the present. (See fig. 2.2.)

Fig. 2.2: God's Power in Creation

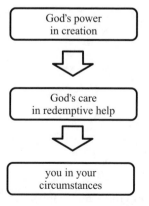

Psalm 121:2 and Isaiah 51:12–13 fit together with many other passages that confirm God's continued involvement with the world:

You [God] *cause the grass to grow* for the livestock
     and *plants* for man to cultivate. (Ps. 104:14)

From your lofty abode you water the mountains;
     the earth is satisfied with the fruit of your work. (104:13)

You make darkness, and it is night,
     when all the beasts of the forest creep about. (104:20)

These [animals] all look to you,
     to give them their food in due season.
When you give it to them, they gather it up;
     when you open your hand, they are filled with good things.
When you hide your face, they are dismayed;
     when you take away their breath, they die
     and return to their dust.
When you send forth your Spirit, they are created,
     and you renew the face of the ground. (104:27–30)

For he strengthens the bars of your gates;
     he blesses your children within you.
He makes peace in your borders;
     he fills you with the finest of the wheat.
He sends out his command to the earth;
     his word runs swiftly.
He gives snow like wool;
     he scatters frost like ashes.
He hurls down his crystals of ice like crumbs;
     who can stand before his cold?
He sends out his word, and melts them;
     he makes his wind blow and the waters flow.
He declares his word to Jacob,
     his statutes and rules to Israel. (147:13–19)

We also find summary statements that affirm God's universal control over what happens:

The LORD has established his throne in the heavens,
  and his kingdom *rules over all.* (Ps. 103:19)

In him we have obtained an inheritance, having been predestined according to the purpose of him *who works all things according to the counsel of his will.* (Eph. 1:11)

Who has spoken and it came to pass,
  unless the Lord has commanded it?
Is it not *from the mouth of the Most High*
  that good and bad come? (Lam. 3:37–38)

For his dominion is an everlasting dominion,
  and his kingdom endures from generation to generation;
all the inhabitants of the earth are accounted as nothing,
  and *he does according to his will* among the host of heaven
  and among the inhabitants of the earth;
and none can stay his hand
  or say to him, "What have you done?" (Dan. 4:34–35)

This universal control is called God's *providence* or his *providential rule.*[2]

PROVIDENCE AND SCIENCE

How does God's rule over the world fit in with modern sciences? Sciences study regularities in the present order of the world. These regularities are the product of God's specification. For example, "God said, 'Let there be light,' and there was light" (Gen. 1:3). By speaking, God not only created the world but also continues to rule it. Note in other verses the key role of God's word:

By the *word* of the LORD the heavens were made,
  and by the *breath of his mouth* all their host. (Ps. 33:6)

He sends out his *command* to the earth;
  his *word* runs swiftly.
He gives snow like wool;
  he scatters frost like ashes.
He hurls down his crystals of ice like crumbs;
  who can stand before his cold?

---

[2] The biblical teaching on God's control, which we discuss in this and the following chapters, is also covered in Frame, *Doctrine of God,* chapters 4 and 14.

He sends out his *word*, and melts them;
> he makes his wind blow and the waters flow. (147:15–18)

He upholds the universe by the *word* of his power. (Heb. 1:3)

Who has *spoken* and it came to pass,
> unless the Lord has *commanded* it?
Is it not from the *mouth* of the Most High
> that good and bad come? (Lam. 3:37–38)

The Bible uses other kinds of descriptions as well, but the descriptions in terms of God's speech are particularly useful as we think about science. God's speech is the *real* law governing the world. Scientific theories approximate God's speech, and so in their theories scientists think God's thoughts after him. God planned the character of the entire universe. His thoughts about the world were in his mind even before he created it. Scientists are made in the image of God, and so their minds have the capability of imitating God's thoughts. They imitate God when they try to reconstruct the laws that originated in God's mind. There is no tension between God's providence and science, when we understand science in harmony with what the Bible says about God's speech.[3]

GOD'S PLAN

The Bible also indicates that God's ongoing providential rule is in accord with a plan that he has already made. Ephesians 1:11 indicates that what happens is in accord with "the counsel of his will":

> In him we have obtained an inheritance, having been predestined according to the purpose of him who works all things according to *the counsel of his will*.

The events have "been predestined," that is, determined beforehand, indicating that God's plan is already in place. Isaiah makes a similar point about God's purposes as he proclaims the superiority of God to all idols:

> for I am God, and there is no other;
> > I am God, and there is none like me,

---

[3] For further explanation, see Poythress, *Redeeming Science*.

declaring the end from the beginning
  and from *ancient times* things not yet done,
saying, "My counsel shall stand,
  and I will accomplish all *my purpose*,"
calling a bird of prey from the east,
  the man of my counsel from a far country.
I have spoken, and I will bring it to pass;
  I have purposed, and I will do it. (Isa. 46:9–11)

Ephesians 1:4 says that "he chose us in him [Christ] *before the foundation of the world*," indicating that God's plan goes back to before the beginning of creation. These verses indicate the magnificence of God's power and wisdom; they also underscore the security of those who are chosen by God, because God's purposes for them will be accomplished.

PRACTICAL TRUST

God's providential rule has practical implications. As we saw from Psalm 121:2, we are meant to trust that he can come to help us. Similar language about trusting God occurs in other psalms:

The Lord is on my side; I will not fear.
  What can man do to me? (Ps. 118:6)

God is our refuge and strength,
  a very present help in trouble.
Therefore we will not fear though the earth gives way,
  though the mountains be moved into the heart of the sea,
though its waters roar and foam,
  though the mountains tremble at its swelling. (46:1–3)

The Bible indicates that our trust in God should extend to all areas of life. We should trust in matters of war:

Some trust in chariots and some in horses,
  but we trust in the name of the Lord our God.
They collapse and fall,
  but we rise and stand upright. (20:7–8)

We should trust when beset by enemies:

O my God, in you I trust;
  let me not be put to shame;
  let not my enemies exult over me. (25:2)

We should trust when we are afraid:

When I am afraid,
  I put my trust in you. (56:3)

We should trust in him for the security of our lives:

Those who trust in the LORD are like Mount Zion,
  which cannot be moved, but abides forever. (125:1)

Psalm 62:8 sums it up: "Trust in him *at all times*, O people."

CHRIST'S CRUCIFIXION AND RESURRECTION

General principles about God's faithfulness and control over the world fit together with many particular examples that the Bible records. The supreme example occurs in Christ's crucifixion and resurrection, which were prophesied in the Old Testament and predicted by Christ during his earthly life (Isa. 53:7–12; Matt. 16:21; 17:11, 22–23; 20:18–19; 21:39; 26:2, 24, 31–32, 45–46). What happened to Christ was "whatever your [God's] hand and your plan had *predestined* to take place" (Acts 4:28). God's commitment to us through Christ gives us security:

If God is for us, who can be against us? He who did not spare his own Son but gave him up for us all, how will he not also with him graciously give us all things? (Rom. 8:31–32)

The book of Romans indicates that since God is committed to people in this way through Christ, all things work for good for those who belong to Christ:

And we know that for those who love God all things work together for good, for those who are called according to his purpose. (Rom. 8:28)

The general principles and the particular cases work together, as shown in fig. 2.3.

Fig. 2.3: God's Universal Control

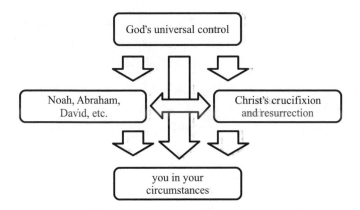

Charles Spurgeon speaks about the security that a Christian should experience from knowing God's power and purposes:

> [The Christian] believes that an invisible hand is always on the world's tiller, and that wherever providence may drift, Jehovah steers it. That re-assuring knowledge prepares him for everything. He looks over the raging waters and sees the spirit of Jesus treading the billows, and he hears a voice saying, "It is I, be not afraid" [alluding to Matt. 14:27 and parallels]. . . . and so, believing that God rules all, that He governs wisely, that He brings good out of evil, the believer's heart is assured, and he is enabled calmly to meet each trial as it comes.[4]

HONORING GOD

We honor God when we trust him, as we respond to him in the way that he deserves. Honoring God includes other aspects of life as well. First Corinthians 10:31 says, "So, whether you eat or drink, or *whatever* you do, do all to the *glory* of God." God is deserving of all glory and praise. Everything we do should serve to honor him and to reflect his glory.

This principle includes within its scope whatever we do in our *thinking*. In the pages that follow, we should honor God and magnify his greatness as we think about issues related to chance. We should look for ways

---

[4] Charles H. Spurgeon, *Morning and Evening: Daily Readings* (McLean, VA: MacDonald, n.d.), 436 (morning, August 5).

to praise him for controlling the world and for displaying his wisdom in the world.

Those of us who follow Christ have a further motivation. The Bible indicates that Christ is now exalted in heaven and rules over everything:

> He [God] raised him [Christ] from the dead and seated him at his right hand in the heavenly places, far above all rule and authority and power and dominion, and above every name that is named, not only in this age but also in the one to come. And he put *all things* under his feet. (Eph. 1:20–22)

> He [Christ] *upholds the universe* by the word of his power. (Heb. 1:3)

Christ is Lord of all. So we should serve him in every thought and in every sphere.

CHAPTER 3

UNPREDICTABLE EVENTS

What about seemingly random events? Does God control them?

THE FLIGHT OF AN ARROW

First Kings 22 contains a striking case. Micaiah, speaking as a prophet of the Lord, predicts that Ahab, the king of Israel, will fall in battle at Ramoth-gilead (1 Kings 22:20–22). Ahab disguises himself in battle to avoid being a special target for enemy attack (v. 30). But God's plan cannot be thwarted. The narrative describes the crucial event:

> But a certain man drew his bow *at random* and struck the king of Israel between the scale armor and the breastplate. Therefore he [the king] said to the driver of his chariot, "Turn around and carry me out of the battle, for I am wounded." (v. 34)

"A certain man drew his bow at random." That is, he was not aiming at any particular target. An alternative translation would be that he drew his bow "in his innocence" (ESV marginal reading). The alternative translation might mean that the man shot at Ahab, but he did not know who it was (he was "innocent" of knowing it was the king). Whichever interpretation we take of this detail, we should notice that the arrow struck in just the right place. Ahab was dressed in armor. If the arrow had struck Ahab's breastplate, it might have simply bounced off. If it had struck his scale armor, it would not have wounded him. But there *happened to be* a small space between the scale armor and the breastplate. Perhaps for just a moment Ahab turned or bent in such a way that a thin opening appeared. The arrow went right in, exactly in the right spot. It wounded him fatally. He died the same day (1 Kings 22:35), just as God had said.

God showed that day that he was in charge of seemingly random events. He controlled when the man drew his bow. He controlled the direction of his aim. He controlled the moment the arrow was released. He controlled the flight of the arrow. He controlled the way Ahab's armor was put on earlier in the day, and the position that Ahab took as the arrow came nearer. He controlled the arrow as it struck in just the right spot and went in deep enough to produce fatal damage to organs. He brought Ahab to his death.

Lest we feel too sorry for Ahab, we should remind ourselves that he was a wicked king (1 Kings 21:25–26). Moreover, by going into battle he directly disobeyed the warning that Micaiah the prophet gave in God's name. It was an act of arrogance and disobedience to God. God, who is a God of justice, executed righteous judgment on Ahab. From this judgment we should learn to revere God and honor him.

Ahab's death was an event of special significance. It had been prophesied beforehand, and Ahab himself was a special person. He was the king of Israel, a prominent leader, a key person in connection with the history of God's people in the northern kingdom of Israel. But the event illustrates a general principle: God controls seemingly random events. A single outstanding event, like the arrow flying toward Ahab, has not been narrated as an *exception* but rather as a particularly weighty instance of the general principle, which the Bible articulates in passages where it teaches God's universal control.

COINCIDENCES

We can find other events in the Bible where the outcome depends on an apparent coincidence or happenstance.

In Genesis 24, Rebekah, who belonged to the clan of Abraham's relatives, *happened to come out* to the well just after Abraham's servant arrived. The servant was praying and waiting, looking for a wife for Abraham's son Isaac (Gen. 24:15). The fact that Rebekah came out at just the right time was clearly God's answer to the servant's prayer. Rebekah later married Isaac and bore Jacob, an ancestor of Jesus Christ.

Years later Rachel, who belonged to the same clan, *happened* to come out to a well just after Jacob arrived (Gen. 29:6). Jacob met her, fell in love with her, and married her. She became the mother of Joseph, whom God later raised up to preserve the whole family of Jacob during a seven-year famine (Genesis 41–46). When God provided Rachel for Jacob, he was fulfilling his promise that he would take care of Jacob and bring him back to Canaan (28:15). Moreover, he was fulfilling his long-range promise that he would bless the descendants of Abraham (vv. 13–14).

In the life of Joseph, after Joseph's brothers had thrown him into a pit, a caravan of Ishmaelites *happened to go by*, traveling on their way to Egypt (Gen. 37:25). The brothers sold Joseph to the Ishmaelites. They in turn *happened* to sell Joseph to Potiphar, "an officer of Pharaoh" (v. 36). Joseph's experiences were grim, but they were moving him toward the new position that he would eventually assume in Egypt.

False accusation by the wife of Potiphar led to Joseph being thrown into prison (Gen. 39:20). Pharaoh *happened* to get angry with his chief cupbearer and his chief baker, and they *happened* to get thrown into the prison where Joseph now had a position of responsibility (40:1–4). While they were lying in prison, both the cupbearer and the baker *happened* to have special dreams. Joseph's interpretation of their dreams led to his later opportunity to interpret Pharaoh's dreams (Genesis 41). These events led to the fulfillment of the earlier prophetic dreams that God had given to Joseph in his youth (37:5–10; 42:9).

After Moses was born, his mother put him in a basket made of bulrushes and placed it among the reeds by the Nile. The daughter of Pharaoh *happened* to come down to the river and *happened* to notice it. When she opened it, the baby *happened* to cry. The daughter of Pharaoh took pity and adopted Moses as her own son (Ex. 2:3–10). As a result, Moses was protected from the death sentence on Hebrew male children (1:16, 22), and he "was instructed in all the wisdom of the Egyptians" (Acts 7:22). So God worked out his plan, according to which Moses would eventually deliver the Israelites from Egypt.

Joshua sent two spies to Jericho. Out of all the possibilities, they *happened* to go to the house of Rahab the prostitute (Josh. 2:1). Rahab hid the spies and made an agreement with them (vv. 4, 12–14). Consequently, she and her relatives were preserved when the city of Jericho was destroyed (6:17, 25). Rahab then became an ancestor of Jesus (Matt. 1:5).

Ruth "*happened to come* to the part of the field belonging to Boaz"

(Ruth 2:3). Boaz noticed Ruth, and then a series of events led to Boaz marrying Ruth, who became an ancestor of Jesus (Ruth 4:21–22; Matt. 1:5).

During the life of David, we read the following account of what happened in the wilderness of Maon:

> As Saul and his men were closing in on David and his men to capture them, a messenger came to Saul, saying, "Hurry and come, for the Philistines have made a raid against the land." So Saul returned from pursuing after David and went against the Philistines. (1 Sam. 23:26–28)

David narrowly escaped being killed, because the Philistines *happened* to conduct a raid at a particular time, and the messenger *happened* to reach Saul when he did. If nothing had happened to interfere with Saul's pursuit, he might have succeeded in killing David. The death of David would have cut off the line of descendants leading to Jesus (Matt. 1:1, 6).

When Absalom engineered his revolt against David's rule, a messenger *happened* to come to David, saying, "The hearts of the men of Israel have gone after Absalom" (2 Sam. 15:13). David immediately fled Jerusalem, where otherwise he would have been killed. During David's flight, Hushai the Archite *happened* to come to meet him, "with his coat torn and dirt on his head" (v. 32). David told Hushai to go back to Jerusalem, pretend to support Absalom, and defeat the counsel of Ahithophel (v. 34). As a result, Hushai was able to persuade Absalom not to follow Ahithophel's counsel for battle, and Absalom died in the battle that eventually took place (18:14–15). Thus, happenstances contributed to David's survival.

When Ben-hadad the king of Syria was besieging Samaria, the city was starving. Elisha predicted that the next day the city of Samaria would have flour and barley (2 Kings 7:1). The captain standing by expressed disbelief, and then Elisha predicted that he would "see it . . . but . . . not eat of it" (v. 2). The next day the captain *happened* to be trampled by the people who were rushing out the gate toward the food (v. 17). "He died, as the man of God had said" (v. 17), seeing the food but not living to partake of it. His death was a fulfillment of God's prophecy.

When Athaliah was about to usurp the throne of Judah, she undertook to destroy all the descendants in the Davidic family. Jehosheba *happened* to be there, and she took Joash the son of Ahaziah and hid him away (2 Kings 11:2). So the line of the Davidic family was preserved, which had to be the case if the Messiah was to come from the line of David, as God had promised. Joash was an ancestor of Jesus Christ.

During the reign of king Josiah, the priests *happened* to find the Book of the Law as they were repairing the temple precincts (2 Kings 22:8). Josiah had it read to him, and so he was energized to inaugurate a spiritual reform.

The story of Esther contains further happenstances. Esther *happened* to be among the young women taken into the king's palace (Est. 2:8). She *happened* to be chosen to be the new queen (v. 17). Mordecai *happened* to find out about Bigthan and Teresh's plot against the king (v. 22), and Mordecai's name then *happened* to be included in the king's chronicles (v. 23). The night before Haman planned to hang Mordecai, the king happened not to be able to sleep (6:1). He asked for an assistant to read from the chronicles, and he happened to read the part where Mordecai had uncovered the plot against the king (vv. 1–2). Haman happened to be entering the king's court at just that moment (v. 4). A whole series of happenstances worked together to lead to Haman's being hanged, the Jews being rescued, and Mordecai being honored.

The book of Jonah also contains events that worked together. The Lord sent the storm at sea (Jonah 1:4). When the sailors cast lots in order to identify the guilty person, "the lot fell on Jonah" (v. 7). The Lord appointed the fish that swallowed Jonah (v. 17). The Lord also appointed the plant that grew up (4:6), the worm that attacked the plant (v. 7), and then the blazing of the sun and the "scorching east wind" (v. 8).

Zechariah the priest, the husband of Elizabeth, happened to be chosen by lot to burn incense in the temple (Luke 1:9). The time was just right, shortly before the conception of John the Baptist and the coming of Jesus (vv. 24–38).

When Dorcas died in Joppa, Peter *happened* to be nearby in Lydda (Acts 9:32, 38). The disciples in Joppa happened to hear that he was there. So they sent for Peter, and as a result Dorcas was raised back to life.

While Paul the apostle was in prison, the son of Paul's sister *happened* to hear about the Jewish plot to kill Paul (Acts 23:16). He passed the news on to the Roman leader, the tribune, who had his soldiers take Paul to Caesarea. Paul was saved from being killed because of a happenstance.

We could multiply instances of this kind. The storm and the fish that the Lord sent to Jonah might be considered miraculous, but for the most part we have focused on incidents where a bystander may not have noticed anything extraordinary. In each case, the narrative as a whole shows that God was accomplishing his purposes. He was in control of these apparently "happenstance" events. We could add to our list many incidents in the Bible of a more extraordinary kind, where God exerted miraculous power. He brought the plagues on Egypt, divided the waters of the Red Sea, gave manna in the wilderness.

We see a supreme exhibition of God's control when we look at some of the apparently "happenstance" events during Jesus's crucifixion and death.

When Jesus was crucified, the soldiers *happened* to cast lots to divide his garments. They thus fulfilled the Scripture,

> They divided my garments among them,
>   and for my clothing they cast lots. (John 19:24; Ps. 22:18)

When Jesus had died, one of the soldiers *happened* to pierce his side with a spear, fulfilling prophecy:

> But one of the soldiers *pierced* his side with a spear, . . . (John 19:34)

> And again another Scripture says, "They will look on him whom they have *pierced*." (John 19:37; quoted from Zech. 12:10)

After the death of Jesus, Joseph of Arimathea, a rich man (Matt. 27:57), took the body of Jesus and laid it in his own tomb, which *happened* to be nearby and which was empty. He thus fulfilled prophecy:

> And Joseph took the body and wrapped it in a clean linen shroud and laid it in his own new tomb (Matt. 27:59–60)

> And they made his grave with the wicked
>   and with a *rich man* in his death (Isa. 53:9)

In Acts, the believers took courage as they reflected on how God had controlled the events of Jesus's crucifixion (Acts 4:25–28). They prayed that God would continue to act in power in their lives:

> "And now, Lord, look upon their threats [from the religious leaders] and grant to your servants to continue to speak your word with all boldness, while you stretch out your hand to heal, and signs and wonders are per-

formed through the name of your holy servant Jesus." And when they had prayed, the place in which they were gathered together was shaken, and they were all filled with the Holy Spirit and continued to speak the word of God with boldness. (vv. 29–31)

God is the same God today. We can infer that God is in control of the apparently happenstance events in each of our lives. All of us have to face events over which we have no control: "time and chance happen to them all" (Eccles. 9:11). It is a great comfort to know that God controls such things, because God knows what he is doing. Romans 8:28 reminds us that "for those who love God all things work together for good, for those who are called according to his purpose." Let us praise God for his majesty. And let us trust God for the future, including "coincidences" and "happenstance." (See fig. 3.1.)

Fig. 3.1: God's Control over Happenstance

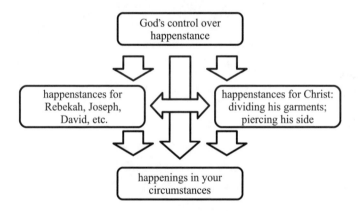

CHAPTER 4

DISASTERS AND SUFFERING

We can confirm the point about God's control over apparently random events with another case, namely the disasters that befell Job.

DISASTERS IN THE BOOK OF JOB

Job 1 describes several disasters. The key passage is worth quoting in full:

> Now there was a day when his [Job's] sons and daughters were eating and drinking wine in their oldest brother's house, and there came a messenger to Job and said, "The oxen were plowing and the donkeys feeding beside them, and the Sabeans fell upon them and took them and struck down the servants with the edge of the sword, and I alone have escaped to tell you." While he was yet speaking, there came another and said, "The fire of God fell from heaven and burned up the sheep and the servants and consumed them, and I alone have escaped to tell you." While he was yet speaking, there came another and said, "The Chaldeans formed three groups and made a raid on the camels and took them and struck down the servants with the edge of the sword, and I alone have escaped to tell you." While he was yet speaking, there came another and said, "Your sons and daughters were eating and drinking wine in their oldest brother's house, and behold, a great wind came across the wilderness and struck the four corners of the house, and it fell upon the young people, and they are dead, and I alone have escaped to tell you."
>
> Then Job arose and tore his robe and shaved his head and fell on the ground and worshiped. And he said, "Naked I came from my mother's

womb, and naked shall I return. The Lord gave, and the Lord has taken away; blessed be the name of the Lord."

In all this Job did not sin or charge God with wrong. (Job 1:13–22)

Some of these disasters seem to be random. For one thing, how come they all happened on the same day? That in itself seems unlikely, because they are not causally connected to one another. One of the disasters was that "the fire of God fell from heaven" (Job 1:16). When and where it would fall was totally unpredictable. Why did it fall when it did on Job's sheep and servants, and not elsewhere? How was it that "a great wind" came (v. 19), and why did it hit the house and not elsewhere, and why did it hit at the moment when Job's sons and daughters were inside the house?

Job was faced with a series of seemingly random events. He was emotionally devastated by the losses. But how did he deal with the question of *why*? Did he think, "Well, things just happen by chance because the world has chance in it"? No, he saw the hand of God: "The Lord gave, and the Lord has taken away" (1:21).

A consistent deist would have to say, "It was all part of the clockwork." Deism might lead to the conclusion that God created the world with both order and randomness. According to deistic thinking, the randomness just has to be accepted. God is not responsible for disasters, because he has walked away from the clock that he made. Other people might still want God to be responsible for the good things and the blessings that come to us. But they cannot stomach the idea that he was responsible for a disaster like Job's. They would say that they want to protect the goodness of God.

Yes, the Bible does teach that God is good and does good (Ps. 86:5; 100:5; 107:1; 119:68). But it flatly contradicts those who want to "protect" him by removing his control over disasters. Job made it clear that he thought God was in control: "The Lord gave, and the Lord has taken away" (Job 1:21). Was Job wrong? From the surrounding narrative in Job 1 we learn that Satan engineered the disasters:

And the Lord said to Satan, "Behold, all that he has is in your hand. Only against him do not stretch out your hand." (Job 1:12)

But Satan did not act without God's permission (see Job 1:10–11). We see *three* distinct causes: God, Satan, and human raiders (vv. 15, 17), all acting within the same events. The plans of Satan do not negate the sovereignty of God.

As we have observed, Job's reaction includes a strong affirmation of the sovereignty of God: "The LORD gave, and the LORD has taken away" (v. 21). It also includes an affirmation of God's goodness: "blessed be the name of the LORD" (v. 21). At this early point in Job's experience, he did not understand the reasons why God had brought the disasters, but he was still willing to affirm God's goodness and to bless his name. God approves: "In all this Job did not sin or charge God with wrong" (v. 22).

Some people would like to "correct" Job if they could. They think Job was wrong to imagine that God brought the disasters. But the Bible clearly indicates that Job is right and they are wrong. The Bible says, "Job did not sin" (v. 22).

Later in the book of Job, we see Job struggling with the mysteries. Why was God doing what he was doing? His three "friends" Eliphaz, Bildad, and Zophar wanted to help. Eliphaz, Bildad, and Zophar wrongly supposed that the disasters must be a consequence of some particular sin or sins that Job had committed. The dialogue goes back and forth between them and Job. At the end of the book, God indicates that the friends were mistaken in their inference about sin. But the friends share with Job a common conviction—that God was behind what happened to Job. No one—none of the three friends, not Elihu, not Job himself—considers the possibility that bad things "just happen" and that God does not control them. Everyone assumes that God is thoroughly in control, even over events of a disastrous and inexplicable kind.

This common conviction among the participants is *never* challenged throughout the book. Rather, it is confirmed by God himself, when he appears to Job and overwhelms Job by a recital of the power and wisdom of his works:

> Where were you when I laid the foundation of the earth?
>   Tell me, if you have understanding. (Job 38:4)

> Have you an arm like God,
>   and can you thunder with a voice like his? (40:9)

Job's reaction affirms the greatness of God's sovereignty:

> I know that you can do all things,
>   and that no purpose of yours can be thwarted. (42:2)

Job's new depth of conviction about God's sovereignty actually gives Job support. Even though Job still does not know the reasons why God brought disasters on him, he has a certain peace, based on trust in God. God knows. God plans wisely. Even when Job does not know, he can trust. The same principle applies to each of us. When we do not know why, we are still called upon to trust God. This view of disasters is not only biblical and true, but spiritually healthy.

The book of Job as a whole contains more dimensions than those of which Job was aware. Job 1–2 introduces God in heaven, and Satan appears before him. Satan accuses Job of serving God only because of the benefits that God gives him. We as readers can understand one reason why God permits Satan to bring disasters. By reading the whole book, we can also see that God's intentions are wholly good, while Satan's intentions are wholly evil. God intends to vindicate his name. He also intends to vindicate Job's integrity, because Job's perseverance shows that he does not serve God merely because of a payoff in prosperity. Finally, God causes Job to grow spiritually through the painful experiences that he goes through.

Satan intends the opposite. He intends to destroy Job's faith and bring him to spiritual disgrace, as well as to undermine God's glory reflected in Job's life. Both sets of intentions—God's and Satan's—come to expression in the very same events, the disasters that befall Job. Thus the book of Job can help us to see that the goodness of God is consistent with his control over disasters.

The book of Job provides extra insight by giving us special access to the discussion with Satan that took place in God's presence. But we also know that in most cases we are in a position like Job's rather than like that of the angels. Most of the time God does not give us any access to angelic discussions. Most of the time we do not hear directly the divine reasoning that lies behind particular events in this world. The book of Job underscores the extraordinary character of the information that it provides in Job 1–2. By doing so, it indirectly implies that when we do not have such information—which is almost all the time—we should not presumptuously claim to know all the reasons why God is doing what he is doing. Job reaches a similar conclusion. When God's confrontation with Job at the end of the book (Job 38–41) reminds Job of how puny his power and knowledge are, he confesses his own limitations:

> Then Job answered the LORD and said:

> "I know that you can do all things,
> and that no purpose of yours can be thwarted.
> 'Who is this that hides counsel without knowledge?'
> Therefore I have uttered what I did not understand,
>   things too wonderful for me, which I did not know.
> 'Hear, and I will speak;
>   I will question you, and you make it known to me.'
> I had heard of you by the hearing of the ear,
>   but now my eye sees you;
> therefore I despise myself,
>   and repent in dust and ashes" (Job 42:1–6)

Like Job, we should move in the same direction. We should take to heart what God tells Job in Job 38–41, and also what Job 1–2 tells us about our limited power and knowledge. Like Job, we should admit that we do not know enough to see why God is doing what he is doing.

We will still have to suffer. We may still go through Job-like experiences, in which God's plan seems inexplicable. Worse, it may seem to limited human judgment as if God is acting cruelly or spitefully or unjustly. The book of Job comes to aid us in such circumstances, by reminding us of our limitations as well as God's greatness.

THE SUFFERING OF CHRIST AND OUR SUFFERING

We should not leave behind the case of Job without reckoning with its forward connection to Christ. The book of Job does not by itself give the fullest answers about suffering and disaster. It looks forward to a future time of salvation (Job 19:25–27).

We should observe that, though Job was not sinlessly perfect, he was fundamentally in the right, while his friends were in the wrong. That is, his friends wrongly claimed that Job must be suffering because he had committed some particular grievous sins of which he should repent. Job rightly claimed that their accusation was not true. Job was not suffering because of particular sins that he had committed. Rather, he was a righteous sufferer. As such, his suffering points forward to Christ. Why did Christ suffer? In Christ's suffering we see the climax of human suffering, and it has a purpose. Christ suffered and died *for sinners, to redeem us*:

> For to this you have been called, because Christ also *suffered for you*, leaving you an example, so that you might follow in his steps. He committed no sin, neither was deceit found in his mouth. When he was reviled, he did not revile in return; when he suffered, he did not threaten, but continued entrusting himself to him who judges justly. He himself *bore our sins* in his body on the tree, that we might die to sin and live to righteousness. By his wounds you have been healed. (1 Pet. 2:21–24)

Christ's suffering was unique, because he died for our sins. But it is also an encouragement for us when we have to suffer. As we see the purpose in Christ's suffering, it gives us greater confidence that God has purposes for our own suffering, even when we cannot see how. Christians "may share his [Christ's] sufferings, becoming like him in his death" (Phil. 3:10), and our sufferings may become an occasion to understand and appreciate more deeply how much Christ suffered for us.

Moreover, God knows our suffering. Christ is able to sympathize with us in our suffering and distress, because he suffered:

> For we do not have a high priest who is unable to sympathize with our weaknesses, but one who in every respect has been tempted as we are, yet without sin. Let us then with confidence draw near to the throne of grace, that we may receive mercy and find grace to help in time of need. (Heb. 4:15–16)

For these reasons, we need not hesitate to believe that God is in control even when suffering comes to us. We can praise God for his wisdom and goodness and compassion, even when we do not understand the reasons for individual cases of suffering.

PURPOSES FOR SUFFERING

Though many times we do not know why suffering comes into people's lives, God does give us passages in Scripture that indicate positive purposes for some instances of suffering. These passages can aid us by reminding us that God can bring good out of suffering.

First, suffering can be used by God to produce godly character:

> Not only that, but we rejoice in our sufferings, knowing that suffering produces *endurance*, and endurance produces *character*, and character produces hope, and hope does not put us to shame, because God's love has been poured into our hearts through the Holy Spirit who has been given to us. (Rom. 5:3–5)

> Count it all joy, my brothers, when you meet trials of various kinds, for you know that the testing of your faith *produces steadfastness*. And let steadfastness have its full effect, that you may be perfect and complete, lacking in nothing. (James 1:2–4; see 1 Pet. 4:1)

Second, suffering can increase our respect for God's word:

> Before I was afflicted I went astray,
>   but now I keep your word. (Ps. 119:67)

> It is good for me that I was afflicted,
>   that I might learn your statutes. (v. 71)

> I know, O LORD, that your rules are righteous,
>   and that in faithfulness you have afflicted me. (v. 75)

Third, suffering can bring glory to God by showing the quality of our faith:

> In this you rejoice, though now for a little while, if necessary, you have been grieved by various trials, so that the tested genuineness of your faith—more precious than gold that perishes though it is tested by fire—may be found to result in *praise and glory and honor* at the revelation of Jesus Christ. (1 Pet. 1:6–7; see 4:12–16)

Fourth, as we indicated, suffering gives us a fellowship in Christ's sufferings, and helps us to appreciate more deeply how he suffered for us (Phil. 3:10; 1 Pet. 2:19–24).

OTHER PASSAGES

The general principle about God's control over disasters comes to expression in other passages:

> I form light and create darkness,
>> I make well-being and *create calamity*,
>> I am the LORD, who does all these things. (Isa. 45:7)

> Is it not from the mouth of the Most High
>> that good and *bad* come? (Lam. 3:38)

> Does *disaster* come to a city,
>> unless the LORD has done it? (Amos 3:6)

In addition, we could multiply instances where the Lord brings specific judgments on people in the form of disaster and death.

> But if you will not obey the voice of the LORD your God or be careful to do all his commandments and his statutes that I command you today, then *all these curses* shall come upon you and overtake you. (Deut. 28:15)

> "Behold, I will remove you from the face of the earth. This year *you shall die*, because you have uttered rebellion against the LORD."
> In that same year, in the seventh month, the prophet Hananiah died. (Jer. 28:16–17)

We conclude that God is in control of suffering, disaster, and death. Sometimes, as in the examples just given, God brings disasters as a judgment on sin. But at other times, as with the suffering of Job and the suffering of Christ, suffering is *not* a judgment on personal sins. Christ bore the judgment for the sins of *others*; he did not sin himself:

> He committed no sin, neither was deceit found in his mouth. (1 Pet. 2:22)

> He himself bore our sins in his body on the tree, that we might die to sin and live to righteousness. By his wounds you have been healed. (v. 24)

AN INITIALLY GOOD CREATION

One other principle helps us in confronting suffering and death. The Bible indicates that when God created the world, it was "very good" (Gen. 1:31). The world that exists today is no longer very good. The entrance of sin has brought about disasters. Present-day disasters are a loud reminder that all is not well with the world. They remind us that the world is no longer what it once was. They remind us of the need for redemption. They also remind us to hope for a future world, the new heaven and the new earth (Rev. 21:1), in which suffering, disaster, and death are completely overcome by God:

> He [God] will wipe away every tear from their eyes, and death shall be no more, neither shall there be mourning, nor crying, nor pain anymore, for the former things have passed away. (Rev. 21:4)

Thus, even the dark events in this world can be used by God to teach us. We can respond by turning to God's promises, and increasing our longing for the new heavens and the new earth, which God will create. We can glorify God in our suffering.

Some disasters, like Cain's murder of his brother Abel, are the direct result of sin. Abel died because sin infected Cain's heart and then Cain's envious and murderous heart led to murderous action. He killed his brother (Gen. 4:5–8). Other kinds of suffering are not the direct result of sin in any way that we can easily see. But the Bible indicates that sin has *indirect* effects. For example, Genesis 3 indicates that after Adam's first sin, thorns and thistles grew up, and man's labor became difficult and sweaty:

> *Because* you [Adam] have listened to the voice of your wife
>   and have eaten of the tree
> of which I commanded you,
>   "You shall not eat of it,"
> *cursed* is the ground because of you;
>   *in pain* you shall eat of it all the days of your life;
> *thorns and thistles* it shall bring forth for you;
>   and you shall eat the plants of the field.
> By the *sweat* of your face
>   you shall eat bread,
> till you return to the ground,
>   for out of it you were taken; . . . (Gen. 3:17–19)

Some people think that the thorns and thistles refer to new kinds of plants that God created after the fall, with the express purpose of making man's life difficult. But that interpretation seems unlikely, in view of the fact that God's work of creating different types of plants was completed during the six days of creation in Genesis 1. It is more likely that the verse means that vegetation types that already existed outside the Garden of Eden would no longer cooperate with man but would appear at times and places that would frustrate his work. A weed is simply any plant that is out of place from the standpoint of human purposes. Weeds will continue to be with us in this life, because the fall into sin has had indirect effects on the relationship of mankind to the plant kingdom. The principle applies not only to weeds but more broadly to all kinds of events that result in disaster and frustrate human life and human purposes. Disasters testify that the world is affected by sin.

Disasters also remind us that a final judgment is coming. Jesus shows us this principle when he comments on disasters that took place during his time on earth:

> There were some present at that very time who told him [Jesus] about the Galileans whose blood Pilate had mingled with their sacrifices. And he answered them, "Do you think that these Galileans were worse sinners than all the other Galileans, because they suffered in this way? No, I tell you; but unless you repent, you will all likewise perish. Or those eighteen on whom the tower in Siloam fell and killed them: do you think that they were worse offenders than all the others who lived in Jerusalem? No, I tell you; but unless you repent, you will all likewise perish." (Luke 13:1–5)

Thus, among other things, disasters can remind us that the final judgment of God is coming, and that we should repent before it is too late.

We would rather live in a world where everything gave us comfort. But we do not. This world is not always pleasant. We do not know all the reasons that God has behind the suffering and disasters that he controls. But we can at least discern that there are sometimes some reasons. (1) Disaster can remind us that this world has been infected by sin and its consequences (Rom. 8:20–22). (2) Disasters that directly result from sin remind us of the terrible character of sin and can teach us to take more seriously the importance of avoiding sin ourselves (Rom. 6:23). (3) Disasters warn us of the coming of God's final judgment (Luke 13:1–5). (4) For Christians, suffering can increase our appreciation for what Christ suffered for us. We suffer *in fellowship with* Christ (Phil. 3:10). (5) Suffering can remind us of the importance of Christ's compassion for us, because he himself suffered (Heb. 4:15; 5:7). He compassionately understands our suffering. (6) Sufferings can be used by God to sanctify our character

(Rom. 5:3–5; James 1:2–4). (7) Sufferings can refine our faith and give glory to God (1 Pet. 1:6–7).

Though the Bible enables us to understand some of God's purposes for some of our sufferings, much remains mysterious. When we confront the mysteries in suffering, we need to trust that God is good even though we cannot see how, because he has proved himself trustworthy in key situations that he describes in Scripture—above all, the situation of the crucifixion of Christ. The Bible calls us to exercise such trust, even when we are in the midst of trials.

In sum, a number of biblical teachings fit together to instruct us about disasters, including disasters that may come to us or to those around us. (1) The Bible affirms as a general principle that God controls disasters. (2) The Bible illustrates the principle with many individual cases, like the case of Joseph and his brothers. (3) The supreme case where God brings good out of evil is found in the crucifixion of Christ, where the Bible clearly affirms God's control. (4) The Bible indicates that we should apply its lessons about disasters to ourselves and our circumstances. (See fig. 4.1.)

Fig. 4.1: God's Control over Disasters

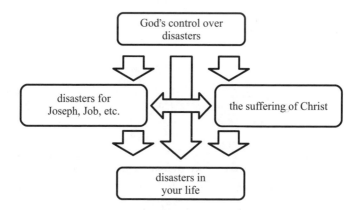

ALTERNATIVES ARE NOT REALLY BETTER

Let us now consider the alternatives. The main alternative is to say that God is not thoroughly in control. It says that some disasters "just happen," apart from God's control. This alternative is superficially attractive, because it appears to protect the goodness of God. It relieves God of responsibility for anything unpleasant that happens to us. But further reflection shows that it is not satisfying—in fact, it is spiritually devastating.

Consider a particular disaster—an auto accident that causes serious injury or death, or a tsunami that causes widespread death and destruction. If God is in control of it, we have to wrestle with a major difficulty, because it is hard to see how a good God could bring such suffering. But we also have a consolation such as the Bible provides, namely, that God is able to bring good out of evil. He brought good out of evil when Joseph's brothers sold Joseph into slavery (Gen. 50:20). He brought good out of evil above all in the crucifixion of Christ, which brought us salvation. We usually cannot see how God can bring good out of present-day evils, but we can have hope if we trust in the wisdom of God and his power, based on what he has demonstrated in cases such as Joseph and the crucifixion of Christ.

On the other hand, what if we say that God is not in control of the disaster? God might still do something good in response. But the disaster itself is still out of control, and inherently unredeemable. There is no comfort to be had for it. We are left with fear for the future. Thus, even in practice, removing disasters from God's control does not actually help at the deepest level.

It is better to follow what God says in Scripture, even if we ourselves do not understand the meaning of events. In the Bible God says,

> Trust in the LORD with all your heart,
>   and do not lean on your own understanding.
> In all your ways acknowledge him,
>   and he will make straight your paths. (Prov. 3:5–6)

PRACTICAL CONSOLATION

We have focused on what the Bible teaches about suffering and disasters, and in particular whether God controls disasters. But much more could be said. Sufferings impinge on people in practical ways, and the Bible gives direction and consolation to people who are in the middle of suffering. Practical books on grief and suffering can help those who are in the midst of it. I recommend J. I. Packer's *A Grief Sanctified*,[1] which includes the entire text of the Puritan writer Richard Baxter's memoir of his wife's life and death.

---

[1] J. I. Packer, *A Grief Sanctified: Through Sorrow to Eternal Hope* (Wheaton, IL: Crossway, 2002).

CHAPTER 5

HUMAN CHOICE

Some happenstance events involve no human agency. For example, in the book of Job, the "fire of God" burned up Job's sheep and servants (Job 1:16); a "great wind" struck the house where Job's children were (v. 19). But other events do involve human agents. The Sabeans fell upon Job's oxen and donkeys, and the Chaldeans raided Job's camels (vv. 15, 17). The Sabeans and the Chaldeans made these raids at just the time when the other disasters were happening to Job.

HUMAN AGENTS

What do we say about these events? Is God still in control? How does God's control mesh with human agency?

Rebekah decided to go out to the well at a particular time, when Abraham's servant happened to be there. Likewise Rachel decided to go out to the well when Jacob was coming. Ruth decided to go out to the field, the field that Boaz owned.

In the battle at Ramoth-gilead, a certain soldier drew his bow and shot at random; then his arrow hit Ahab in the crack between pieces of his armor.

Likewise, the story of Joseph, the son of Jacob, mentions events involving human agents. Pharaoh got angry with his chief cupbearer and his chief baker and decided to put them in custody (Gen. 40:2–3). Another agent, the keeper of the prison, put Joseph in charge (39:22–23). He then appointed Joseph to take care of the cupbearer and the baker (40:4). There was nothing remarkable about any of these actions, taken by themselves. But the whole series of actions worked together to put Joseph in the right place at the right time. Joseph then became the crucial human agent whom

God used to save his people, the family of Jacob, as well as the Egyptians, from the coming famine.

In these cases and many others, human agents were acting in normal ways, and their actions contributed to the eventual outcome. The outcome *happened* to advance the purposes of God. But we can imagine how the events could have turned out very differently. What if Rebekah had not come to the well? What if the soldier at Ramoth-gilead had shot in another direction or at another time? What if the Sabeans and the Chaldeans had decided to relax that day, or to conduct raids in a different direction? What if Pharaoh had decided just to send away the cupbearer and the baker, rather than imprison them? What if, what if?

GOD'S SOVEREIGNTY OVER HUMAN CHOICE

What should we think about cases that involve human choice? Is God in charge? Is he in control? And if he is in control, is he in control merely in some kind of vague, broad way, a way that actually leaves out of his control various specific human choices, in order to create space for free human action? On the other hand, if he controls specific human choices, does his control abolish human responsibility?

These are important questions. A full exploration of the questions could easily take up a whole book. We must direct readers elsewhere for a full discussion.[1] Here we will give only a summary.

God's ways are higher than our ways (Isa. 55:8–9). We cannot expect to receive an exhaustive answer to the profound questions about human choice. God knows fully. But for us there remains mystery.

Nevertheless, Scripture has not left us in the dark about the basic issues. In the course of working out history, God uses human choice for his own purposes. The choices are genuine. At the same time, the result comes out exactly as God planned it. God controls human choices, without dissolving the reality of those choices. The choices are real choices by real human beings. The examples given above fit into this pattern. And there are many others. Joseph says,

> As for you [his brothers], you meant evil against me, but *God meant it for good*, to bring it about that many people should be kept alive, as they are today. (Gen. 50:20)

---

[1] See John M. Frame, *The Doctrine of the Word of God* (Phillipsburg, NJ: Presbyterian & Reformed, 2010), 119–159.

Joseph affirms the genuine responsibility of his brothers, when they sold him. "You meant evil against me." The actions were real, and the intention—in this case, a sinful intention—was real. The brothers chose to sell him when they had other alternatives. They were responsible for their choice, and they rightly felt guilty when the close questioning and harsh-looking treatment by the governor of Egypt brought their guilt to mind:

> Then they said to one another, "In truth we are *guilty* concerning our brother, in that we saw the distress of his soul, when he begged us and we did not listen. That is why this distress has come upon us." (Gen. 42:21)

At the same time, Joseph affirms the reality of God's control. God exercised his control in the *very same events* where the brothers were sinning and making their crucial choices: "God meant it [these events] for good."

The supreme case of God's control over human choices took place with the crucifixion of Christ. Note how the Bible describes the relation of human choice to God's control:

> This Jesus, delivered up according to the *definite plan* and foreknowledge of God, you crucified and killed by the hands of *lawless* men. (Acts 2:23)

The expression "definite plan" (as well as "foreknowledge") shows that God controlled the events. Far from being simply one more death of a common criminal, the crucifixion of Christ took place in order that God might accomplish his climactic act of salvation through it. At the same time, the expression "lawless men" indicates the sin and responsibility that belong to Pontius Pilate, Herod, and the Jewish leaders who brought about the crucifixion on a human level. The text clearly affirms the sovereignty of God over the events and at the same time the normal human responsibility for human actions. Both are true.

Moreover, both sides *need* to be true in order for the crucifixion of Christ to have the meaning that it actually does have according to biblical teaching. On the one hand, we have God, not man, to thank for our salvation. We have to say that God was in control of these events. At the same time, it is theologically important that Christ was innocent and that the crucifixion was unjust. His innocence was necessary in order that he could bear the punishment for our sins. He had no sin (2 Cor. 5:21; 1 Pet. 2:22). Pilate and the leaders were *guilty* for what they did.

Can any Christian bring himself to say, "Since human beings were involved, God did not control the outcome. So I really cannot thank God for what happened and for my salvation. I have to thank men." It is clear that we are supposed to thank God. God does claim to control the events—these events above all. The situation is parallel to the case with Joseph in Genesis 50. In a manner parallel to Genesis 50, we can say, "Pontius Pilate and the Jewish leaders meant it for evil, but God meant it for good." The goodness of God is not compromised in any way, since we can see that his intentions were good, even in the midst of horrible human sins that led to the crucifixion.

Acts 4:24–28 is similar. After quoting from Psalm 2, Acts applies it to the crucifixion, showing that the crucifixion is a fulfillment of God's plan as articulated long beforehand in Psalm 2:

> "Why did the Gentiles rage,
>   and the peoples plot in vain?
> The kings of the earth set themselves,
>   and the rulers were gathered together,
>   against the Lord and against his Anointed"—
>
> for truly in this city there were gathered together against your holy servant Jesus, whom you anointed, both Herod and Pontius Pilate, along with the Gentiles and the peoples of Israel, to do whatever *your hand and your plan had predestined to take place.* (Acts 4:25–28)

The final expression, "your hand and your plan had predestined to take place," makes plain the complete control of God, both during the events and beforehand (his plan). God accomplished his plan through the sinful rebellion "against the Lord and against his Anointed" in which "the Gentiles and the peoples of Israel" engaged. God used human sin to accomplish salvation: ". . . you meant evil . . . , but God meant it for good."

Scripture contains other, more minor instances of the same principle. God used Assyria as a "rod" to punish Israel, but afterward judged Assyria for its sinful attitude (Isa. 10:5–7, 12). He raised up Pharaoh to resist him, in order to exhibit his power (Ex. 9:16; Rom. 9:17). God fulfilled his prophecy against David's wives (2 Sam. 12:11–12) when Absalom sinfully went into the tent with them on the rooftop (16:22). Note God's strong assertion of his sovereignty in this event:

> Thus says the LORD, "Behold, *I will raise up evil* against you out of your own house. And *I will take* your wives before your eyes and *give them* to your neighbor, and he shall lie with your wives in the sight of this sun. For you did it secretly, but *I will do this thing* before all Israel and before the sun." (2 Sam. 12:11–12)

How can we understand how God's sovereignty is compatible with human responsibility? Theologians use the term *concursus*, which in Latin means "running together." God's action and human action run along together. God's action and God's control happen in addition to and alongside human action and influence. We have abundant examples in the Bible of such divine action. But it remains mysterious to us exactly *how* God's action relates to human action in such a way that God is fully in control and human agents are at the same time fully responsible.

John Frame uses the analogy of a human author who creates fictional characters.[2] God's governance of human action is like an author's governance over the characters in his story. God and the human author are completely in control, but it is also true that the human actors in God's history and in an author's story make decisions that lead to consequences. (See fig. 5.1.)

Fig. 5.1: Analogy of Human Author

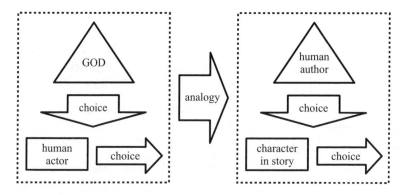

---

[2] Ibid., 156–159.

This analogy stems from the fact that God made human beings in his image. God's power to write the "story" of world history is analogous to a human being's power to write a story with human characters in it. The analogy goes back to the fact that God creates and governs the world by *speaking* (chapter 2). Because a human author is made in the image of God, he can control the fictional "world" of his characters by writing, which is a form of speaking.

THE ORIGIN OF CREATIVITY

We may consider the reality of God's speech more deeply. God's speech has a trinitarian character. John 1:1 calls the second person of the Trinity "the Word." God the Father is the speaker, and God the Son is the speech. In addition, the Holy Spirit is like the breath of God, carrying the speech to its destination and giving it powerful effect (note the representation of the Spirit as breath in Ezek. 37:10, 14).[3]

These personal relationships within the Trinity are the original pattern, which forms the basis for God's speech governing the world. John 1:1 invites us to see a relationship of God to the creation of the world, because the phrase "in the beginning" alludes to Genesis 1. So does the language about creation in the next verses, John 1:2–4. In Genesis 1 God creates the world by speaking. For instance, he creates light by saying, "Let there be light" (Gen. 1:3). These particular speeches of God have their ultimate roots in the eternal speaking where God the Father speaks his Word, which is God the Son.

This trinitarian communication is the expression of the character of God the Father. It is always consistent with his character. At the same time, God the Father expresses something distinct from himself, namely his Word, who is God the Son.

The original trinitarian reality within God is analogically expressed when God creates the world. His acts of creation conform to his character—they express his goodness, wisdom, truth, and power. That is, they display the character of God the Father. At the same time, they bring forth something new. (God has a plan from before the foundation of the world, but the execution of his plan takes place at particular times.) The words of

[3] Vern S. Poythress, *Redeeming Science: A God-Centered Approach* (Wheaton, IL: Crossway, 2006), 24–26.

command, such as "Let there be light," are new words. And they produce something new in the world—in this case, they produce light. This new product reflects the creativity of God's word, which has its foundation in the original creativity of God the Son. In addition, the Holy Spirit is present when God creates the world (Gen. 1:2). By the Spirit's presence and power, the light that comes into being conforms to God's word that calls it into existence. The creation reflects the power and control of the Holy Spirit.

We have associated the character of God especially with God the Father, who is the original speaker. We have associated creativity with the Son, and control with the Holy Spirit. But all these characteristics also belong ultimately to all three persons of the Trinity. The persons of the Trinity are in harmony with one another. God's work of creation is the work of all three persons, who have goodness and creativity and control.

Now we may consider the incarnation. When Jesus Christ became man, he continued to be fully God. He was both God and man, in one person (John 1:14). On earth, he acted in harmony with the will of his Father. As the eternal Word become flesh, he acted in harmony with his Father's character and will:

I always do the things that are pleasing to him. (John 8:29)

For I have not spoken on my own authority, but the Father who sent me has himself given me a commandment—what to say and what to speak. (John 12:49)

He did not act independently, but in subjection to the Father's commandment. At the same time, he acted with the full creativity of God. He did "the works that no one else did" (John 15:24). He acted with divine power, in communion with the power of the Holy Spirit (Luke 4:18).

Jesus in his human nature is the model for what we are to become, as we are transformed into his image (2 Cor. 3:18). "Freedom" comes in personal communion with the Spirit: "and where the Spirit of the Lord is, there is freedom" (v. 17). In communion with Christ, we find satisfaction, goodness, wisdom, and creativity, because we are in communion with the goodness, wisdom, and creativity of God the Father, God the Son, and God the Holy Spirit.

In short, we can understand human creativity—and thus also the reality of human choices—by using analogy. We begin with the divine character and creativity and control in the Trinity. Then we have the expression of creativity in God's acts of creation. Then we have expression of creativity in the incarnate Son, with respect to both his divine nature and his human nature. And then we have expression of creativity in our own human nature. Our choices are free and responsible precisely because they take place in communion with God through Christ, who is the source of all creativity. (See fig. 5.2.) The alternative is slavery to sin (John 8:34–36).[4]

Whatever analogy we use, it does not dissolve mystery. God is God, and his relation to his creation is unique. We cannot understand him fully without being God. We must be content to *believe* what Scripture teaches, even though we do not *master* God or his teaching. We believe that God sovereignly controls events. We believe also that God gives to human beings genuine choices and that he holds them responsible for their choices. We believe both of these clear teachings of Scripture without being able to see for ourselves exactly how his control is compatible with human responsibility and genuine human choice.

This mystery should stimulate our praise. We praise God and honor him by confessing how great he is, and that "his greatness is unsearchable" (Ps. 145:3).

---

[4] See further Vern S. Poythress, *Redeeming Sociology: A God-Centered Approach* (Wheaton, IL: Crossway, 2009), 51–56; Vern S. Poythress, *In the Beginning Was the Word: Language—A God-Centered Approach* (Wheaton, IL: Crossway, 2006), 42–49, and appendix J.

Even human beings enslaved to sin do not escape God's presence (Acts 17:28). We can see a striking illustration with Caiaphas, whom God used to utter a prophecy, in spite of the wickedness of his heart (John 11:49–53). Caiaphas's speech was empowered and made creative by the work of God.

Fig. 5.2: Analogy for Creativity

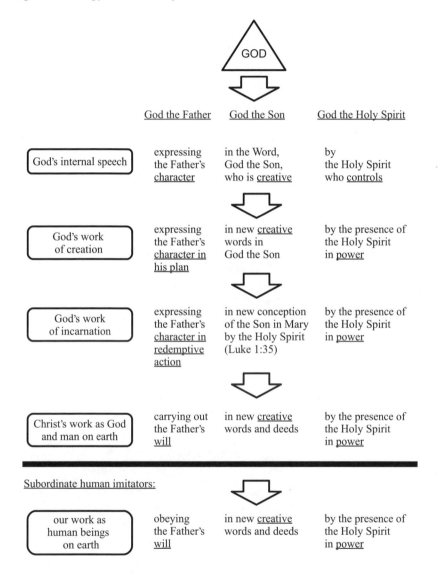

CHAPTER 6

SMALL RANDOM EVENTS

We have studied God's comprehensive control over events of historical significance. But what about minor events? What about small things, so small that we seldom pay attention to them? Should we imagine that God is too great to be involved, that small things are somehow "beneath his dignity"?

BIBLICAL PASSAGES ABOUT DETAILS

We cannot presume just to postulate beforehand how God will interact with details. We need to look at what the Bible says, rather than just presuming to imagine on our own what sort of thing God will or will not do. So what does the Bible say? The Bible makes it clear by any number of cases that God involves himself in details:

> Are not two sparrows sold for a penny? And not one of them *will fall* to the ground *apart from your Father.* (Matt. 10:29)

> But even the *hairs* of your head are all numbered. (Matt. 10:30)

> . . . to bring rain on a land where no man is,
>   on the desert in which there is no man,
> to satisfy the waste and desolate land,
>   and to make the ground *sprout with grass*? (Job 38:26–27)

> Lift up your eyes on high and see:
>   who created these?
> He who brings out their host by number,
>   *calling them all by name,*

by the greatness of his might,
> and because he is strong in power
> *not one is missing.* (Isa. 40:26)

In the verses following Isaiah 40:26, Isaiah uses God's power over each one of the stars, individually, as an argument for his involvement with Israel:

> Why do you say, O Jacob,
>> and speak, O Israel,
> "My way is hidden from the Lord,
>> and my right is disregarded by my God"?
> Have you not known? Have you not heard?
> The Lord is the everlasting God,
>> the Creator of the ends of the earth.
> He does not faint or grow weary;
>> his understanding is unsearchable. (vv. 27–28)

God's involvement in details has a practical bearing. If we deny his involvement, it undermines the practical affirmation that he is involved intimately with his people. Both affirmations are based on the infinitude of his power and "his understanding" (v. 28).

Jesus makes a similar point in the Sermon on the Mount:

> Therefore I tell you, do not be anxious about your life, what you will eat or what you will drink, nor about your body, what you will put on. Is not life more than food, and the body more than clothing? Look at the birds of the air: they neither sow nor reap nor gather into barns, and yet your heavenly Father *feeds them.* Are you not of more value than they? And which of you by being anxious can add a single hour to his span of life? And why are you anxious about clothing? Consider the lilies of the field, how they grow: they neither toil nor spin, yet I tell you, even Solomon in all his glory was not arrayed like one of these. But if God so *clothes the grass of the field*, which today is alive and tomorrow is thrown into the oven, will he not much more clothe you, O you of little faith? Therefore do not be anxious, saying, "What shall we eat?" or "What shall we drink?" or "What shall we wear?" For the Gentiles seek after all these things, and your heavenly Father knows that you need them all. But seek first the kingdom of God and his righteousness, and all these things will be added to you.

Therefore do not be anxious about tomorrow, for tomorrow will be anxious for itself. Sufficient for the day is its own trouble. (Matt. 6:25–34)

Jesus appeals to detailed works of God: "your heavenly Father feeds them [the birds]"; "God so clothes the grass . . ." How much more, he says, will God care for your needs, even the most prosaic needs: "all these things will be added to you." Jesus tells us to be free from anxiety. Why? Because God not only controls these details, but does so as a heavenly Father who cares for his children. Practical living in faith without anxiety depends on the fact of God's control, a control that extends not merely to broad generalities of the universe but to details in providing for each bird, each lily, each human child.

We may also observe that, at a practical level, details can have big effects. The Bible gives us a "detail" about where a soldier aimed his arrow and where his arrow traveled in the battle at Ramoth-gilead. The "detail" resulted in the death of Ahab, the king of Israel, and so affected the course of an entire kingdom. The "detail" of Pharaoh sending his cupbearer and baker to prison eventually affected the survival of both Egypt and the surrounding nations during the years of famine. We cannot neatly cordon off so-called "details" and claim that they do not make a difference.

So much can depend on a detail. That is precisely why people want to pry into the future and go to fortune-tellers. God forbids fortune-telling and calls on us instead to trust in him (Deut. 18:14, 15–22). This exhortation does not have its proper force unless God controls the details for which people think they need to consult fortune-tellers.

A CLASSIC RANDOM EVENT

Consider now a classic case of a random event: the roll of dice. When we roll dice, no one can predict what numbers will come up. The result is a matter of pure "chance." Here is what the Bible says:

> *The lot* is cast into the lap,
>   but its *every* decision is *from the* LORD. (Prov. 16:33)

The expression "the lot" designates some kind of random event. It covers a range of possible means. People can roll dice, or flip a coin, or spin a top, or spin a dial with markings on it. Or they may throw down sticks and observe whether they form a pattern of some kind. The fact that the lot "is cast into the lap" suggests in this case something more like dice. Whatever the means used, "its every decision is from the LORD." "Every decision," it says, not just some. Every time the dice come up, they come up as the Lord directs. The Lord controls the outcome of this random event.

A skeptic might still claim that Proverbs 16:33 covers only a few "special" events. The proverb envisions primarily a situation where people cast a lot in order to make a decision based on the outcome of the lot. They might have an important religious or political decision to make.

In Joshua 7:14 we see a significant incident where lots are used. Someone in Israel has taken things out of Jericho that were "devoted" to God, which God had claimed for himself and told the people not to take. Joshua then uses lots to find out which tribe and which member of the tribe has done the deed. The outcome of the lots does take place under the Lord's control, because they find out that Achan is the culprit (Josh. 7:18).

In more pleasant circumstances, in 1 Samuel 10:20–21, the casting of lots singles out Saul the son of Kish as the new king of Israel. A lot also singles out Jonah as the person responsible for the storm at sea (Jonah 1:7). A lot is used by the apostles in Acts 1 to determine whether Joseph called Barsabbas or Matthias should be appointed as an additional apostle, to fill the place left empty by the death Judas Iscariot (Acts 1:23–26). The successor to Judas must be the one whom the Lord has appointed, and the will of the Lord comes to expression when the apostles cast lots. "The lot fell on Matthias, and he was numbered with the eleven apostles" (v. 26). The apostles clearly understand that the outcome for this casting of lots is controlled by the Lord.

We can see a similar kind of thing in modern times when a group of people draw straws or flip a coin to see who goes first. Sometimes the result may be humanly important, if they are risking their lives in a dangerous mission. Sometimes the result may be of small importance, if they are just determining which person plays first in a game.

So, the skeptic wonders, does God's control over dice or lots take place *only* when some weighty decision is needed? Or, even more narrowly, does his control apply *only* to intense *religious* situations in Israel, such as selecting Achan or Saul or Matthias? Or does God's control extend to other instances?

The verse in Proverbs 16:33 does not have any qualification. It does not say, "When an important decision has to be made, the decision is from the Lord." The formulation is a general one: "the lot is cast into the lap." The natural meaning is, "any lot whatsoever." It includes the lot cast by the pagan sailors on Jonah's ship. "Every decision," not merely a decision once in a while, is "from the Lord." It is true that the proverb *focuses* on lots that have some significance, because such lots are the ones in which people are most interested, and where it is most important that they understand the Lord's control. But the principle is a general one: every lot. Every lot has its outcome determined by the Lord in his sovereignty, and in accord with his eternal plan. We can generalize further: the Lord controls every random event, whether it is deliberately brought about by a human action of rolling dice or flipping coins, or is just a happenstance, like a hair coming out of someone's head and falling to the ground.

How do we know this? We know this because Proverbs 16:33 is a general principle. It has no qualifications that would limit the power of God over details. The absence of limitation agrees with the verses that we have already seen that teach the complete universality of God's control:

> . . . having been predestined according to the purpose of him who *works all things according to the counsel of his will.* (Eph. 1:11)

> Who has spoken and *it came to pass,*
>   unless the Lord has commanded it?
> Is it not from the mouth of the Most High
>   that *good and bad* come? (Lam. 3:37–38)

As usual, the various passages of the Bible fit together to reinforce one another. We can listen to (1) passages affirming the universality of God's control; (2) passages illustrating his control over tiny events like the casting of lots; and (3) passages indicating his control over tiny events during the crucifixion of Christ, such as the soldiers' casting lots or the piercing of Christ's side with a spear. All these passages together imply that God takes care of the tiniest events in each of our lives. (See fig. 6.1.)

Fig. 6.1: God's Control over Tiny Events

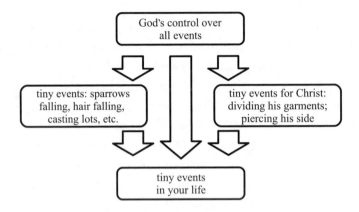

GOD AS UNLIMITED

Let us consider an objection to the idea of God's controlling details. If we compare God to a human manager over a factory or a business, we might think about the fact that a human manager delegates responsibility to his inferiors. He may do so out of pride, but he may also do so out of realism. He would be wasting his time if he attended to all the details. His time and his energy are limited. He must forgo attention to details in order to devote attention to major issues.

But God is not limited in the way that human managers are. One of the glories of God is that he not only rules the whole universe but he cares intimately for his children. His knowledge and his energy are unlimited. There is no tension between attention to major issues and intimate involvement in details.

A human manager has another motivation for delegating responsibility. He trusts his subordinates to do their jobs even when he is not looking over their shoulders and giving them directions for every move they make. Of course, some of his workers may need training and experience and wise advice before they consistently do their job well. Other workers, through laziness or incompetence, may never do well when they are unsupervised. But if a manager has good workers, he can leave them to themselves most of the time. If he interferes, he may actually distract from their concentration, lower their morale, breed resentment, and foul up their productivity. So does the human manager provide us implications for how God rules the world? Does a principle of "noninterference" imply that God should practice a hands-off policy and not interfere?

We cannot draw such a conclusion. The analogy with a human manager does not work when we focus on alleged "interference." As the previous chapter has reminded us, God's sovereignty does not destroy human action, but works in and through human action. God is not on the same level as a fellow human being. His presence is not an insult to our intelligence or our competence. Rather, his power and presence give us whatever competence and energy we have. He empowers rather than "interferes." He is not an outsider whose presence we resent.

Or at least we ought not to resent his presence. Human sin and rebellion has at its root the desire to be independent, to be gods ourselves. In our sin we *do* resent God. But that is our problem, not a problem with God's "management." God can be present in the details as well as the broad features of our decision making and our activities. The same goes for his presence in events that do not involve human beings.

PRACTICAL IMPORTANCE

God's control over small, seemingly unimportant events has practical value. If he is in control even of what is small, he is obviously in control over what is big. If he is in control over the hairs of our head, he clearly cares about everything in our lives, even if we are "small" people in the eyes of the world.

We can also see that small events can have big consequences. The small event of the flight of a single arrow had a big effect on the life of Ahab in the battle of Ramoth-gilead. The same is often true in modern times. What if your parents had never met? What if a cosmic ray had damaged the DNA in the sperm or egg that later was going to become you?

Look at it another way. Practically speaking, would you rather have ultimate randomness or chance determine the fate of your DNA, or would you rather have your destiny in the hands of an infinitely wise God? When we ask a question like that, the practical meaning of God's control becomes obvious. It is better to be in God's hands. We should thank him that we are in his care rather than in danger from events that no one controls.

CHAPTER 7

REFLECTING ON CREATION AND PROVIDENCE

The Bible's teaching about God's sovereignty has practical value. We have already seen this from Psalm 121:2 and Isaiah 51:12–13 (chapter 2). God's creation of the world exhibits his wisdom and his power. We can rely on that same wisdom and power today. In particular, we should rely on his wisdom and power when we think about so-called chance events. We are secure if we place ourselves in God's hands. We can praise him. Isaiah 51:12–13 says that God comforts us and that we do not need to be afraid. In particular, we do not need to be afraid of chance events.

Reflection on God's power in creation and in providence should lead to increasing our trust in God today, and increasing our confidence in God's control today. In particular, we should apply this confidence to the details of our lives and the details about which we are tempted to worry:

> Therefore, I tell you, do not be anxious about your life, what you will eat or what you will drink, nor about your body, what you will put on. . . .

> But seek first the kingdom of God and his righteousness, and all these things will be added to you.

> Therefore do not be anxious about tomorrow, for tomorrow will be anxious for itself. Sufficient for the day is its own trouble. (Matt. 6:25, 33–34)

This confidence should increase our praise. Listen to Spurgeon praise God for the wisdom and comprehensiveness of his plan:

> Our belief in God's wisdom supposes and necessitates that He has a settled purpose and plan in the work of salvation. What would *creation* have been without His design? Is there a fish in the sea, or a fowl in the air, which was left to chance for its formation? Nay, in every bone, joint, and muscle, sinew, gland, and blood-vessel, you mark the presence of a God working everything according to the design of infinite wisdom. And shall God be present in creation, ruling over all, and not in *grace*? Shall the new creation have the fickle genius of free will to preside over it when divine counsel rules the old creation? Look at *Providence*! Who knoweth not that not a sparrow falleth to the ground without your Father? Even the hairs of your head are all numbered. God weighs the mountains of our grief in scales, and the hills of our tribulation in balances. . . . He sees in its appointed place, not merely the corner-stone which He has laid in fair colours, in the blood of His dear Son, but He beholds in their ordained position each of the chosen stones taken out of the quarry of nature, and polished by His grace; He sees the whole from corner to cornice, from base to roof, from foundation to pinnacle. . . . At the last it shall be clearly seen that in every chosen vessel of mercy, Jehovah did as He willed with His own; and that in every part of the work of grace He accomplished His purpose, and glorified His own name.[1]

In light of the practical value of God's sovereignty, we can reread biblical texts about creation, such as Genesis 1, Psalm 8, Psalm 104, and Psalm 148. We could spend a long time going through these passages, verse by verse. For each verse, we could praise God for his power, and for each verse, we could confess our confidence in God's wisdom and in his control. For each verse, we could exhort ourselves and others to have confidence today. Here we will give only a sketch of what could be done.

GENESIS 1

Consider what God says in Genesis 1. Many people today have questions about the relation of Genesis 1 to modern science. But discussion of those

---

[1] Charles H. Spurgeon, *Morning and Evening: Daily Readings* (McLean, VA: MacDonald, n.d.), 430 (morning, August 2).

questions belongs to other books.[2] Let us consider its practical value for our comfort and edification.

"In the beginning God created the heavens and the earth" (Gen. 1:1). Praise God for his power! Praise him for his wisdom! He did not need any starting material with which to work. He created "from nothing" (*ex nihilo*). So what he created offers no resistance to his will. Let us trust him because his will prevails.

"The earth was without form and void, and darkness was over the face of the deep" (Gen. 1:2a). Human beings cannot live in a formless, empty waste. But it is not a threat to God. God confidently rules over it, and over the darkness, and over the deep. In his wisdom he works on this original situation, and brings it to where he wants. He is sovereign over time and over process, the movement from formlessness to order. By implication, he can bring order to our lives. He can protect us when we confront formlessness and disorder, either internally in our souls, externally in our circumstances, or externally in our enemies. Let us trust him for his mastery over formlessness and waste and darkness.

"And the Spirit of God was hovering over the face of the waters" (Gen. 1:2b). By analogy, God can send his Spirit to hover over us and work on us and in us. Those who trust in Christ have the Holy Spirit dwelling within them (Rom. 8:9–11). Praise God for his intimate presence in our lives. Let us trust him for the gift of his Spirit and the power of his Spirit.

"And God said, 'Let there be light,' and there was light" (Gen. 1:3). Light can be beautiful. We owe this beauty to God. Praise God for beauty in this world! Praise God for light, by which we can see our way physically. Praise God for spiritual light from his word, by which we can find our way spiritually: "Your word is a lamp to my feet and a light to my path" (Ps. 119:105). Let us trust him for his majestic beauty displayed in the light.

Consider the work on the second day:

> And God said, "Let there be an expanse in the midst of the waters, and let it separate the waters from the waters." And God made the expanse and separated the waters that were under the expanse from the waters that were above the expanse. And it was so. And God called the expanse Heaven. (Gen. 1:6–8)

---

[2] Vern S. Poythress, *Redeeming Science: A God-Centered Approach* (Wheaton, IL: Crossway, 2006); C. John Collins, *Science and Faith: Friends or Foes?* (Wheaton, IL: Crossway, 2003); C. John Collins, *Genesis 1–4: A Linguistic, Literary, and Theological Commentary* (Phillipsburg, NJ: Presbyterian & Reformed, 2006).

God has established heaven, and it remains firmly there to this day. He separated the waters, inaugurating the structure by which rain comes down from heaven to water the earth (Deut. 11:11; 1 Kings 8:35; Isa. 55:10). God controls the rain and snow, the weather, and the crops. Praise the Lord for weather, including rain and snow (Ps. 147:15–18; Isa. 55:10). Praise him for provision for crops and food (Acts 14:17). He has established and maintains the distinct regions in the world—the sky above and the earth and waters beneath. His power reassures us that he can care for us, both in the weather that he gives and in the food that he gives.

These words of praise may sound strange to people who are accustomed to think of "nature" as independent of God. But the idea of an independent nature needs to be abandoned. Genesis 1 indicates that events in the world reflect the faithfulness and wisdom of God. Some people attribute the dependability of the world to "natural law," which they understand mechanistically. But that is a misunderstanding of the character of "law." The real law is God's speech governing the world. When scientists make their formulations, they are depending on and expressing the consistency and faithfulness of God. So praise is the appropriate response.

Consider the work on the third day:

> And God said, "Let the waters under the heavens be gathered together into one place, and let the dry land appear." And it was so. (Gen. 1:9)

Praise God for the dry land, which provides a place for human beings to live. Praise him that he has promised not to send a flood again that will wipe out mankind. (8:21–22)

> And God said, "Let the earth sprout vegetation, plants yielding seed, and fruit trees bearing fruit in which is their seed, each according to its kind, on the earth." And it was so. (1:11)

Praise the Lord for giving us plants and trees, for their fruit, for the regularities of growth, for seed by which we can enjoy the next generation of plants. Thank him that we can depend on his goodness in agriculture.

We can thank the Lord also that food is edible and good-tasting. God set up the various kinds of plants in the beginning, and by his rule the plants continue to produce grains and fruits that sustain us. The food we put on the table comes from him. And our ability to digest it comes from him. Thank the Lord for the working of our digestive systems.

We could continue through Genesis 1 and 2. Instead, let us turn to Psalm 104.

PSALM 104

Psalm 104 is like an inspired version of what we have just been doing imperfectly as we traveled through Genesis 1. It is full of praise, and includes themes that come from all six days of Genesis 1.

"Bless the LORD, O my soul!" (Ps. 104:1a). Yes, let each of us address our own soul, and summon ourselves to bless the Lord, who is worthy of all blessings.

"O LORD my God, you are very great!" (v. 1b). The Lord is great. He is great as displayed in creation. So he is great as displayed in providence. He is great as displayed in caring for each of us and in caring for the hairs of our head.

"You are clothed with splendor and majesty" (v. 1c). Lord, you are majestic and splendid. The heavens reflect your splendor. Their majesty reflects your majesty. The beauty of the sky and the clouds comes from you. You are splendid and majestic today, and you take care of us in accordance with who you are.

And so we may proceed through the psalm.

OTHER PASSAGES

In a similar way, we may reflect on and respond to other passages about creation and providence: Psalm 8, Psalm 147, Psalm 148, and Job 38–41. Then we may move to psalms about the record of God's care in past generations: Psalms 78, 105, 106, 107. The entire book of Psalms gives us inspired examples of the prayers of God's people in the past and reminds us of God's sovereignty over people's lives.

The Psalms give us examples of trust in God and expressions of faith in God. They point forward to Jesus Christ, who is both God and man. As God, he is the One in whom we are to trust. As man, he himself perfectly trusted in God during his entire life on earth. His trust was mentioned in mockery by the religious leaders:

> He trusts in God; let God deliver him now, if he desires him. For he said, "I am the Son of God." (Matt. 27:43)

But Christ's trust in God was vindicated in his resurrection. We who are Christian believers are to trust God as people who are united to him, whom the Spirit empowers to exercise trust in "him who raised Jesus from the dead" (Rom. 8:11).

The resurrection of Christ from the dead is the supreme demonstration of God's faithfulness, and should draw us to trust:

> What then shall we say to these things? If God is for us, who can be against us? He who did not spare his own Son but gave him up for us all, how will he not also with him graciously give us all things? (Rom. 8:31–32)

The Bible is full of instruction that should draw us to praise God and trust him.

CHAPTER 8

GOD'S SOVEREIGNTY AND MODERN PHYSICS

The examples where the Bible describes unpredictable events cover the kind of thing that can be observed by ordinary people. In modern times, scientific instruments like the telescope and the microscope have given us access to events on an extended scale, from the very large to the very small. What do we say about such events?

We have every reason to believe that the Bible's general statements about God's sovereignty apply to these realms as well. The general principle, that "his kingdom rules over all" (Ps. 103:19), still applies. (See fig. 8.1.)

Fig. 8.1: God's Universal Control

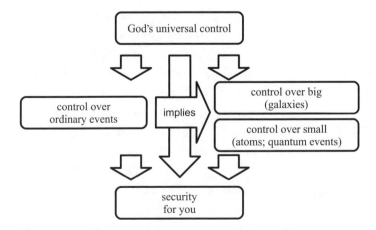

LARGE-SCALE EVENTS

On the scale of the very large, Isaiah 40:26 points the way by declaring that

> [God] brings out their host [of stars] by number,
>   calling them all by name,
> by the greatness of his might,
>   and because he is strong in power
>   not one is missing.

God governs the whole expanse of heaven.
    Likewise Psalm 147:4–5 affirms that

> He [God] determines the number of the *stars*;
>   he gives to all of them *their names*.
> Great is our Lord, and abundant in power;
>   his understanding is beyond measure.

If we acknowledge God's control over each star, we should also acknowledge his control over galaxies and cluster of galaxies and galactic dust clouds and black holes and quasars, which have become known to mankind only in the twentieth century.

MICROSCOPIC EVENTS

The principle of God's control logically extends to the level of the very small as well. The region of the very small offers a special interest, because unpredictability crops up there.

In the region of the very large, the behavior of stars is in many respects well understood and predictable on the basis of current understanding of physical laws. Astronomers cannot, of course, predict every detail, but they can predict overall behavior, because for many situations the overall behavior depends on averages rather than knowledge of every detail. The same is *not* true, however, at a microscopic level, the level of the very small. If we travel down far enough, to the level of atoms, the behavior of individual atoms cannot be exactly predicted, for two reasons.

First, our knowledge is limited by practical constraints. Because of the limitations in present-day measuring apparatus, we do not have absolutely precise information about the position, velocity, and electronic state of each individual atom. This limitation to the knowledge that we have about the situation at one particular time "propagates" forward in time. The uncertainties with which we started grow bigger and bigger over time, when we try to calculate the motions of the atoms.

We can see a simple analogue to this difficulty if we think about billiard balls moving on a pool table. A very slight change in the angle of a cue stick produces a small change in the direction of motion of the starting cue ball. This small difference at the start may make a big difference in the final position of the balls. Small differences enlarge into big differences over the passage of time.

Similarly, when atoms move around, the growth in uncertainty makes the distant future of the locations of atoms highly unpredictable. The equations governing the motions of atoms and their interactions show that typical complex physical systems involving many atoms have properties something like the situation with billiard balls. The interaction of atoms over time gradually magnifies the uncertainty about the position and velocity of any one atom in the system, until finally only averages can be estimated. The exact position of any one atom is totally unpredictable. From a human point of view, it is *random*.

Depending on the situation, unpredictability at the atomic level can also have large-scale, macroscopic effects. Many physical systems are such that a tiny change in initial conditions radically affects the future. These systems are called "chaotic" systems because they are unpredictable. Scientists have a special name for an effect in which a tiny change in an initial situation causes a big change in outcome. They call it "the butterfly effect." A small change, like a butterfly flapping its wings in the Amazon River basin, may produce a radical difference in the weather pattern of North America weeks later.

Scientists can make short-range weather predictions about temperature and precipitation. They can predict weather for tomorrow and the next day, because their data have enough accuracy to allow it. But beyond about a week into the future, predictions become progressively more difficult and less accurate, because the butterfly effect takes its toll. Finally, prediction breaks down completely. Detailed long-range weather predictions are permanently impossible. (Scientists can sometimes predict *tendencies* toward cooling and warming, but these are averages. They cannot predict the location of next month's tornadoes.)

QUANTUM EFFECTS

Unpredictability has a second source. Current physical theory includes quantum mechanics, which appears to indicate that there are innate physical limits to measurement. The limits arise from the very nature of the world, not just from temporary limitations in the apparatus that we are using to make measurements. Within quantum mechanics, the famous *Heisenberg uncertainty principle* says that if you pick out a direction, let us say straight up, and then try to measure at the same time both the position and velocity of an atom in that direction, the uncertainty d in the position, when multiplied by the uncertainty s in velocity, will always be greater than or equal to a certain minimal quantity u, which is inversely proportional to the mass of the atom. In mathematical terms, $d \times s \geq u$.[1]

If we try to determine the position of the atom with very great accuracy, we are making d very small. As it becomes smaller, the uncertainty s in the velocity becomes greater and greater. There is *always* some uncertainty, both in position (d) and in velocity (s). And the uncertainty of the two together cannot be diminished below the specific amount u, no matter what measuring apparatus we use and no matter what experimental setup we put in place. There is a *fundamental* and *absolute* limitation on our ability to make precise measurements and obtain precise information about a physical system.

The Heisenberg uncertainty principle applies to elementary particles like electrons and large objects like baseballs as well as to atoms. But baseballs have a large enough mass so that the minimum quantity u for a baseball is incredibly small. In practice, we cannot detect any difficulty with baseballs. Atoms and electrons, on the other hand, can exhibit notable effects from the Heisenberg uncertainty principle, because they have very small masses in comparison to a baseball. A baseball has a mass of about five ounces, or 140 grams. An electron has a mass of about 9.1×10^{-28} grams, so a baseball is 1.5×10^{29} times as massive. That is 150 billion billion billion times more massive. Only large increases in accuracy of measurement,

---

[1] In modern notation, $\Delta z \times \Delta p_z \geq \hbar/2$, where Δz (d above) is the uncertainty in position along the z-axis, Δp_z is the uncertainty in momentum along the same axis, and $\hbar = h/2\pi$ is Planck's constant h divided by 2π. The velocity plays a role in this situation because, for low (nonrelativistic) speeds, the momentum p_z is the velocity v_z in the z-direction times the mass m of the particle. The uncertainty s in velocity is $\Delta p_z/m$ and the value u is $\hbar/2m$. (See Jan Hilgevoord and Jos Uffink, "The Uncertainty Principle," *Stanford Encyclopedia of Philosophy (Spring 2011 Edition)*, ed. Edward N. Zalta, http://plato.stanford.edu/archives/spr2011/entries/qt-uncertainty/, §2.5, accessed January 5, 2012.)

due partly to the use of complex and delicate measuring apparatus, have allowed us in the twentieth and twenty-first centuries to appreciate more directly the reality of these effects.

THE PHILOSOPHY OF PHYSICAL DETERMINISM

So what difference does it make? Ordinary people do not worry about such things, because they have to deal with baseballs and not with electrons or single atoms. But the presence of even minute uncertainty has a deeply disturbing influence on some non-Christian philosophical positions. After Isaac Newton wrote out for the first time the fundamental equations for the motion of physical particles, some scientists began to think that the world was physically *deterministic*. They argued that the future could in principle be calculated precisely, for distant times as well as for small time periods, if only we had precise enough information about the positions and velocities and interactive forces of all the physical particles at just one moment in time. The whole world, according to the philosophy of *physical determinism*, is determined mechanically by the past.

We can use the analogy with billiard balls. Imagine a billiard player with superhuman ability. With one precise shot on a pool table, he might make all the balls go into pockets. Or, if there were no pockets and no friction, he could calculate out the position of all the balls at all future times, if he began with perfectly precise information about their present positions and about the shot that would set them all in motion. By analogy, physical determinism postulates that atoms are like billiard balls, and that the future can in principle be calculated from the past.

According to this view, causes of an essentially mechanical type, operating in the interaction of atoms, completely determine the future, not only for a few moments but for all future times. This philosophy seems to drain all meaning out of human actions, because these actions along with everything else are absolutely determined by the physical motions of the particles that make up the bodies of human beings.

Once physicists became convinced that quantum mechanics was true to the world, the Heisenberg uncertainty principle put the philosophy of physical determinism in retreat. But the advocates of determinism did not immediately accept defeat. Some of them maintained that quantum mechanics must be a temporary, incomplete theory. The final theory, it was hoped, would move beyond or underneath the uncertainties in the Heisenberg uncertainty principle. We would finally arrive at a perfectly deterministic theory, and the Heisenberg uncertainty principle would be only a secondary, superficial result. It would be an expression of the temporary incompleteness in our knowledge about the way the world functions "down underneath" the measurements that we make. Some people hoped that the final deterministic theory would have so-called "hidden variables," extra information in addition to the information about positions and velocities, and this extra information would dissolve the uncertainties that appeared in quantum mechanics as currently formulated.

In the early days of developments in quantum mechanics, many physicists and philosophers preferred a deterministic theory, for aesthetic, philosophical, and other personal reasons. Other scientists and philosophers, however, *prefer* a picture in which the world has permanent uncertainty. Later we will consider why. But our preferences, one way or the other, do not determine the real nature of the world that we live in. We cannot dictate to God how the world must be.

Our investigation of the Bible has shown that God has no uncertainty about what will happen. He not only knows what will happen, but controls what will happen. But we still need to consider a question about the knowledge of human beings: could human beings through experiments and through gathering enough data eliminate uncertainty from their own minds and arrive at exact predictions about the future? There is no indeterminacy with respect to *God's* knowledge. But is there unavoidable indeterminacy with respect to *human* knowledge?

In some cases, even in the context of quantum mechanics, human beings can make exact predictions about the outcome of a carefully controlled experiment;[2] but in many other cases they cannot. If God has created a world in which human beings must permanently live with uncertainty, we cannot dissolve the uncertainty just by preferring it to be otherwise. Scientists are forced to wrestle with the possibility that the world does not match their preferences.

---

[2] For example, a hydrogen atom in an excited electronic state emits electromagnetic radiation of a definite frequency when it falls into its ground state. By measuring the frequency, the experimenter can be certain that the hydrogen atom is now in its ground state, and a subsequent measurement will confirm this inference. But at no point does the experimenter obtain enough information to predict deterministically the results of an arbitrary experiment on the hydrogen atom.

ARE WE STUCK WITH PERMANENT UNCERTAINTY?

The latter half of the twentieth century has seen technical developments in quantum theory that seem to have made human indeterminacy unavoidable in any future theory. We cannot enter into the technical details. The evidence for a permanent indeterminism has come from a combination of two kinds of research, the one theoretical and the other experimental.

On the theoretical side, John Stewart Bell derived a result called *Bell's theorem*, which has proved to have decisive weight. What does it say? The details are technical, but the basic idea can be explained in simple terms. Suppose someone were to come up with a future theory that has some similarities to quantum mechanics. This new theory offers to account for the same physical phenomena that are the focus of quantum mechanics. But it also has extra variables, that is, additional mathematical quantities, which represent *additional* information about individual particles.[3] The additional information supplements the information represented by quantum mechanics in its current form. Suppose also that these extra variables are intended to dissolve the uncertainties in quantum mechanics. While current quantum mechanics involves innate uncertainties, this new theory will in principle allow exact predictions, provided that at the start we have the additional information represented by the extra variables. Using a few minimal assumptions, Bell's theorem establishes that no such theory can exactly match the experimental predictions of quantum mechanics; it also specifies some particular cases where the lack of a match will occur.

The second, experimental side of the work has consisted in experiments checking whether the predictions of quantum mechanics actually hold in practice in situations designed to test Bell's theorem experimentally. As of 2012, experiments have not closed every possible loophole, but they have decisively confirmed quantum mechanics in contrast to the possibilities for purely deterministic theories. A lack of mechanical determinism of this kind seems to be with us permanently.

These results do not affect the question of whether God determines and controls the future. The results contradict *physical* determinism, not *divine*

---

[3] In the more technical language of quantum mechanics, these variables are called *local hidden variables*—local because they describe information about the states of individual particles located within small regions of space. Bell's theorem is not relevant if we allow *nonlocal* variables. By postulating a sufficient number of nonlocal variables, and giving them carefully chosen character, theorists can always "rescue" an ultimate determinism. But a physical determinism of this kind is counterintuitive, and not very "physical" because the information is not "located" in space. It might just as well be information that resides only in the mind of God!

determinism. The results say something about the limitations of human knowledge, not the limitations of divine knowledge.

PRACTICAL EFFECTS

Physical indeterminism holds at the atomic level, the level of the very small. But does it make any practical difference? As noted earlier, we do not directly observe Heisenberg uncertainty or indeterminism with baseballs. The flight of a baseball is determined once it leaves the pitcher's hand. That is, it is determined for practical purposes. But, according to quantum theory, human beings *cannot* determine it with infinite precision.

As usual, a small amount of human uncertainty at the beginning propagates in time, and eventually produces large-scale uncertainty. A famous illustration comes from Erwin Schrödinger, one of the pioneers in quantum mechanics. He imagines a situation in which a cat is placed in a box. Alongside the cat is a Geiger counter and a small amount of radioactive material. The Geiger counter is also linked to a flask containing poisonous gas, in such a way that if the Geiger counter fires, the flask breaks and the cat dies.[4] The Geiger counter will fire only if a radioactive atom disintegrates.

The timing of the radioactive disintegration of a single atom is a standard case for quantum mechanics. The exact time when it disintegrates is completely uncertain to human beings. All that quantum mechanics can give us is a probability estimate for how long *on the average* it will take. Schrödinger's setup as a whole links the quantum mechanical uncertainty at the atomic level to a large-scale uncertainty about the fate of the cat. We as human beings cannot know whether the cat is alive or dead unless we open the box and observe it.

This case has become known as "Schrodinger's cat."[5] Its significance has been vigorously debated. At the very least, it shows that quantum mechanical uncertainty can have effects on ordinary life.

---

[4] Animal lovers naturally find this example unpleasant. But we must remember that Schrödinger was discussing a "thought experiment," not an experiment that he proposed actually to carry out.

[5] Erwin Schrödinger, "The Present Situation in Quantum Mechanics: A Translation of Schrödinger's 'Cat Paradox Paper,'" trans. John D. Trimmer, http://www.tu-harburg.de/rzt/rzt/it/QM/cat.html, §5, accessed July 19, 2011; originally published in *Proceedings of the American Philosophical Society* 124 (1980): 323–338. Schrödinger produced the illustration partly to illustrate some other counterintuitive aspects of quantum mechanics. Quantum mechanics includes mathematical expressions that represent a "superposition" of quantum mechanical states; the mathematics can apparently represent a situation in which the cat is neither alive nor dead with certainty. Is it then half alive?

A MISTAKEN THEORY OF LIMITED SOVEREIGNTY

Some people, emboldened by the message of quantum indeterminacy, have claimed that quantum indeterminacy limits not only human knowledge but God's knowledge. They allege that the uncertainty about the decay of a radioactive atom encompasses God as well as man. Allegedly God does not know, because there is nothing to be known until the atom actually does decay. Once the atom decays, God comes to know and we can come to know. Until it happens, the moment of decay is an absolute metaphysical unknown. The decay represents absolute chance.

But such reasoning is not only overbold but at odds with the Bible. The Bible indicates that God knows the future:

> I am God, and there is no other;
> > I am God, and there is none like me,
> declaring *the end* from the beginning
> > and from ancient times *things not yet done*,
> saying, "My counsel shall stand,
> > and I will accomplish all my purpose." (Isa. 46:9–10)

This passage indicates not only that God can "declare" or describe the future, but that this future happens in accordance with his "counsel" and "all my purpose" (v. 10). He not only *knows* the future but plans it and *controls* it. Ephesians 1:11 states the general principle: he "works *all things* according to the counsel of his will."

The bold reasoning that restricts God's knowledge or his control makes the mistake of putting God on the same level as man. According to quantum theory, *we* as human beings do not know and cannot know exactly when a radioactive atom will decay. But God does know. He plans, specifies, and controls the decay and its timing. God is the author of quantum theory, not its victim.

More precisely, according to the Bible God authors the laws for the universe. He speaks the universe into existence and specifies all its regularities. His speech is the real law (chapter 2). Quantum theory as we know it is a human approximation, our best human guess as to what God's law looks like. The innate uncertainties that crop up in quantum theory show us our human limitations in measurement. God is not so limited. The decay of each radioactive atom belongs within his comprehensive plan for history.

DETAILED CONTROL

God is thoroughly in control. His plan is comprehensive, and his execution of his plan during the course of history is comprehensive. But is this really so? Some people have doubts.

In discussing God's relation to the details of history, I once heard someone say, "God does not micromanage the world." He meant that God does not control every detail, every atom. He would have admitted that God controls the big things, the overall course of history. But atoms, presumably, just take their own course. Having created them, God sustains them in being. But like a human manager who gives his subordinates scope for independent decision making, God opens up space for small events that just happen, more or less on their own initiative and without divine "interference."

Where is the justification for this picture of limited divine control? Is it in the Bible? Where in the Bible is there some passage or verse that teaches that some one event takes place *outside* of God's plan and control? There is no such verse. Instead, as we have seen, we have verses aplenty that give us specific examples of God's detailed control. And we have further verses that make general statements about the universality of God's control. So where does the idea of limited control come from?

It comes, I think, partly from the desire to protect the goodness of God. People want to say that he is not involved in disasters. We have discussed this challenge earlier (chapter 4). But there is a second reason why people want limited control. We human beings *do not like* the prospect of an all-controlling God. Ever since the fall of human beings into sin, sin has pervaded the human heart. And sin includes at its roots the desire for independence from God. "You will not surely die," says the serpent. In other words, the serpent claims that God is not universally in control. And the serpent says, "You will be like God, knowing good and evil." That is, you will be independent. You will take charge of your own decision making, independent of God. You will do what you decide to do, not what God directs you to do. Such is the voice of Satan, who speaks through the serpent and instigates human rebellion against God. Such also becomes the internal voice in our hearts, when our hearts are corrupted by sin.

We earlier mentioned that some people prefer an ultimate indeterminacy to determinism. Why? Maybe there are several possible reasons. But for some people, their preferences are sinful. They prefer indeterminacy because they hope to escape God. They prefer a world of absolute chance, because absolute chance would be a limitation on God, or even an indication that God does not exist. They prefer to have God dethroned—in effect, no longer to be God.

I suspect in addition that the word *micromanage* evokes the idea of a human manager who supervises workers under him. God, it is suggested, is like a human manager. We have already seen the limitations and perils of this comparison (chapter 5). In fact, God is *not* like a human manager. He is unlimited, and he is on a divine rather than a human level. His control does not mean "interference," that is, interference with an allegedly original "independent" action on the part of man. His control means sustenance.

God works his will *through* human agents, even sinful, disobedient agents. "As for you, you meant evil against me, but *God meant it for good*, to bring it about that many people should be kept alive, as they are today" (Gen. 50:20). We need as our model the life of Joseph, and—even more important—the events of the crucifixion of Christ, rather than the picture of a limited human manager who introduces a radical "independence."

On the other hand, suppose that we make for ourselves a picture where God is merely a limited general manager. What have we done? We have produced a picture without any warrant from God's revelation of himself in Scripture. We have simply followed our own imagination. Moreover, this new picture, this product of our imagination, opposes the teaching of the Bible. It is an idol, a false god. We make ourselves idolaters, who worship this false god of our imaginations but who nevertheless pretend that this false god is God, the true God. We prefer our own notions to God's teaching. And we blaspheme God by making claims about him that dishonor his majesty, power, and sovereignty. We involve ourselves in multiple sins of a grievous kind. No, let us repent and return to God, the God who describes himself faithfully by speaking to us in Scripture.

By returning to Scripture, we reap not only the long-range benefits of submitting to God and learning from him, but also some immediate benefits in our ability to appreciate and praise him. We learn about the immensity of his majesty and his wisdom. "His understanding is unsearchable" (Isa. 40:28). Praise God that his power is so great that he can rule the galaxies and rule the hairs on my head and rule the atoms in the keratin molecules in one hair. We can glorify God for what we see, in the small things as well as the great. We can confidently see the hand of God in the moment when a radioactive atom decays. We can praise him for the marvel of radioactivity. We can praise him for quantum mechanics and the mysteries in the behavior of electrons and the puzzles of Schrödinger's cat.

I can thank God for delivering my family and me from an auto accident on our vacation. I do not need to know first whether God worked a supernatural miracle with the cars, or whether an angel intervened, or whether the motions of the cars and the reactions of the drivers operated according to purely "normal" ways in which God governs the world. I do not know all the answers about how God did it, and in a way it does not matter. One way or another, God was there and he was totally in control.

We conclude, then, that God is indeed a "micromanager," if we must use that term. He is not merely a "micromanager," who controls microscopic events in individual living cells in our bodies, but a nanomanager, a zeptomanager, who controls events far more minute than what we can observe even through a microscope. He controls it all. Since the word *manager* may create difficulties by suggesting false comparisons with human managers, we might say simply that God rules over all events, great and small.[6] "His kingdom rules over *all*" (Ps. 103:19). (See fig. 8.2.)

---

[6] Scripture itself regularly uses comparisons between God's action and human action. The word *rule* exhibits this comparison, since human rulers act in a manner analogous to God's rule. God has made it so, and had designed language so that it may communicate truly about God using analogies. Our point is that we should use analogies along the lines that God has provided for us in Scripture, rather than in antagonism to what he says about himself in Scripture.

Fig. 8.2: God's Control over All Events, Great and Small

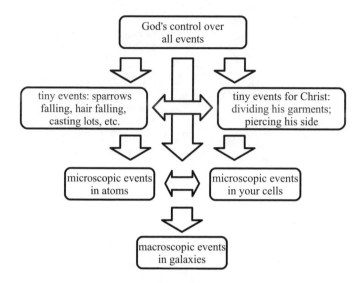

CHAPTER 9

WHAT IS CHANCE?

So what is "chance"? What should we think?

TWO DEFINITIONS OF CHANCE

In English the word *chance*, like many words, has a range of uses. The uses that most concern us are the first two options in Merriam-Webster's dictionary:

> **1 a** : something that happens unpredictably without discernible human intention or observable cause **b** : the assumed impersonal purposeless determiner of unaccountable happenings : LUCK[1]

Merriam-Webster's first definition (1a) talks about unpredictability. The examples that we have previously discussed, from the Bible and from modern life, conform to this description.

One part of the description could use clarification. It says, "without discernible human intention." Human beings may be involved in "chance" events. Rebekah and Rachel both intended to go to the well. Pharaoh intended to put the cupbearer and the baker in prison. The soldier at Ramoth-gilead intended to shoot an arrow. But in these cases the way in which various events came together did not have a "discernible human intention or observable cause." Neither Rebekah nor Abraham's servant nor any other human being on the scene urged Rebekah to come to the well because he had previous knowledge that Abraham's servant was there, finishing his prayer. Similarly, Rachel did not go out to the well with the intention of

[1] *Merriam-Webster's Collegiate Dictionary* (11th ed.).

meeting Jacob. The meeting took place "by chance," we could say, according to definition 1a.

In these events human beings did not control the outcome, and no human being could have predicted the outcome. God controlled the outcome. Of course Webster's definition of *chance* does not say one way or the other what God's role is; but the definition is clearly compatible with the Bible's teaching about God's control. Human intentions and human predictions are indeed limited, and the word *chance* gives a label for those limitations. We can still affirm that God's intentions and God's knowledge are unlimited, even in cases when we do not know in detail what he knows and what he intends.

Merriam-Webster's second definition, 1b, presents us with a different analysis of "chance": "the assumed impersonal purposeless determiner of unaccountable happenings : LUCK." This definition includes the assumption that some events are "impersonal" and "purposeless" in an absolute sense. In other words, the definition implies that God is not involved and that he is not in control.

Chance in this sense does not exist. There is no such thing as luck. This kind of "chance" fits into a larger worldview that contains erroneous assumptions about God. It assumes either that God does not exist or that he is uninvolved. Granted such an assumption, unaccountable events have no purpose. They are impersonal. But the starting assumption is wrong; it does not match the nature of the world. People with this assumption substitute "chance" for God. "Chance" becomes a kind of idol, because in human thinking it becomes a substitute explanation that replaces God.

TRANSCENDENCE AND IMMANENCE OF GOD

So there are two main views of chance, rather than just one. These two views correspond to two views of God. John Frame has helpfully summarized human views of God in a diagram, which has come to be known as "Frame's square." (See fig. 9.1)[2]

The left-hand side of the square represents the biblical, Christian understanding of God's transcendence (corner 1) and his immanence (corner 2). God's transcendence means that he controls all things. "The

---

[2] John M. Frame, *The Doctrine of the Knowledge of God* (Phillipsburg, NJ: Presbyterian & Reformed, 1987), 14.

LORD has established his throne in the heavens, and his kingdom rules over all" (Ps. 103:19). The reference to God's throne indicates that he has the authority or right to rule. The expression "his kingdom rules over all" indicates that he actually *does* rule; he controls what happens. Both his authority and his control express his transcendence. God's immanence means that he is everywhere present and is intimately involved in the events in this world. This principle is illustrated many times in the Bible. We may choose one:

> Behold, I am *with you* [Jacob] and will keep you wherever you go, and will bring you back to this land. For I *will not leave you* until I have done what I have promised you. (Gen. 28:15)

Both transcendence and immanence are illustrated in Jesus's earthly life. For example, when Jesus stills the storm in Matthew 8:26–27, he shows divine power, illustrating God's transcendence by his control over the storm (compare Ps. 107:23–32). At the same time, as God he is *with* the disciples and takes care of them, illustrating God's immanence.

Fig. 9.1: Frame's Square

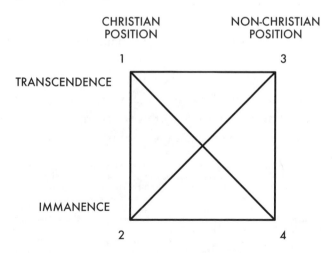

NON-CHRISTIAN VIEW OF GOD

The right-hand side of the square represents the non-Christian understanding of God. At a superficial level, non-Christians have many different views of God. There are atheists, agnostics, pantheists, spiritists, polytheists, and so on. At a deep level, however, non-Christian thinking shows a common pattern, because all non-Christians know God, according to Romans 1:18–21, but suppress the truth.

The non-Christian view of God's transcendence (corner 3) says that God is either nonexistent or distant and uninvolved. Atheists directly deny the existence of God. Spiritists and polytheists multiply the gods. These gods may be accessible, but they are petty gods, not truly transcendent. Ultimate reality, transcendent reality, therefore must be above and beyond the limitations of the gods. Then it becomes distant and inaccessible.[3]

The non-Christian view of God's immanence (corner 4) says that God either is identical with the world or, when he is involved, is subject to the limitations of the world. Pantheism makes God identical with the world, while in spiritism and polytheism the gods are limited, subject to limitations of the world.

We can sum up the two views in a second diagram that fills in the contents of the four corners. (See fig. 9.2.)

John Frame has represented the two positions in a square in order to point out relationships between the two positions. The diagonal lines in the square represent contradictions. The non-Christian view of immanence (corner 4) contradicts the Christian view of transcendence (corner 1). Christian transcendence says that God controls events, while non-Christian immanence says that God is part of the events or is subject to the events.

---

[3] Judaism and Islam deserve separate discussion. Significant variations in viewpoint exist within both of these religions, so that the situation is complicated. Both are monotheistic religions, and both are influenced by the Old Testament, which presents God as a personal, infinite God, who is all-powerful and involved in the world. To the degree to which they follow the teaching of the Old Testament, they agree with the basic outline of the Christian view of transcendence. Moreover, practicing Jews and Muslims pray to a being whom they call "God." Their practice of prayer might seem to imply that this "God" is transcendently powerful and able to answer prayer, and also that he is immanent, accessible, and concerned to listen to prayer.

But on what can we rely when we try to approach God in prayer? According to Old Testament typology and prophecy, and according to New Testament teaching, Christ is the mediator between God and man; he is the one who opens access to God. Since Jews and Muslims do not accept this mediation, God may in practice seem to grow distant and uninvolved.

Moreover, religious thinking and practice get corrupted by human sin. Prayers become a matter of rote, and then there is no real contact with God as a personal God. On the other hand, prayer may be used to try to manipulate God, to get him to do what the worshiper wants. In this case, the attempt is being made to bring God down to a human level, and this attempt represents a non-Christian view of immanence. These failings occur not only among Jews and Muslims, but among professing Christians. They too can fall into essentially non-Christian ways of thinking and praying, if they are not taking to heart the instruction of the Bible.

Non-Christian transcendence (corner 3) contradicts Christian immanence (corner 2). Christian immanence says that God is present, while non-Christian transcendence says that he is absent.

The horizontal lines in the square represent non-Christian counterfeiting. The non-Christian view of transcendence (corner 3) sounds superficially similar to the Christian view of transcendence (corner 1). Indeed, they both use the same word, *transcendence*. The two positions have enough similarity so that the non-Christian position sounds plausible, and may show verbal similarities to biblical teaching. But it is a counterfeit, a subtle substitute that is close enough to the truth to be appealing. We can see its counterfeit character if we notice that it contradicts biblical teaching about God's immanence (corner 2). Similarly, non-Christian immanence (corner 4) may sound like Christian immanence (corner 2). But it is merely a counterfeit, a deceiving substitute. We can also say that the horizontal lines represent "formal similarity." The "form" of the language is similar, sometimes even identical, when we compare the two sides. But the *content* is radically different.

Fig. 9.2: Frame's Square with Explanations

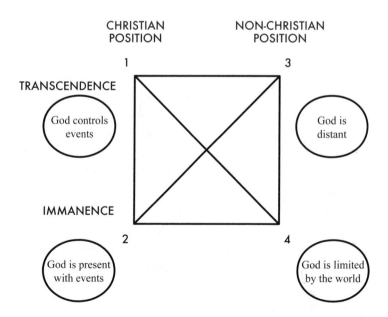

APPLICATION OF TRANSCENDENCE AND IMMANENCE TO THE QUESTION OF CHANCE

Now that we have before us Frame's square, we can apply it to the particular issue of chance events. What do the two sides of the square imply about chance?

Christian transcendence says that God fully controls chance events. They are unpredictable and inexplicable *for human beings*, but not for God. When they look at chance events, human beings cannot see a definite, simple, meaningful pattern of secondary causes, that is, causes within the world. God, however, knows his purposes even if we do not. He brings about the events even if we as creatures cannot see a cause.

Christian immanence says that God is present with so-called chance events. He has his purposes. He is involved for the sake of his people. Romans 8:28 says that "for those who love God all things work together for good, for those who are called according to his purpose."

Non-Christian transcendence says that chance events come about for no reason at all. They are "impersonal" and "purposeless." The word *chance* itself can be used to designate an alleged ultimate impersonal origin. People say, "Chance brought it about." That is, chance rules. Chance is a substitute for God. Chance contradicts God's personal purposes that are expressed according to the Christian view of immanence.

Non-Christian immanence says that we as human beings can be the judge of meaning. If *we* see no meaning in an event, there is no meaning. The position also implies that if there is a God, God confronts chance events that he must put up with and react to as best he can. He must deal with things that he does not control. For example, the person who denies that God "micromanages" events implies that microevents are just there and that they have not been brought about by God's control. Likewise, the person who talks about "luck" usually means that luck, and not God, brings about the event. These views are both expressions of a non-Christian view of immanence, where God is limited in practice by chance or luck.

We can sum up the two views as a whole in a diagram. (See fig. 9.3.)

The diagram represents the challenge for us to honor God as we think about the nature of chance. We honor God when we confess his power and his purpose in chance events. We dishonor God if we replace him with an idea where chance is an "impersonal purposeless determiner."

Fig. 9.3: Frame's Square for Chance

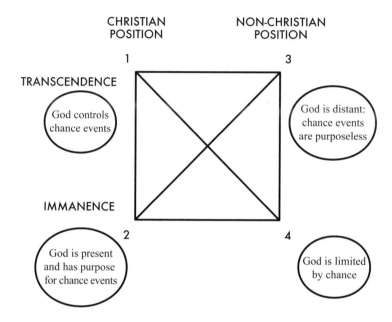

PART II

GOD AS THE FOUNDATION FOR CHANCE

CHAPTER 10

REGULARITIES AND UNPREDICTABILITIES

We have said that God controls small, unpredictable events as well as big patterns and regularities in history. But we can say even more. In the world that he has created, God in his wisdom has given us the whole tapestry of regularities and unpredictabilities and their connections with one another. This tapestry, along with many other features we see in creation, reflects his wisdom and his character, as Romans 1:19–20 indicates:

> For what can be known about God is plain to them, because God has shown it to them. For his invisible attributes, namely, his eternal power and divine nature, have been clearly perceived, ever since the creation of the world, in the things that have been made.

Are God's "invisible attributes" shown also in chance events? They are. What we call "chance" concerns unpredictable events. These unpredictable events arise in the midst of predictable regularities. For example, the well to which Rebekah regularly walked had water in it. She could predict that she would find water when she arrived. She could not predict that she would meet Abraham's servant. Unpredictable and predictable go together. Let us think about them both.

DIVINE SPEECH

We may begin by recalling the fact that God governs the world by speaking (see chapter 2). By speaking he establishes the regularities that we see in the world. "Let the earth sprout vegetation, plants yielding seed, and fruit trees bearing fruit in which is their seed, each according to its kind, on the earth" (Gen. 1:11). In an act of creation he specifies the regular pattern for plants and trees bearing seed and reproducing according to their kinds. The process still goes on today. So God's speech in creation establishes the regularities about the events that we see.

WEATHER

Does God speak to establish each unpredictable event? We have examples:

> He sends out his command to the earth;
>> *his word* runs swiftly.
> He gives snow like wool;
>> he scatters frost like ashes.
> He hurls down his crystals of ice like crumbs;
>> who can stand before his cold?
> He sends out *his word*, and melts them;
>> he makes his wind blow and the waters flow. (Ps. 147:15–18)

God's word of command, which Psalm 147:15, 18 calls simply "his word," specifies when snow and frost come, when ice and cold come, and when they melt. They melt when "he sends out his word." God's word not only specifies particular events; it also *controls* them. His word is powerful. Speaking of creation rather than providence, Psalm 33:9 says simply,

> he *spoke*, and it came to be;
>> he *commanded*, and it stood firm.

The same principle holds for God's providential rule. He speaks, and it happens. What happens? Each individual thing, each event that happens. Unpredictable events like the coming of snow, ice, frost, and wind take place because he commands them to happen.

Weather is an instructive example for us, because it *combines* elements of predictability and unpredictability. Human beings cannot predict long in advance a particular individual instance where snow or ice comes. But they can predict that the seasons will continue to come at regular times. God promises to Noah,

> While the earth remains, seedtime and harvest, cold and heat, summer and winter, day and night, shall not cease. (Gen. 8:22)

God produces regular patterns of weather in the succession of seasons. He also produces irregularities or unpredictable events in the details of weather, day by day. The "great wind" in Job 1:19 that knocked down the house with Job's children in it is an example of unusual, unpredictable weather.

HARMONY

What is regular and what is unpredictable actually fit together harmoniously. A large number of individual events of weather fit together in succession to make up a whole season—let us say, the winter season. The season does not exist except by being composed of all the individual events. Conversely, the individual events of weather have meaning because from the beginning God designed them to be part of a larger pattern, the pattern of seasons. And he uses this pattern to affect the well-being of human beings: "Yet he did not leave himself without witness, for he did good by giving you *rains* from heaven and fruitful *seasons*, satisfying your hearts with food and gladness" (Acts 14:17). He has special care for his people Israel. In Deuteronomy 28 he indicates that he will send rain as a blessing on obedience (28:12), or a period of drought as a judgment on Israel's disobedience (vv. 23–24). (See fig. 10.1.)

Fig. 10.1: Regularities and Unpredictabilities

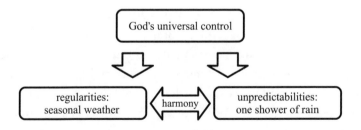

Once we have noticed the joint operation of predictability and unpredictability in the weather, we can see that the same occurs over and over again in God's works. For example, Newton's law of gravitation is a human approximate formulation of the universal pattern that God has specified for falling objects and gravitating objects. Each fall of a sparrow, as mentioned in Matthew 10:29, exhibits the general principle of gravitation. In addition, the fall of a sparrow is a particular instance of gravitation, unpredictable as to exactly when it will take place.

Similarly, God has specified in his word of power a general pattern for how birds will get the nourishment that they need to live (see Gen. 1:30). At the same time, the details concerning where there will be food for any particular bird are unpredictable (Matt. 6:26).

In the case of each human life, God has planned both the overall course of life and the details:

> Your eyes saw my unformed substance;
> in your book were written, every one of them,
>> the days that were formed for me,
>> when as yet there was none of them. (Ps. 139:16)

We may consider an analogy between God and human beings. Using language, we as human beings can talk about both the generalities and the specificities, the predictabilities and the unpredictabilities. We can talk about the seasons, and we can talk about today's weather.

In cases where we give directions, we can choose to give general directions or specifics. The mother may say to her son, "Make your bed every morning." She gives a general directive that will hold every morning. Or, on a particular occasion, she may stand over her son and issue detailed directions, either because she is showing him for the first time or because the bed needs *these special* sheets, tucked and folded in *this special* way, perhaps to prepare for a particular guest who is coming.

Normal human beings have these capabilities. God's capabilities, of course, are infinitely greater. Human managers and mothers avoid over-elaborate instructions and fussy interference with unnecessary details. But their limited management does not compare with God's unlimited rule. God has unlimited energy and unlimited attentiveness. His control is not an "interference" with a situation that is allegedly operating purely under its own autonomous power. We may conclude that his speech specifies both the generalities and the details, the predictabilities and the unpredictabilities. He specifies it all. And because his word has his power, his specification is effective. By *speaking* his will, he brings about what he specifies.

God's speech expresses his wisdom. He has a plan for history. He has thought it through. One event goes together with another. Everything harmonizes, that is, it works coherently according to plan. Thus, the particulars of weather go together with the generalities of the seasons, and the particulars of making one bed at one time go together with the generalities about making beds. The particulars about one roll of the dice go together with the generalities about all dice rolls. Why? God specifies it all, and it all expresses his wisdom, in the particulars and in generalities. We can praise him for it all.

CHAPTER 11

TRINITARIAN FOUNDATIONS FOR CHANCE

The wonderful interlocking between the general and the particular has its ultimate foundation, its ultimate archetype or original pattern, in God himself. We can see relationships to God as the foundation in several ways.

GOD'S SPEECH GOVERNING CHANCE

We saw earlier (chapter 5) that trinitarian communication is the basis for God's speech governing creation and providence. It therefore forms the basis in particular for chance events. God the Father has a plan, which he articulates through the speech of God the Son, and which he brings into realization by the power of the Holy Spirit. It snows because God has planned for it to snow; he "sends out his command" that brings snow (Ps. 147:15–16). Through the power and presence of the Holy Spirit the word takes effect, and snow comes.

By analogy we may say the same things about a flip of a coin. God the Father plans the flip and its result. He speaks through the speech of God the Son, sending out his command to govern the coin. The Holy Spirit is present, applying the word of command to the coin. The coin comes up heads, according to his plan and his speaking and his power. According to God's wisdom, the process and the result for the coin cohere with all other events in his plan.

UNITY AND DIVERSITY IN THE TRINITY

As a second way of seeing foundations in God, we may consider the unity and diversity in the Trinity. God is one God in three persons. God has unity in being one God. He has diversity in being three persons. The two go together. This unity and diversity is the ultimate unity and diversity, because it belongs to God himself rather than merely to creation. God's plan for creation also includes unity and diversity. God's capability to plan unity and diversity together has its root in God's own inner unity and diversity. The unity and diversity within creation is to be explained on the basis of who God is. Because God is one, the plan that he produces has unity. Because God is three persons, with diversity in himself, he has diversity in thought, and therefore diversity in plan. The diversity in his plan gets manifested in the diversity of the working out of his plan in time and space.[1]

The principle of unity and diversity applies to chance events like rain. We see unity in the pattern of weather and the pattern of rain over a whole season. We see diversity in the particular instances when God sends rain.

We can also see the interlocking of unity and diversity at a lower level. A single shower of rain on a plot of ground has unity as a single event. Within this event, we can observe the diversity involved in the fall of each distinct raindrop. The fall of each drop works together with the fall of all the other drops, and together this diversity in the drops forms a unity, namely, the shower of rain as a whole.

What about coin flips? We see unity in the general motion of a coin as it is thrown into the air. It goes up in the air and comes down in agreement with the general principle of Newton's law of gravitation. It spins at a regular speed. These are regularities. They are unities that belong to all the coin flips.

At the same time we have unpredictabilities, which are a kind of diversity. We see diversity in the results of different coin flips. One comes up heads. Another comes up tails. Then tails again, three times. Then heads. And so on. There are only two possible results for any one flip of the coin, which is itself a regularity. But each result comes at a particular time. And the whole sequence of results could be any of a large number of possibilities. For two flips in a row, there are a total of four different (i.e., diverse)

---

[1] Vern S. Poythress, *Redeeming Science: A God-Centered Approach* (Wheaton, IL: Crossway, 2006), 26; Cornelius Van Til, *The Defense of the Faith*, 2nd ed., rev. and abridged (Philadelphia: Presbyterian & Reformed, 1963), 25–26.

possibilities: two heads (HH), a head and then a tail (HT), a tail and then a head (TH), and two tails (TT). For three flips, there are a total of eight possibilities:

HHH
HHT
HTH
HTT
THH
THT
TTH
TTT

In the midst of the diversity of possibilities, we can immediately see one more regularity. The total number of possibilities for three tosses is fixed—there are eight possibilities in all. The total number of different possibilities resulting from a greater number of flips can also be calculated.

Let us work out the calculation for the total number of possibilities. For a single flip of a coin, there are two possibilities, heads (H) and tails (T). If the first flip comes up heads, there are two possibilities for the second flip. So we have in all two patterns of results, HH (heads followed by heads) and HT (heads followed by tails). Likewise, if the first flip comes up tails, there are two possibilities for the second flip. We could have TH (tails followed by heads) or TT (tails followed by tails). Hence, there is a total of $2 + 2 = 4$ possibilities if we have two coin flips.

Now add a third coin flip. If the first flip comes up heads, there are still 4 possibilities for the next two flips. Likewise, if the first flip comes up tails, there are 4 possibilities for the remaining two flips. So there is a total of $4 + 4 = 8$ possibilities. The argument can continue for any number of flips. Each additional flip results in twice as many possibilities as before. There are $8 + 8 = 8 \times 2 = 16$ possibilities for a sequence of 4 flips. There are $16 + 16 = 16 \times 2 = 32$ possibilities for 5 flips. And so on. We have here an exact, regular pattern. The pattern has unity, and each possibility within the pattern is part of the diversity.

There is a further unity of pattern. If we take the average over a large number of coin flips, we will find that about 50% come up heads. Though any one flip of the coin is unpredictable, the average is roughly predictable.

God plans and controls both the unpredictable and the predictable aspect. We will think more about these patterns when we discuss probability in later chapters.

THE RELATION OF UNITY AND DIVERSITY

We can see a foundation for generalities and particularities in another way. The generalities about how coin flips take place are related to the *class* of all coin flips. The class of all coin flips has common characteristics, and these common characteristics allow the classification of all coin flips into one group. Each coin flip within the class is an *instantiation*. We can also introduce a third category, the category of *association*, to designate the relationship between the particular instances and the class of instances to which they belong, or to designate relationships between different kinds of events and things within the overall plan of God.

The three categories, namely, classification, instantiation, and association, form a natural triad that has its ultimate roots in the Trinity.[2] All God's works involve all three persons of the Trinity, because they are the work of one God, and the three persons indwell one another. Yet we can more closely associate the general *class* of works with God the Father, because his plan gives unity to the class. In this sense, God the Father is the source for *classification*. God the Son became incarnate, and as the incarnate Son uniquely manifested God in time and space. He is the unique instantiation of God for revealing God to us. He is the ultimate source for the phenomena of *instantiation*. Third, God the Holy Spirit in his presence expresses the love and communion between God the Father and God the Son. He binds together *classification* and *instantiation*. He guarantees that they are closely associated with one another and live in harmony with one another. He also gives us an association, a communion, with God the Father through the Son. He is the source of *association* between the generality of *classification* and the particularity of *instantiation*.

All three categories, classification, instantiation, and association, belong together. They presuppose one another. A classification, such as the class of all coin flips, presupposes individual coin flips that make up the class. That is, it presupposes instantiations in individual coin flips. Conversely, any flip

---

[2] See Vern S. Poythress, *Logic: A God-Centered Approach to the Foundation of Western Thought* (Wheaton, IL: Crossway, 2013), chapter 14.

of a coin, to be a flip of a coin rather than some other event, presupposes a classification. It belongs to the class of all coin flips. Class and instantiation hold together by *association*. (See fig. 11.1.)

Fig. 11.1: Archetype for Regularities and Unpredictabilities

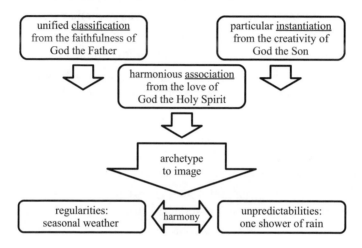

DIVINE ATTRIBUTES

Romans 1:20 indicates that God reveals himself in the things that he has made:

> For his invisible attributes, namely, his eternal power and divine nature, have been clearly perceived, ever since the creation of the world, in the things that have been made.

We can apply this general truth to chance events. Romans 1 indicates that God's nature is displayed in chance events like rain and coin flips. We can see that a number of his attributes are displayed.

Regularities in the long-range patterns of weather and coin flips display God's *faithfulness*. God specifically promised Noah that he would continue to enjoy a regular pattern of seasons (Gen. 8:22). God is faithful to his promise. He faithfully brings the seasonal cycle. Likewise, he faithfully maintains the regularities that we call the laws of gravity and the physical laws governing the motion of a coin as it goes up into the air and then down to the ground. He maintains the general pattern that says that a coin will come up heads roughly half of the time (50%). He is faithful in his sustenance of the world as a whole and coin flips in particular.

The particularities and unpredictabilities in the coming of rain and the result of individual coin flips manifest God's creativity. God is not constrained by any laws or regularities *above* him, regularities that would force him into a particular outcome. Any alleged government that was *above* God would, in fact, be the real "God," the real governor, a more ultimate governor than God himself. Such government would demote God into a small god, with the real control taking the form of some impersonal principle or principles above him. The Bible contradicts the idea of such an impersonal government by indicating that God is in control, and that his government over the universe is personal.

God always acts in accordance with his character. God is faithful to his character. So, as we have said, there is regularity in the world that he created. At the same time, God has choices that are not simply a logical outcome of his character. God is sufficient to himself. He did not *need* to create a world. But he did so. It was his choice. Having decided to create a world, he still had many choices about just what kind of world to create. He created earth with horses and *not* unicorns, with bugs but *not* with bug-eyed intelligent monsters. He created sea horses that look like horses, not like pigs.

God's creativity finds expression not only in his large-scale acts of creation, but in everyday "chance" events. Let me flip a coin. It comes up tails. Once I see that it has come up tails, I know that God has exercised creativity by including in his plan the decision that this particular flip of this particular coin should come up tails. It did not have to be so. God has within his plan many instances of creative choices, where he could have planned otherwise and could have done otherwise.

God displays his wisdom and his love through his acts of providence. But we can see a particular case of it when we look at the harmony between God's creativity and his faithfulness in governing rain and coin flips. God's exercise of wisdom produces harmony in the whole of his plan. He produces harmony between the course of an individual coin flip and the general pattern.

Or we may use God's love as a starting point to arrive at the same result. We know from Scripture that the Father loves the Son through the

Holy Spirit (John 3:35).[3] His love is the bond of his inner harmony. As a consequence, God's love reflects itself in the harmonies that he specifies and brings about in the world. And among these harmonies are the harmonies in the way coins flip. In other words, we can see that God is loving from coin flips, which manifest the effects of his love.

God reveals his faithfulness, creativity, wisdom, and love in the flip of a coin.[4] We could extend the list. He reveals his power. He controls what happens, even down to the details. Someone might object that the unpredictability of a coin flip suggests instead that no one is in control, perhaps not even God. But, as we observed in the previous chapter, the flip of the coin exhibits regularities in the motion of the coin, due to gravitation and other laws governing physical behavior. The laws express the personal will of God and reveal his power. They reveal his truth as well.

The very unpredictability of the flip of a coin shows the unique greatness of God. God knows the result from all eternity, but we do not know until it happens. God controls the outcome, while we cannot control it.

When we wake up to the display of God's character through chance events, such unpredictable events along with the regularities should lead us to praise him.

---

[3] Vern S. Poythress, *In the Beginning Was the Word: Language—A God-Centered Approach* (Wheaton, IL: Crossway, 2006), 252.
[4] We can observe at least a rough correlation between God's attributes of faithfulness, creativity, and love on the one hand and the Christian virtues of faith, hope, and love on the other hand. Faith is the appropriate response to God's faithfulness; hope is the appropriate response to God's creativity, which God will express in the future for which we hope; and love on our part is the appropriate response to God's love.

CHAPTER 12

RESPONDING TO CHANCE

How should we respond to chance events? What should we think of them, and what should we learn from them?

OUR RESPONSE

In every chance event God provides for us an example of his greatness. We should respond with worship. We should praise him for his power, his wisdom, his love, his faithfulness, and his creativity. It is easier to do so when we deal with happy events that we cannot predict. For example, by happenstance we may meet a long-lost friend, or we may receive an inheritance from an obscure great-uncle. Our response should be to praise God for this blessing. We should acknowledge that God brought it about. God showed his care for us by bringing us into contact with the long-lost friend, whom God knew that we would enjoy meeting.

It is not so easy for us to respond faithfully when the events involve pain and grief. God designed us and the world around us in such a way that pain and grief are not pleasant. And they are not normal to human beings in the good world with which human life began (Gen. 1:31). But because of the fall into sin, pain and grief are common experiences now. And they too are under God's control. However painful they may be, they still display God's greatness. Job understood this when he praised God even in the midst of pain:

> And he said, "Naked I came from my mother's womb, and naked shall I return. The LORD gave, and the LORD has taken away; blessed be the name of the LORD."
>
> In all this Job did not sin or charge God with wrong. (Job 1:21–22)

Chance events give us an opportunity to learn humility. Chance confronts us with our limitations in comparison to God. A chance event, by definition, is one that we as human beings cannot predict. God, by contrast, knows it beforehand, plans it, and brings it about by the greatness of his power. God calls us to depend on him and his wisdom and his knowledge and his plan, because we cannot depend on ourselves when it comes to chance. Our wisdom and our knowledge and our planning fail us.

In this light, we can see how people sin when they seek fortune-tellers and palm readers and other channels to secret knowledge. To begin with, they are disobeying God's direct command *not* to seek out these means:

> There shall not be found among you . . . anyone who practices divination or tells fortunes or interprets omens, or a sorcerer or a charmer or a medium or a necromancer or one who inquires of the dead, for whoever does these things is an abomination to the LORD. . . . for these nations, which you are about to dispossess, listen to fortune-tellers and to diviners. But as for you, the LORD your God has not allowed you to do this. (Deut. 18:10–12, 14)

In addition, when people seek fortune-tellers, they misuse the opportunities that God gives us to seek him. They avoid God's call to humility, and instead they invest their trust in the arrogance of the fortune-teller who claims to find out secrets.[1] They also crave security in the secret knowledge that they receive, rather than humbling themselves before God. They crave God-like knowledge instead of admitting that they do not know and they cannot know what he knows in his secret plan. "The secret things belong to the LORD our God, but the things that are revealed belong to us and to our children forever, that we may do all the words of this law" (Deut. 29:29).

REVELATION AND EVASION

The revelation of God's character through events in the world conforms to the key description found in Romans 1:18–21:

> [18] For the wrath of God is revealed from heaven against all ungodliness and unrighteousness of men, who by their unrighteousness suppress the

---

[1] It is arrogant to claim to have secret access to the future. Some fortune-tellers might admit that they do not always know. But even then, there is a basic underlying arrogance in their proceeding with an activity that God has forbidden. In fact, there is arrogance in all sin.

truth. [19] For what can be known about God is plain to them, because God has shown it to them. [20] For his invisible attributes, namely, his eternal power and divine nature, have been clearly perceived, ever since the creation of the world, in the things that have been made. So they are without excuse. [21] For although they knew God, they did not honor him as God or give thanks to him, but they became futile in their thinking, and their foolish hearts were darkened.

The passage indicates that God's character, "his eternal power and divine nature" (v. 20), "is plain to them, because God has shown it to them" (v. 19). His invisible attributes "have been *clearly* perceived" (v. 20). "They knew God" (v. 21). If these things are "plain," why do people not acknowledge them and take them to heart? Romans 1 gives the answer. People "by their unrighteousness suppress the truth" (v. 18). "Their foolish hearts were darkened" (v. 21).

Romans 1:22–23 goes on to indicate the way in which people suppress the truth:

> Claiming to be wise, they became fools, and exchanged the glory of the immortal God for images resembling mortal man and birds and animals and creeping things.

People make substitutes for God in the form of idols. In the ancient context, idols took the form of statues that people worshiped and that were supposed to mediate the presence of a god. In modern life in the Western world, idol statues and talismans are returning in some quarters, but more often people worship desirable goals: pleasure, wealth, fame, power, health, personal well-being, humanity. Natural laws, rather than being seen as the speech of God who is personal, are reinterpreted as an impersonal mechanism.[2] (See fig. 12.1.)

SUPPRESSION OF THE TRUTH ABOUT CHANCE EVENTS

What do people do when they come to consider chance events, like rain and coin flips? Some people—those with a deterministic philosophy—think that chance could be eliminated if we just knew enough. They think that the world is governed by mechanistic, deterministic laws. We have already

---

[2] Vern S. Poythress, *Redeeming Science: A God-Centered Approach* (Wheaton, IL: Crossway, 2006), 19–20, 27–28.

discussed this position briefly in chapter 8. For these people, mechanism becomes an impersonal substitute for God, but it is inadequate.[3]

Today, many more people believe in the ultimacy of chance. Unpredictable events are described simply as the product of "chance." People do not see them either as revealing God or as controlled by God. They just happen. When these people say "chance," they mean "chance" in the second sense given in Merriam-Webster's dictionary: "the assumed impersonal purposeless determiner of unaccountable happenings: LUCK."[4] "Chance" in this sense is a substitute for God. "Chance" rather than God, it is alleged, is "the impersonal purposeless determiner." Note that there is still a "determiner." So "chance," as a substitute, is close to the character of God. People are alleging that it has power to bring about events. In fact, people are implying that the power of chance is more comprehensive than God's power, because it is controlling events *outside* of God's power—if God exists at all. "Chance" in this sense might be called Chance, with a capital C, to emphasize that it is a substitute god.

Fig. 12.1: Responses to Regularities and Unpredictabilities

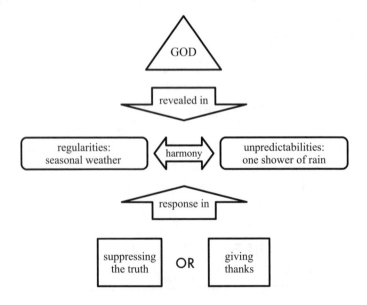

"Chance" is not only a substitute for God, but a *counterfeit*. It is enough like God to be plausible. People assume that it has power. It is present in all places and times, and it is an invisible and immaterial and transcendent source behind the phenomena. At the same time, it is impersonal and purposeless. That is a convenient change, because a *personal* God can hold us responsible. If God brings about chance events, we have to praise him and glorify him for those events. And we have not done so. We are guilty. If, on the other hand, Chance brings about the events, we are free from responsibility to respond. We have no guilt.

People have here a convenient way of avoiding the spiritual pain of dealing with guilt. They avoid also the prospect of being judged on the basis of guilt. As sinners and rebels against God and ungrateful creatures, we have powerful hidden motivations for preferring Chance to God as an explanation.

However, in the end Chance is a poor substitute for God, because it is an explanation that does not really explain. Let us consider. The word *chance* first gets associated with events that we as humans cannot predict or explain. The word *chance* acts like an empty word to label our ignorance. We are saying that we do not know the causes, and we do not know the reasons that would explain how and why an event came about. Our ability to explain fails us. So far, this situation corresponds to Merriam-Webster's first meaning, "something that happens unpredictably."

Then, in a second step, we convert this empty word *chance* into the word *Chance* with a capital C. The empty word suddenly becomes a label that we offer as the new explanation for the unpredictable event. But this new "explanation" has no real content. We just have a word to label what we do not know. We say, "Chance brought it about," but the word *Chance* translates into saying, "What we do not know brought it about." If Chance is a kind of god, it is a classic case of an unknown and unknowable god. It expresses a non-Christian view of transcendence.

Moreover, an appeal to Chance does not explain how chance events fit coherently into the larger patterns of this world. Rain fits into patterns of seasonal weather, and coin flips fit into patterns where heads come up half of the time. Rain is water, and conforms to the laws governing the behavior of water. Coins thrown into the air conform to the laws of gravitation and rigid-body motion. Even chance events have rationality to them.

Moreover, these events, even in their uniqueness or unpredictable character, can be described in language. Rationality and language belong to persons and the thinking of persons, not to the thinking of rocks and subpersonal creatures. We show by the way we act that we know that chance events conform to personal thinking and speech. We show that we know, deep down, that God specifies them and controls them. We know that the unpredictability in chance events shows God's creativity and the superiority of his greatness to our wisdom. We are suppressing what we know when we declare that these events are a result merely of Chance, the impersonal substitute.

TRUTH REVEALING GOD

We can arrive at the same conclusion by considering the issue of truth. It is true that when I flipped the coin, the result was tails. The truth about the result, and the truths about the processes leading to the result, show divine attributes. Truth is immutable, invisible, immaterial, everywhere present. It is also rational and language-like. All these are attributes of God. Why? Because truth belongs first to God's mind. Truth is what God knows. God's mind is divine, and all his attributes are expressed in everything he thinks, everything he plans, and everything he says.[5] We see the imprint or reflection of God and his attributes when we deal even with one truth, namely, the truth that the coin came up tails. We know God and his attributes, because they are "plain" in the things that he has made. But we will not acknowledge God. We do not give him thanks. We rebel.

Rebellion against God is deep within us. It is so deep that it covers its tracks. We do not realize the depth of our rebellion because we make excuses. And we make substitutes, like Chance as a substitute, or fortune-tellers as a substitute source for security, without even realizing that we are betraying God in the process. Romans 1:21 has said it: "their foolish hearts were darkened."

How shall we escape? Human beings do not escape by intelligence or insight. Rather, they use their intelligence and their insights to help cover their tracks. The clever person produces clever reasoning for excusing his rebellion and hiding it from himself as well as others.

---

[5] Poythress, *Redeeming Science*, chapter 14.

THE REMEDY

The Bible indicates that God has intervened to provide a remedy. We did not deserve it. We deserved his wrath and his just retribution for our betrayal: "For the wrath of God is revealed from heaven against all ungodliness and unrighteousness of men" (Rom. 1:18). But wrath is not the end of the story. "But now the righteousness of God has been manifested . . . the righteousness of God through faith in Jesus Christ for all who believe" (Rom. 3:21–22). God the Father sent Christ into the world on a mission to bring salvation from sin and rebellion (John 12:47). Christ has borne the penalty for our sins, and through faith in him we may receive forgiveness from God and be welcomed into his arms as his children (Rom. 3:23–26; 1 Pet. 2:24–25; 2 Cor. 5:17–21).

We need not only forgiveness but renewal in our minds and hearts. And this also God accomplishes through Christ. He makes us a new creation (2 Cor. 5:17) and renews our mind (Col. 3:9–10; Rom. 12:1–2). We must leave it to others to expound at greater length the rich nature of God's salvation.[6] Our point here is that salvation in Christ includes a "renewal" or change in our minds. We have to learn to think differently about the world. And this change in thinking includes a change in thinking about chance. We must take to heart the fact that God is in control of unpredictable events. In reality, Chance is not a god. The word *chance* is properly used to describe the limitations of human knowledge, not the limitations of God's power.

---

[6] See, for example, J. I. Packer, *Knowing God* (Downers Grove, IL: InterVarsity Press, 1993); John Blanchard, *Right with God: A Straightforward Book to Help Those Searching for Personal Faith in God* (Edinburgh/Carlisle, PA: Banner of Truth, 1985).

CHAPTER 13

CHANCE IN EVOLUTIONARY NATURALISM

We should consider one particular case where chance has a key role in human thinking: the philosophy of evolutionary naturalism. What is evolutionary naturalism? We need to clarify what we mean. We do not simply mean all forms of theory that postulate gradual origins of living things. First of all, evolutionary naturalism is a form of *naturalism*. Naturalism or *materialism* says that the universe is nothing but matter and motion and energy. *Evolutionary naturalism* combines this basic belief with the claim that all living things originated and differentiated into their present diversity by chance physical processes, without purpose.

EVOLUTIONARY NATURALISM AS PHILOSOPHY

Evolutionary naturalism clearly leaves God out. It says that the universe is matter and motion and energy. It implies that either there is no God or he is distant and uninvolved. It also says that life appears and propagates itself *without purpose*. Personal purposes of God are excluded.

Evolutionary naturalism needs to be distinguished from all the views that ascribe to God the control over apparently chance processes. Some people who believe that God exists may think that God brought life about through gradual processes, more or less the way that current evolutionary biology describes the process, but that God has continuously been in charge and in control of all the details. Hence, all the details have purposes—

though we as human beings may not be able to discern the purposes. Others who believe in God may believe that God created each major kind of living thing separately. Or they may believe that God used gradual processes quite a bit of the time, but that he created Adam and Eve separately. We must leave it to other books to sort through the various viewpoints that affirm God's involvement.[1]

Evolutionary naturalism is different from all these views because it eliminates God's involvement. In place of God, it has "chance." I have called evolutionary naturalism a *philosophy* because it is a speculation that goes far beyond normal science and scientific evidence. It postulates a whole view of the universe in which there is no purpose. It arrives at its view not by gradually building up evidence, but by a leap. It simply *interprets* the evidence according to its own pre-chosen assumption—that the universe is *only* matter and motion and energy and nothing more. Of course, if you assume this, you endeavor to fit science into your framework. But others, against the background of their own assumptions, see science as testifying to the wisdom and power of God. God's rule over the universe is the very foundation for scientific investigation of the universe. God guarantees both the regularities and the unpredictabilities (which we then call "chance"; see chapter 10).

THE ROLE OF CHANCE

Chance obviously plays a key role in evolutionary naturalism. Evolutionary naturalism sees the presence of chance all through the picture that it presents of the gradual evolution of living things. Life originated "by chance." Each living thing that survives long enough to reproduce survives by chance. Chance mutations lead gradually to new forms of life.

DOES CHANCE FUNCTION AS A GOD-SUBSTITUTE?

The word *chance* in these contexts floats ambiguously between the two meanings that we discussed earlier (chapter 9). At first it seems only to represent *unpredictability*, which is outside the scope of human ability to predict. It is a confession of ignorance: a scientist may say, "I do not know why this mutation took place at this particular time and place, and I do not

---

[1] Vern S. Poythress, *Redeeming Science: A God-Centered Approach* (Wheaton, IL: Crossway, 2006), 252–258.

suppose that anyone can know, given the present state of our knowledge." But then the word comes to play a positive role in explaining evolution. "Chance" brought about the origin of vertebrates, fish, reptiles, whales, and so on. In this kind of context, "chance" appears to be moving toward being a substitute god. It is Chance with a capital C. A blank space in our knowledge now becomes a positive explanation. As we already observed, this explanation does not explain. It is religiously motivated by the need for a substitute for God. The word *Chance* appears to do the job until we ask whether we know what it is. It simply represents what we do not know!

Chance is somewhat of an embarrassment to evolutionary naturalism, because as a philosophy naturalism aspires to give a rational, humanly intelligible explanation of life. Its approach is a form of rationalism, because it wants to exercise reason independent of God. But at the heart of the explanation is Chance, which is irrational.

Moreover, what is left as irrational is a potential source of divine action. Every instance of "chance," according to a theistic point of view, is an instance of divine control, and so injects purpose into a cosmos, even though philosophical naturalism must dogmatically assert that the events are without purpose.

Within a Christian approach, as we have seen (chapter 10), we affirm God's sovereignty over both the regularities—the laws to which evolutionary naturalism appeals—and the unpredictabilities—what evolutionary naturalism ascribes to Chance. In both cases, evolutionary naturalism is assuming, rather than proving, its own essentially atheistic starting point.

CHANCE IN THE ORIGIN OF THE UNIVERSE

Similar difficulties confront evolutionary naturalism when it talks about the origin of the universe rather than the origin of life. The fundamental physical constants for the universe, such as the speed of light and the strength of the force of gravitation, have values that turn out to be "just right" so that the atomic building blocks for complex life become available. Is this "just-right" fit a pure accident, a matter of "chance"? From the point of view of philosophical materialism, the chances are just too low. That is to say that Chance with a capital C does not result in a plausible enough explanation. So cosmologists have postulated multiple universes. Some of the role of Chance can be eliminated if we speculate that all possible values of the fundamental constants and all possible forms of fundamental laws are embodied in *some* universe. But this paring down of the role of Chance has a price. We must invest confidence in some other source. In this case, the confidence is placed in the postulate of multiple universes. Who says that all possible values are necessarily embodied (not just conceivable)? And why is it so (if indeed it is so)? From where does this necessity come? Where do the laws themselves come from? At the bottom of the whole process of explanation is still a dark blank. Some things are just accepted—by faith, we might say. Those things play part of the role of a God-substitute.

DIFFICULTIES WITH DETERMINISM

The use of Chance as a substitute god produces other difficulties, akin to the difficulties with physical determinism. Let us see how.

Physical determinism undermines the significance of human choice. If the entire future can be precisely calculated from the positions and velocities of the material particles in the universe, real human choice seems to be an illusion. The calculation appears to show that we are simply "fated" to walk through a future that is already written in stone by the properties of the particles that make up our bodies and the environment around us.

As we observed in chapter 8, quantum mechanics, at least in its current state, suggests a picture that contains an ultimate indeterminism instead of physical determinism. Our human fates cannot be predicted simply by mechanical calculation. Some microscopic events cannot be predicted at all, but happen "by chance." So have we escaped deterministic fate?

Suppose we try to make Chance a substitute god. Chance plays a role that determines the outcomes of all the otherwise unpredictable events. Chance plus the equations of physics produce the series of outcomes for each human being. But Chance by definition is supposedly purposeless. And the equations of physics, according to materialist thinking, are just "there" rather than being the speech of God the Creator.

If so, there is no purpose or innate meaning either in Chance or in physics. So there is no innate meaning in the motions of the particles in our bodies. Genuine human purpose again becomes an illusion. We are fated to walk through the future by Chance and physics taken together, rather than by deterministic physics taken by itself. The addition of Chance does nothing to improve meaning. If anything, it makes our situation worse.

The equations of physics can at least have a kind of wonderful beauty and harmony to them, but Chance represents blank meaninglessness.

It is no wonder that the French existentialists, having given up believing in God, struggled with despair over the meaninglessness of human existence. Their best response was to exhort themselves and others to *produce* meaning temporarily in their lives by acts of will. The same goes for the current forms of evolutionary naturalism. According to naturalism, there is no innate personal meaning in the universe, its laws, or its chance events. So, individually and corporately, the best we can do is generate our own personal meanings.

Unfortunately, even this level of personal acts of will and personal creation of meanings is undermined if these very acts of will and acts of creativity are *fated* by the interaction of particles, energy, and Chance. Not only are you and I accidents, but your act of will and your creation of meaning is an accident. Where are *you*, the real person who makes responsible decisions? You are evaporated into a mechanistic, meaningless fate. Your fate is the joint effect of impersonal matter, impersonal law, and impersonal Chance. (See fig.13.1a.)

Fig. 13.1a: If Chance Rules

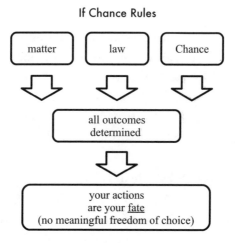

We may contrast this bleak impersonalist picture with the personal character of God's rule. God as a personal God has created human persons in his image. Therefore, human beings have personal significance and have ability to make choices and act as personal agents. Our actions are not *fated*, either by Chance or by mechanisms. (See fig.13.1b.)

Fig. 13.1b: When God Rules

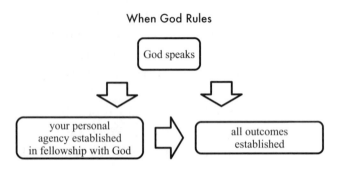

When God Rules

More consequences follow from believing in Chance as a substitute god. If Chance rules, the actions of naturalists themselves are fated. According to their own position, the naturalists are merely fated to make the claims they do in favor of naturalism. Fate undermines the significance of the arguments themselves.[2]

By its philosophical commitments, evolutionary naturalism has made for itself a desert devoid of meaning, in which it proposes that human beings live. And of course, if they are consistent, the advocates of naturalism must themselves live there, along with the rest of humanity.

Surely we can find some irony in the fact that the advocates of naturalism still cling to the hope that they can make convincing arguments for naturalism while living in this desert. The desert is so barren that it furnishes no nourishment to support any argument whatsoever.

WIDER IMPLICATIONS FOR SCIENCES

Evolutionary naturalism is the most prominent example in which scientific insights are mixed with philosophical commitments that substitute Chance for God. But analogous issues crop up in every kind of science. Scientific insights are based on experiments, and experiments always include instances

---

[2] See also Alvin Plantinga's argument against naturalism (Plantinga, *Where the Conflict Really Lies: Science, Religion, and Naturalism* [Oxford: Oxford University Press, 2011], chapter 10).

of chance variations. Even the most respected scientific laws have come to be accepted because of evidence, and the evidence in its details always includes not only regularities but unpredictabilities. Each experimental instance illustrating Newton's laws of motion or the laws of fluid flow is unrepeatable when we include minute details. So how do we include chance events within our view of science?

The Bible says that God controls all chance events. God is wise and rational; God's faithfulness and his creativity harmonize. And so, even though we do not ourselves control the chance variations, we can confidently proceed to grow in knowledge of the world, including the insights that sciences offer. Without God, however, there is no foundation to limit the suspicion that Chance is an irrational piece in the universe. If it were the case that Chance ruled, science would have irrationality at its foundation. Such is not a desirable platform from which to try to launch a rational claim that we can dispense with God.

REVISITING METHODOLOGICAL NATURALISM

We may also consider what meaning belongs to the principle of *methodological naturalism*. *Methodological naturalism* designates the principle that in their methods scientists look only for *naturalistic* explanations for events.[3] Certainly it makes sense for scientists to focus on secondary causes, because these characterize God's regular government of the world. Such scientific investigation is legitimate.

But methodological naturalism means more. It says that scientists are supposed to assume the uniformity of natural law and that they exclude "supernatural" or "preternatural" influences. This kind of recipe has coherent meaning if we already know what is "natural." We have to know (1) what the laws are (thereby specifying what is in accord with "nature"), (2) that there are no exceptions, and (3) that everything in principle is determined by law.

But we know none of these things. First, current sciences give us useful guesses about law or approximations to it. With only an approximate view of law, we cannot say for sure what is and is not natural rather than supernatural. If we see an unusual event, is it due to supernatural influence or to

---

[3] See Poythress, *Redeeming Science*, chapter 19.

a failure in our approximation or to some as-yet-unknown "natural law"? We cannot tell for sure.

Moreover, a biblically based worldview breaks down the hard-and-fast distinction between natural and supernatural, because God, a supernatural being, is continually involved in what we consider most "natural." In addition, the idea that there are no "exceptions to a law" has two different meanings, depending on whether our concept of law is impersonalistic, or whether we think of law as God's personal speech. In the latter case, exceptions to normal patterns are specified by God's speech. So they are under God's law, but are surprising to us and to our approximate estimates as to what the law is.

Worst of all, the whole scheme works well only with deterministic "laws." Consider the decay of a radioactive nucleus, which cannot be predicted by scientific laws as we know them. The individual event of decay, in contrast to statistical predictions for many instances of decay, lies outside the domain of "law," and so there is no way of saying whether it is "natural" or "preternatural" or "supernatural."[4] Biblical teaching indicates that God does it. And scientists cannot find a deterministic secondary cause, so they have no "natural" explanation at all. An event that has no secondary cause but only a primary cause, namely God, is usually considered "supernatural." And yet myriads of such quantum mechanical events are happening every second. In terms of frequency, they are "normal" and "natural." Conceptually, the distinction between natural and supernatural threatens to breaks down. This breakdown implies that the recipe for "methodological naturalism" has difficulties.[5]

But methodological purists may attempt a rescue operation: Chance with a capital C fills the gap in naturalism. Chance is treated as a part of

---

[4] Alvin Plantinga in a similar way notes that indeterminism of quantum mechanics leaves wide scope for divine action: "given contemporary quantum physics, there isn't any sensible way to say what intervention *is*, let alone find something in science with which it is incompatible" (Plantinga, *Where the Conflict Really Lies*, 97; also 108–121).

[5] Conceivably, methodological naturalism might be construed as simply a recipe for tight verbal restraint: a scientist may have a personal opinion about supernatural causes, but his or her official report includes only explanations in terms of secondary causes—it is silent when such explanations run out. But this is not the usual understanding of methodological naturalism. Methodological naturalism is usually proposed not as a verbal muzzle but as a positive guide to research programs. It guides how scientists are supposed to think about the world during the course of their research, not merely how they write up conclusions. To serve as a guide, it needs to supply a clear concept of what is "natural."

There is an additional difficulty. Causal explanations have already run out when we come to the word *chance*. Chance with a small *c* is not a causal explanation but a confession of the absence of explanation. Since chance is an integral element in scientific practice and all experimental science, scientists in fact are not silent: they do talk about chance. In doing so, they refer to divine action (without specifically acknowledging it).

"nature." That is one way of choosing to talk. But it is easy to miss the fact that the word *chance* can slide between two meanings: *chance* as a label for the unknown and *Chance* viewed as "natural" and explanatory. The latter begs the question of God's involvement in chance events. And it also raises the question of whether methodological naturalism, in some forms, involves intrinsically the appeal to Chance as a substitute god. Such a move presupposes the absence of God, rather than presenting a coherent argument.

In sum, the idea of methodological naturalism is difficult to stabilize without making a religious commitment to excluding God. Appeals to chance within science are problematic, unless we put chance itself within the framework of a Christian worldview. Those of us who are Christians need to live with an awareness of God, and not compromise with the prevalent atmosphere that ignores him.

CHAPTER 14

CHANCE AND IDOLATRY

We have said that Chance with a capital C can function as a substitute for God. Instead of giving God the glory for unpredictable events, people can say that it was "chance" or "luck." But issues related to chance can lead to idolatrous substitutes in more subtle ways. Let us consider some of them.

SPIRITS

Fortune-telling and divination and some other occult practices claim to give people an advantage by giving them secret information about the future. The secret sources may be of two kinds, "spiritual" or "natural." In Acts 16, Paul and his companions "were met by a slave girl who had a spirit of divination and brought her owners much gain by fortune-telling" (Acts 16:16). She had "a spirit of divination." That is, she was in touch with or manipulated by a spiritual being, who provided her with secret information. The spirit, not the girl herself, was the source of secret knowledge.

What about these spiritual beings? In modern societies many sophisticated people are secular and materialistic in orientation. They think that there are no such things as angels or evil spirits. In their view, the idea that such things exist is mere superstition. We can agree that superstition is indeed widespread. But how do these people know that such superstition may not be an exaggeration and distortion of something real?

Natural sciences, by focusing on the material aspect of the world,[1] leave out the world of spirits in their foundational orientation. So the fact that natural sciences have not detected spirits proves nothing. What is most

---

[1] I simplify here. Biology focuses on living things, and life is purposeful; in this respect, it is not strictly reducible to physics and chemistry.

persuasive in modern society is rather a cultural atmosphere, a set of assumptions or a philosophy of nature that is materialistic. This philosophy appeals to the successes of science. But in the process, it wrongly infers from scientific success (which describes the material aspect) that the material must be all that there is rather than only one aspect of what there is. The cultural sophisticates, by accepting this atmosphere at face value, are simply allowing themselves to be naive victims of cultural propaganda. The propaganda happens to be popular among the elite, and gives them a feeling of superiority over the masses who are still in the clutches of various "superstitions." But their confidence in their superior knowledge is an illusion.

As a follower of Christ, I have confidence in the instruction in the Bible, and so I also have confidence in the existence of angels and evil spirits. The Bible describes these spirits in matter-of-fact ways. There is no incompatibility with science, because science focuses on only one aspect of the whole.

If supernatural spirits exist, and they have great power, they may have more knowledge than human beings. Moreover, the spirits behind human attempts at divination are evil spirits, and may lie. They may deceive or manipulate human recipients, so that in various ways some of the pronouncements based on divination can make the human recipients feel as if they have received something of value.

In sum, the Bible teaches that the world of spiritual beings is real. Angels and demons are real. But the Bible forbids us from trying to access spirits in order to gain secret knowledge (Deut. 18:9–14). The desire for such access substitutes the world of spirits for God, and is a form of idolatry.

SECRET KNOWLEDGE IN "NATURAL" SOURCES?

Some forms of divination may not make claims to have contact with the spirit world. Rather, they may claim to be "natural" in orientation. They seek out secret knowledge not from personal, spiritual forces, but perhaps from natural forces. For instance, astrology claims to seek out information based on the influences of the planets and stars on human beings.[2] Or maybe people think that influence or information can be obtained from certain special objects.

---

[2] However, there may still be *forms* of astrology that believe that the influence of planets is mediated through spirits associated with the planets.

The Old Testament describes a case that may be of this kind. Ezekiel 21:21–22 describes the king of Babylon using divination:

> For the king of Babylon stands at the parting of the way, at the head of the two ways, to use *divination*. He shakes the arrows; he consults the teraphim; he looks at the liver. Into his right hand comes the divination for Jerusalem, to set battering rams, . . .

What was the king of Babylon doing? The passage in Ezekiel is describing a known practice of the time, so it does not go into details. The lack of detail leaves us with questions. Who or what did the king of Babylon think he was consulting? How did he go about it? What exactly are the "teraphim"? They may be some kind of occult object, perhaps an idol that is supposed to have spiritual force. What does it mean to "look at the liver"? Perhaps the king hoped that by slaughtering a chicken or a cow in the proper circumstances, with the proper procedures and the proper invocation of gods, he might gain information from inspecting its liver. He might have thought that the shape or structure of the liver would provide a secret source of advice about which road to take in his program of conquest ("the parting of the way").

So was the king's source natural or supernatural? In paganism and poly-theism, gods and spiritual forces can be confusedly identified with certain natural forces, so that the very distinction between natural and supernatural is blurred.

The blurring of the distinction between gods and nature, and the un-dermining of the real distinction between Creator and creature, is char-acteristic of many false religions. False religions are inevitably *counterfeit* religions, which combine some fragments of truth into an overall view that corrupts both worship and the human beings who engage in it. God— the true God—no longer receives the exclusive honor and worship that he deserves. Honor goes instead to various spirits or gods, or to natural or quasi-natural forces. The forces are regarded as self-sufficient, rather than under the control of the one true God. So these ways of seeking for secret knowledge, whatever they are, amount to forms of idolatry.

SECRET KNOWLEDGE FROM GOD

People sometimes seek secret knowledge not only from spirits or from nature but from God. If we acknowledge, as we should, that God is in control of all unpredictable events, we may be tempted to use some un-predictable event that we select in order to obtain secret information from God. For example, a person wants to know whom to marry, or whether he will get married, or how many children he will have, or how long he will live—the list of questions about the future is endless. He flips a coin or rolls a die,[3] after asking God to give him an answer. Is this kind of procedure legitimate?

God controls the outcome of the coin flip or the roll of the die. And God does know the future. But these realities about God do not give us an authorization to try to pry into the unknown future, or to demand that he give us knowledge by means of chance events. Rather, everyone should be content: "I have learned in whatever situation I am to be content" (Phil. 4:11). We should trust God rather than grasping for human security:

> Trust in the LORD with all your heart,
>   and do not lean on your own understanding.
> In all your ways acknowledge him,
>   and he will make straight your paths. (Prov. 3:5–6)

We should recognize that the future belongs to God, and is secret:

> The secret things belong to the LORD our God, but the things that are revealed [in God's written word] belong to us and to our children for-ever, that we may do all the words of this law. (Deut. 29:29)

We have seen in the Bible some instances where God authorized lead-ers to obtain information by lots (Josh. 7:14–18; 1 Sam. 10:20–21; Acts 1:23–26). But these events were exceptional. They involved special circum-stances and special authorization. In our circumstances today, we must not use a random event to try to *force* God to reveal information that we think we need. In such an act we are trying to put ourselves in charge, rather than being content to have God in charge, revealing information in the ways and at the times that he chooses. God may show mercy to immature believers who do such things, but he may also justly refuse to provide an answer. In such a case, the person who depends on a lot or a random event may walk away misled. He does not realize that God is not under obligation to provide an answer. The person's presumption misleads him.

---

[3] "Die" is the singular form of "dice."

Some people have tried practices like "Bible dipping" or "lucky dipping," in which they open a Bible at random, and, with eyes closed, put their finger on the page. Then they look at the verse to which their finger points. They expect the verse to speak directly to them. The verse, they hope, will answer their question or give them a hint to guide a crucial decision. They are using random events.

They are right that God controls all such events. They are also right in believing that the verses of the Bible are all inspired by God; the verses *do* speak to anyone who reads them. The verses are all valuable (2 Tim. 3:16–17). But the Bible dipper is not really relying simply on those valid principles. Rather, he is hoping to get some secret information, based on *which* verse he finds under his finger. Rather than reading the verse in its context, he reads it in isolation, as if it were a secret message to him alone. That shift toward a secret message is already a distortion of the verse's meaning. God gives us each verse, not in isolation, but in the context of the surrounding paragraph and the particular book of the Bible in which it is found. God intends us to read and understand the verse by taking into account the context. And God addresses all his people, not just one individual.

Typically the Bible dipper wants a way to take control, to force God to speak to a particular need. The practice is superstitious, even though it uses the holiness of the Bible in the hope of "baptizing" its superstitious character. The motive of trying to force an answer makes the practice very different from another experience, in which a believer is reading the Bible in an ordinary way and some verse stands out and impresses its meaning on his mind. In this latter case, the reader is aware that God must take the initiative, and that the reader should not try to force an answer. We see here the difference between being legitimately empowered by God and taught by the Holy Spirit, and trying to take power over God's secrets by our own manipulation.

MAGIC

People may also try to gain an advantage by magic. In this case, they are not seeking secret knowledge but secret power. Both knowledge and power belong ultimately to God. So here again idolatrous corruption creeps into the process. One of the most obvious ways of seeking to gain an advantage is by sacrificing to gods. Before taking a sea voyage, a person may sacrifice to the god of the sea. Before a battle, one may sacrifice to the god of war. Before seeking a wife, one may sacrifice to the goddess of love. One hopes to obtain success by having the power of the god on one's side. All of these are obviously substitutes for allegiance to the true God of the Bible.

These acts of idolatry characteristically take place because people are insecure about the element of chance that they see in their future. A storm may or may not come up while they are at sea. Whether a storm comes up, and whether it swamps or destroys their ship, is a matter of "chance," they think. Similarly, no human being can be certain beforehand about the outcome of the next battle. Special circumstances and "happenstances" can have an influence. Sometimes a small force may defeat a much larger army—as in the case of Gideon and his three hundred men (Judges 7).

So what should we do? If we confront uncertainty about the future, the proper course is to pray to God for his blessing, and to trust his power, not the alleged power of chance.

The desire for secret power can take other forms. People sometimes seek communion with the spirit world in order to invoke the power of spirits, or to have a powerful spirit inhabit them.

SUPERSTITIOUS POWER

The dangers of superstitious practices are real. What about wearing a talisman to protect oneself from evil spirits? What about carrying a rabbit's foot for "good luck"? What about having a good-luck charm on a bracelet? In their usual uses, these things are substitutes for trust in God. At root, the use of them is idolatrous.

The person who uses them probably knows that they do not always work. Still, he thinks to himself, "I am better off with them than without them. There is some chance that they may *sometimes* work." But a person with this kind of thinking has a divided allegiance. His allegiance and his trust are *partly* in the rabbit's foot, even though he knows better than to put total confidence in it. This divided allegiance is wrong. God is a "jealous" God, who is worthy of our *exclusive* allegiance. We must trust in him *alone*:

> You shall worship the Lord your God
>> and him *only* shall you serve. (Matt. 4:10)

What about wearing a cross for protection from demons? The cross is a Christian symbol, and many people wear crosses as a sign of their Christian faith. They want other people to know that they are Christians. They know that they are protected by God, not by the physical cross in itself.

To rely on the physical cross apart from God is superstition. People who trust in the physical object on their neck are trusting in the cross as if it had a magical power built into it. But to trust in God, and in the work of Christ to which the cross points, is no superstition, but true worship of the true God. We should have trust in God on the basis of the promises and commitments to us that God himself has made through Christ.

RITUALS

People sometimes have rituals that they go through. Professional athletes may make sure that they put on their equipment in a certain order. They may have a "lucky shoe" or a "lucky mark" on the shoe or a "lucky tattoo." They go through certain fixed rituals when they begin to warm up. A businessman has a "lucky shirt" or a "lucky tie" that he wears to important meetings.

But, as we have said, "luck" does not exist. Most of these practices constitute subtle forms of idolatry. In reply, we should say, "Give up these things, and trust in God *alone*."

On the other hand, we should not too quickly judge motives. Does an athlete put on his equipment in exactly the same order because he is superstitious? Or is it because he knows that this order is efficient, because the sameness of order helps to make sure that he does not forget anything, and because the sameness of order enables him to focus on other things, such as his faith in God and the calling that God has given him? There may not be any superstition in it. Does the athlete go through the same steps in warming up just because it is a good way to warm up? He knows that God has made his body in such a way that he is less likely to strain a muscle or get injured if his muscles are warm, and his warm-up is then a positive way of honoring the wisdom of God in the way that God made his body.

Some athletes can be seen crossing themselves before a game or before a play. Are they using this act as a kind of talisman, with the idea that it gives them more "luck"? Then they are acting superstitiously, even though the act of crossing oneself is a Christian symbol. Or do they use the act as a physical expression of a prayer in which they are consecrating themselves to serve God during the athletic contest? Are they praying to thank God for the opportunity and for the outcome, whatever it may be? Again, people's motives matter. (See fig. 14.1.)

Fig. 14.1: Spirits and Powers

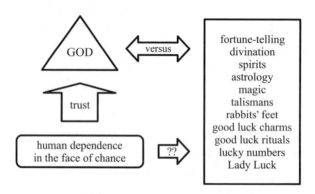

GAMES OF CHANCE

We can see similar dangers of superstitious practices creeping in when it comes to gambling and games of chance—with cards, dice, a roulette wheel, or some other kind of wheel with a spinner. Some players may develop superstitious habits. They blow air on the dice before rolling them— "for good luck," they might say. They may talk to the dice, "Come up six, six, six," as if they could *command* the dice to obey their will. They know, of course, that they cannot really do that, and they may be doing it as a kind of joke, but they may also be doing it because they hope that somehow they can exert magical influence. It makes six more likely, they hope.

People may make sure that they wear their "lucky shirt" or "lucky charm" when they go to play a game. They may pay attention to a radio announcement or a newspaper or some other source that provides them with "lucky numbers" for the lottery that day. They may bet on a horse because the horse has a name that they perceive as "lucky for them." They may be careful to shuffle a deck of cards in a certain way. Motives may differ, of course. One person shuffles in a certain way because he has never been able to succeed in shuffling a deck any other way! But many times, these practices represent allegiance to "luck" that substitutes for allegiance to God.

Gamblers may talk about "Lady Luck," an expression that suggests they are making "luck" semipersonal, ascribing governing power to it, and using it as a substitute for God.

In addition, the whole practice of gambling is attractive to people because they hope for a lucky day or a lucky lottery number or a lucky series of wins that will set them up, if not for life, at least for a year or for the near future. By contrast, they should be trusting in God to provide them their daily bread: "Give us this day our daily bread" (Matt. 6:11). Of course, some people might make the excuse that they are trusting in God to give them their daily bread *through* their act of gambling. But they should read the book of Proverbs, which commends diligence in work rather than a "quick" win:

> Wealth gained hastily will dwindle,
>   but whoever gathers little by little will increase it. (Prov. 13:11)

> A slack hand causes poverty,
>   but the hand of the diligent makes rich.
> He who gathers in summer is a prudent son,
>   but he who sleeps in harvest is a son who brings shame. (10:4–5)

> Whoever works his land will have plenty of bread,
>   but he who follows worthless pursuits lacks sense. (12:11)

> The hand of the diligent will rule,
>   while the slothful will be put to forced labor. (12:24)

I conclude that seeking to gain wealth through games of chances represents disobedience to the Lord. It shows disrespect for him concerning the means that he has established in this world to make one's living. It shows idolatrous trust in luck rather than in God, who has shown us the true way of righteousness and the true way of serving him. It is driven by greed, which is ungodly lust for wealth.

As we have seen, the temptation to give allegiance to luck crops up not only in games of chance but in ordinary life, with good-luck charms and good-luck rituals. We should recognize these things for what they are: substitutes for God. The remedy, however, lies not merely in knowledge of the dangers, but in the allegiance of the heart. Let us give ourselves to Christ, and follow him alone. In following him, we will have spiritual security, and we need not worry about anything at all. Listen to the assurance and confidence that Christ gives us:

> Therefore I tell you, do not be anxious about your life, what you will eat or what you will drink, nor about your body, what you will put on. Is not life more than food, and the body more than clothing? Look at the birds of the air: they neither sow nor reap nor gather into barns, and yet your heavenly Father feeds them. Are you not of more value than they? And which of you by being anxious can add a single hour to his span of life? And why are you anxious about clothing? Consider the lilies of the field, how they grow: they neither toil nor spin, yet I tell you, even Solomon in all his glory was not arrayed like one of these. But if God so clothes the grass of the field, which today is alive and tomorrow is thrown into the oven, will he not much more clothe you, O you of little faith? Therefore do not be anxious, saying, "What shall we eat?" or "What shall we drink?" or "What shall we wear?" For the Gentiles seek after all these things, and your heavenly Father knows that you need them all. But seek first the kingdom of God and his righteousness, and all these things will be added to you.
>
> Therefore do not be anxious about tomorrow, for tomorrow will be anxious for itself. Sufficient for the day is its own trouble. (Matt. 6:25–34)

God will take care of all the chance events of all kinds. Jesus indicates that the key to security is serving God: "Seek first the kingdom of God and his righteousness, and all these things will be added to you" (v. 33).

PART III

PROBABILITY

CHAPTER 15

WHAT IS PROBABILITY?

What is "probability"? We may say, "Edith will probably come to the party."
Or, "Edith will probably not come." In both cases we are not certain. But
in the first case we think that Edith is more likely to come than not. We
also have language concerning "possibility": "Possibly Edith will come to
the party." Or, "possibly it will rain today." All these formulations express
our uncertainty. By using different expressions we acknowledge that there
is a range of relative uncertainty. A "probable" event is more likely than an
event that is "not probable."

Questions of uncertainty become particularly weighty in court cases.
Suppose a person is on trial for murder. Is the defendant guilty of murder?
The prosecution and the defense may both present evidence and arguments.
But the evidence on the two sides is not absolutely conclusive. Some of the
evidence may be circumstantial. One or more of the witnesses may be lying.

The jury has to make up its mind. The standard guideline says that the
jurors should convict the defendant only if he is guilty "beyond a reasonable doubt." It does not say, "only if a juror has absolute certainty." The
guideline recognizes that in court cases human beings never have exhaustive
information, and that they can never be absolutely certain about the reliability of the human witnesses. They must deal with situations where they
think that the defendant is probably guilty, or probably innocent.

The guideline weighs the decision in favor of the defendant when it
speaks of "reasonable doubt." A defendant is treated as "innocent until
proven guilty." A jury is not supposed to convict a defendant merely because
it thinks that the defendant is more likely to be guilty than not. The jury
must continue to weigh the evidence. The total weight of evidence must

make it very probable that the defendant did the deed—"beyond a reasonable doubt."

The challenges of court cases and of determining guilt have been with us for many centuries. Analysts have discussed how to weigh evidence. In the process, they have been discussing issues related to probability.

NUMERICAL PROBABILITY

In addition to this broader kind of probability, a more precise use for the word *probability* has developed. From the sixteenth century onwards, a number of writers—Gerolamo Cardano, Pierre de Fermat, Blaise Pascal, Christiaan Huygens, Jacob Bernoulli, and others—developed a mathematical treatment of chance events and games of chance.[1] This mathematical treatment has now become a vast subject, the *theory of probability*. We will consider only its most elementary parts.

We can attach a numerical value to our estimate of how likely we think an event is. Consider the flip of a coin. The coin is equally likely to come up heads or tails. One half of the time it will come up heads. Or we can say that it comes up heads 50% of the time. The numerical value of 1/2 or 50% is called the *probability* that heads will come up. Or we can write the fraction 1/2 as a decimal, as 0.5. Or we can say that it comes up heads one out of two times, on the average. Fractions (1/2), decimals (0.5), percentages (50%), and expressions in the form "one out of two" can be translated into one another, so the four expressions are equivalent. The probability of the coin coming up heads is 1/2, and the probability of the coin coming up *tails* is also 1/2.

People also use the word *odds* to talk about chance events. The *odds* for heads are the number of times heads is likely to come up in comparison to the number of times it does *not* come up. Since these two chances are equally likely, we say that the odds of heads are one to one.

We can assign numerical probabilities because of the nature of the world that God created. As we have seen, the world shows both regularities and unpredictabilities. It is the unpredictabilities that compel us to study probability. We assign a number because we cannot predict the outcome. The unpredictabilities, as we previously indicated, go back to God's creativity.

---

[1] On the history of probability, see Maria Carla Galavotti, *Philosophical Introduction to Probability* (Stanford, CA: Center for the Study of Language and Information, 2005), 7–27.

Without the activity of God's creativity, there would be nothing new, and nothing to which to assign a probability.

God's creativity makes sense only in the context of his faithfulness and his love. God's faithfulness creates the regularities, which are the background for recognizing something new, something beyond the regularities. And the regularities include regularities among instances of what is new.

Consider the case of tossing a coin. The claim that there is a probability of 1/2 of the outcome being heads means that half of the time it will come up heads. The other half of the time, it will not come up heads. Since there is only one alternative to heads, namely tails, we can deduce that the outcome will be tails 1/2 of the time.

The structure of only two outcomes is already one regularity. In addition, when we talk about "1/2 of the time," we presuppose that we can picture many outcomes in succession. We can flip the coin 10 times, or 100 times, or 1,000 times. All these instances have a common pattern: we take the coin in our hand. We flip it into the air with our thumb in such a way that it spins in the air. It continues to spin as it goes up and then comes down to the ground according to the principles of gravity. We then inspect which side of the coin faces up. All these actions together constitute regularities about what it means to flip a coin. The common pattern or regularity belongs to any of a large number of cases in which we flip the coin. The regularity expresses and reflects God's faithfulness.

We assume that the coin has different markings on the two faces—perhaps a picture of the head of a political figure on one face, and some design on the other face. We assume that the markings on the two faces remain the same while the coin is in the air. If, hypothetically, some scientist had the power to make both faces into heads while the coin was in the air, he could obviously ruin the prediction that heads will come up 1/2 of the time. Equally, if a scientist had special power to manipulate the speed of rotation of the coin, and special powers of quick action, he could theoretically make an ordinary coin come up heads all the time, even without changing its markings. His interference with the spin of the coin would again ruin our prediction of heads 1/2 of the time.

Clearly, we depend on a whole host of regularities that govern the operation of coin flipping. The regularities must be there in order to provide a stable context in which the outcome is unpredictable in the right way, rather than being manipulatable by way of some kind of interference. The regularities, in a word, must cohere with the unpredictabilities in a complex way, and this coherence is one expression of God's love. God's love guarantees his coherence with himself. And his coherence with himself guarantees the coherence of his plan for the world, a plan that includes the subordinate coherence in the patterns of coin flips.

ARRIVING AT PROBABILITY ESTIMATES

Coming up with precise numerical values to express probability also depends on regularities and unpredictabilities. On what basis do we say that the probability that a coin will come up heads is 1/2, rather than 1/3 or 1/4 or 7/9?

To begin with, we observe that there are only two possible outcomes, heads or tails. People sometimes talk about the possibility that the coin could land on edge and just stay there, delicately balanced. If the coin is thrown so that it lands on dirt or clay or sand, it is possible that the impact of its edge, coming down nearly vertically, could create a depression in the dirt, and the dirt on the two sides of the depression could prop up the coin so that it does not fall to one side. We could contemplate various other unlikely scenarios. The coin could fall into a pool of liquid metal, and melt before clearly taking on any final orientation.

In an ordinary analysis of coin flips, we simplify and leave out such unlikely possibilities. Because they are very unlikely, they do not affect our estimate of 1/2 very much at all. In reckoning with and then excluding these unlikelihoods, we show again our dependence on regularities appointed by God in his wisdom. We should praise God that he has appointed a world in which we are able to have a kind of "controlled" approach to unpredictabilities because of the stabilities of the environment.

We should also reflect on how we treat the two main outcomes, heads and tails. One or the other will happen. On what basis do we conclude that each outcome has a probability of 1/2? Why not say that heads has a probability of 1/7 and tails comes up the rest of the time?

CONDUCTING TRIALS

We can arrive at the figure of 1/2 in two ways. First, we can actually take a coin and flip it a large number of times, keeping track of each outcome. Each such flip is called a *trial*. Suppose we flip 10 times. 7 are heads, while the other 3 are tails. Heads have come up 7/10 of the time. So the probability of heads is 7/10, is it? Well, roughly it is. But if we do only a relatively small number of flips of the coin, the result need not come out exactly what we would have with a larger number of flips. Try a sequence of 100 trials, 100 flips of the coin. 48 come up heads, while 52 are tails. So the probability of heads is 48/100, roughly. If we do 1,000 trials, we might find 491 come up heads, and 509 tails. This works out to a probability of 491 out of 1,000, or a fraction 491/1,000, as the probability of heads. We can also write the probability as a decimal: 0.491 for heads. Now suppose we do 10,000 trials. 5,030 come up heads, for a probability estimate of 5,030/10,000, which in decimal form is 0.503. We are getting close to a value of 1/2 or 0.5. But clearly it would be an accident if we came up with exactly 0.5 on the button. In fact, the bigger the number we select as our total number of trials, the less likely we are to hit the result 0.5 exactly on the button. If, for example, we make 10,000 trials, the number of heads could be exactly 5,000, which would be an exact "hit." But it could also be 5,001, or 5,002, or 5,003, or 5,011, or 4,997, or any number near the vicinity of 5,000. When the number of trials is large, the number of "near misses" to an exact ratio of 0.5 is also large.

We can notice regularities in this situation. The number of tails is always what is left over. If there are 100 trials and 48 are heads, exactly 52 are tails. The total number of heads plus the total number of tails must come out to 100: 48 + 52 = 100. That must be so because heads and tails are the only two alternatives, and if one occurs the other does not occur. We say that the two alternatives are *mutually exclusive*.

Using the situation with 100 flips, we can get rough estimates of probability. In our example, the probability of a head is roughly 48/100 or 0.48 and the probability of a tail is roughly 52/100 or 0.52. Together these add up to 0.48 + 0.52 = 1.00. Is this an accident? It is not. The total number of trials is 100. For 48 of these coming up heads, and 52 tails, 48 + 52 = 100. Now divide both sides of the equation by 100. 48/100 + 52/100 = 100/100 = 1. The probability of heads, roughly 48/100, plus the probability of tails, roughly 52/100, add up to a total probability of 1. In 100 out of 100 cases, the result will be one out of the two cases, heads or tails.

We are seeing another regularity: the total probability of all the outcomes together is always 1. A probability of 1 represents complete certainty.

We can see certainty as a kind of limit situation. If we know that a particular outcome happens 9/10 of the time, that is, 9 times out of 10, we are pretty confident that it will happen. But there is still 1 time out of 10 when it will not happen. If the outcome happens 999 times out of 1,000, that is, with a probability of 999/1,000 or 0.999, we are very confident. The number 1 is clearly the limit case, when we consider an event perfectly certain. The number 0 is the limit case in the other direction, when we are certain that an event will *not* happen. In between are numbers like 0.9, which say that 9 out of 10 cases have the outcome in which we are interested.

SYMMETRY

In addition to the process of conducting trials, there is a second way to come up with a figure for probability. We look at the coin, and think about the process of flipping a coin. We know that we cannot control with perfect precision the amount and direction of forces applied to the coin when it takes off from our hand. Nor can we control the air currents and their effects. By the time the coin reaches the ground, it could have virtually any orientation in space. Because the coin is *symmetrical* in shape, there is no reason to suspect that a result of tails up or a result of heads up would be more likely. Neither result receives any kind of intrinsic preference. So the probability of heads should equal the probability of tails. That one conclusion, based on symmetry, allows us to do a numerical calculation about probability.

We first have to assume that the probability of heads is some specific number, say h. That assumption presupposes that God has ordained regularities for the whole series of outcomes of different tosses of the coin. If we toss it today, the probability of heads will be h. If we toss it tomorrow, or a week from now, the probability remains h. That is a stability ordained by God.

Now, we consider the fact that the coin is symmetrical. When we flip it over to its other side, it has the same shape as before. Neither the head nor the tail of the coin has an intrinsic preference. We then conclude that the probability t of tails is the same as the probability of heads. That is, $t = h$.

Because God has made a world in which the physical outcomes with coins are in coherent harmony with numbers and counting, we can also reason numerically. Here is how we do it. We know that heads and tails are the only two outcomes, and they are mutually exclusive. The total probability will be 1. So $t + h = 1$. We have also seen why it seems reasonable to say that the probability h of getting heads is the same as the probability t of getting tails. So $t = h$.

Substituting h for t in the equation $t + h = 1$, we get $h + h = 1$. So $2h = 1$. Dividing both sides by 2, $h = 1/2$. Since $t = h$, $t = 1/2$. The probability of heads is 1/2, and the probability of tails is also 1/2.

Consider another situation, where we roll a die. An ordinary die has a cubical shape, with six faces. On each of the faces there are dots. The first face has one dot; a second face has two dots; and so on, up to six dots on the sixth face. What is the probability that when we roll the die, the face with four dots will end up on top?

Suppose that we let the letter f designate the probability that the face with four dots will come up. The die is symmetrical. And when we throw the die, we cannot precisely control the forces or the starting orientation of the die. So we would guess that each of the other faces will have the same probability of coming up. So the probability that a one will come up is f, because of the symmetry. Similarly for the probability of a two, a three, a five, or a six. Together, these six possibilities (including four) are the only ones. So the total probability of one of them happening must be 1 (certainty). We can write out:

$$f + f + f + f + f + f = 1.$$

$$6f = 1, \text{ or } f = 1/6.$$

The probability of the die coming up four is 1/6.

THE ADDITIVE PRINCIPLE

In this reasoning we have used a principle of *additivity* for probability. The principle of additivity or the *additive principle* says that if two or more events are mutually exclusive, the probability that at least one of them will occur is the sum of the individual probabilities of each case separately. We can see that this principle is true by thinking about the meaning of probability. If four comes up 1/6 of the time, and five comes up 1/6 of the time, the total number of times when either four or five comes up is $1/6 + 1/6$. The total number of times when either a four, five, or six comes up is $1/6 + 1/6 + 1/6$. And so on for the other cases.

The additive principle also holds with respect to a situation where we group together all the possible outcomes. With a die, one out of the total of six outcomes will certainly happen. That is, the probability of getting one of the six outcomes is 1. By the additive principle, this total probability can also be calculated by adding up the probabilities f for each face. So $f + f + f + f + f + f = 1$, as before.

ODDS

We can also talk about the odds that four will come up on a die. The odds are the number of favorable cases compared to the number of unfavorable ones. The number of favorable cases is one case: when four comes up. The number of unfavorable cases is five. So the odds of four coming up are one to five. (People sometimes also say that the odds are five to one *against* the possibility of four coming up. That indicates that there are five unfavorable cases for every favorable one.)

Language about odds is convenient in contexts where people may be about to place bets. Suppose that Rita is invited to place a bet on whether the die will come up with four on top. She will win a dollar if the die comes up four, but will lose her bet if the die comes up with any other number on top. How much money could she bet and still not lose money on the average? Could she bet 5 cents per roll? 10 cents? 25 cents? One dollar?

There are five cases where she will lose her bet for every one case where she will win. If she bets an amount of b cents each time, she will lose on average five times, for a total loss of $5b$ cents, for each time she has a favorable case and wins 100 cents. In order to break even, she would have to bet in such a way that the losses ($5b$) exactly balance the wins (100). To find out the "break-even" point, we should equate the total losses to the total wins: $5b = 100$. Dividing by five we see that $b = 20$ cents. If she bets anything more than 20 cents, she will lose on the average. The odds of one to five match the amounts of her "break-even" bet of 20 cents in relation to the "payoff" of 100 cents.

In a second case, suppose Rita will win one dollar if anything other than a four comes up on the die, while she will lose her bet if four comes up. How much could she bet and still not lose on the average? In this case, the odds are five to one in her favor. She could bet up to $5 and still not lose on the average. Once again, the odds of five to one match the ratio of her "break-even" bet to the payoff of $1. (But see appendices A and B on the foolishness of gambling.)

UNDERLYING PRINCIPLES

In all these cases, our reasoning has relied on coherence between numbers on the one hand and events in the world on the other. And the events in the world are unpredictable. It is all the more remarkable that there are nevertheless stable coherences between these events and the stabilities in numbers. God has ordained both. And he has ordained them *in relation to* each other. He has ordained harmony. As usual, the harmony reflects the inner harmony of his own nature. The Father loves the Son, and he causes this original harmony to be reflected in the world. In particular, his faithfulness, creativity, and wisdom are reflected in the patterns involving chance events. The glory of God is displayed in the glories in probability.

CHAPTER 16

PREDICTIONS AND OUTCOMES

We should note one particular form of coherence: the coherence between predictions and outcomes. With dice rolls, we predict that a four will come up about 1/6 of the time. We can then proceed to roll a die 10 times, or 100 times, or 1,000 times, and keep track of how many times we come up with a four. We call this type of record a *trial*. So we can conduct a trial consisting in 10 rolls, or 100, or 1,000. The term *trial* is also used for a single event: one roll of a die is a *trial*, that is, an experiment. For a trial of 100 rolls, a four will come up about 1/6 out of the total of 100 cases, or 100/6 = 16.666 ... That is, a four will come up about 16 or 17 times. Of course, on any one trial, it may come up as few as 3 times, or as many as 40 times. But both of these outcomes are unlikely. I tried rolling dice one hundred times, and four came up 23 times. Not that close to 17. But if I tried 10,000 rolls, I could be reasonably confident that something close to 1,667 would come up with four on top.

COHERENCE IN THEORY AND EXPERIMENT

We may call this coherence a coherence between theory and experiment. The theory says that a four will come up 1/6 of the time. The experiment consists in rolling a die a large number of times, and seeing if the frequency is 1/6. These two approaches agree with one another. But the agreement is of course always approximate, because there is uncertainty about any one roll of the die.

We can describe the situation in another way. There are two distinct ways to arrive at a numerical figure for probability. In the first, we begin with an "experiment." We run a trial by flipping a coin a large number of times. This approach is called the *a posteriori* approach to probability (in Latin, *a posteriori* means "from the later"). An *a posteriori* estimate of probability is an estimate based on empirical investigation. It is derived from or "posterior" to (later than) observations about facts. We first conduct trials by flipping a coin. Only afterwards do we propose a generality, a "theory" if you want, which says that a coin will come up heads about 0.503 of the time, because 0.503 is the result of this particular "experiment."

The second method takes a more theoretical route. We think about the symmetry of a coin or a die. We reason it out, and decide from the symmetry that the coin will come up heads 1/2 of the time. Perhaps we come to our conclusion without ever flipping an actual coin even once. This kind of probability is called *a priori* probability, because the number produced for the probability is supplied *prior* to the events, the flips of the coin. (In Latin, *a priori* means "from the earlier.")

If things work well, *a priori* probability and *a posteriori* probability match. They cohere. This coherence, as usual, goes back to God. It is God who governs the world and everything in it. On the basis of his inner harmony he ordains this harmony within the world.

In this case, the two approaches cohere within the limits of accuracy that we can expect from trial flips of a coin. With a large number of flips, we may see that heads come up, let us say, 0.503 of the total number of flips. But if we repeated the whole series of trials again, we would come up with a slightly different number, maybe 0.501. By contrast, the *a priori* approach enables us to obtain an exact and permanent value, 0.5. Moreover, the theory of probability, when more fully developed, even allows us to predict the amount of variation that we will find when we repeat an empirical trial several times, in the form of 10,000 or even 100,000 coin flips.

BENEFITS FROM *A POSTERIORI* PROBABILITIES

The *a priori* approach is clearly cleaner and simpler when a symmetry in a coin or in a die allows us a simple calculation. But in other cases there is no easy route. For instance, we may ask, "What is the probability that a 75-year-old woman will die within the next year?" Can we produce a probability based on a simple symmetry? There is no obvious way to do it. Whether a person dies within a year depends on a huge number of factors.

A priori reasoning will not give us a number. But we can still get a number if we look at death statistics and statistics for life expectancy. This is an instance of an *a posteriori* approach.

In this case, the death or nondeath of a particular individual woman during the next year can be treated as an individual outcome. The death of one individual cannot be predicted, but we can consider averages. One way of conducting a trial involving many individual outcomes is to choose a large number of women who are 75 years old, wait a year, and then count how many have died. If we want to shorten the wait, we can look at statistics already gathered from previous years.

Actuaries who work for insurance companies engage in this kind of study. They are able to come up with figures that show just how much a life insurance company should charge its customers for life insurance. The customer pays a monthly or yearly fee, called a "premium," to buy and then maintain life insurance. The life insurance policy specifies how much money will be paid to the beneficiaries when the insured person dies. For a life insurance policy that pays $100,000 at death, there may be a yearly premium of $2,000 or $5,000 or $10,000, depending on how much risk there is that the person in question will die during the next year. The insurance company wants to receive enough in premiums so that *on the average* it will break even when it has to pay the beneficiaries at the time the insured person dies.

For insurance companies, of course, there are added layers of complexity. The insurance company wants not just to break even, but on the average to get some extra money from its customers, so that it can pay its employees, make a profit for the owners, and invest for the future. But if the premiums that it charges its customers are too high, it will not be able to compete with other insurance companies, who will try to offer the same amount of insurance for a lesser premium. In addition, when an insurance company receives money temporarily from its customers in the form of premiums, the money gets invested and, if invested well, gets an additional return. The company wants to estimate, again by probabilities, how much additional return it can expect to get over how many years, and how much of this return should go back to customers in order for the company to stay competitive. The other insurance companies, after all, are going to be doing the same thing.

Insurance companies confront a large number of uncertainties. And the customers confront uncertainties. No one knows for sure when he will die. From the standpoint of the customer, insurance is attractive because it enables him to protect his children from the nasty side of his uncertainties—in particular, the possibility that the major breadwinner of the family may die while the children are still young and unable to support themselves.

The insurance company has the same uncertainty. It does not know anything more about the customer's future than he knows himself. But by having a large number of customers, it *averages* over the uncertainties for all the customers together. It can therefore protect each customer from uncertainty, while at the same time remaining confident that the averages will allow it to maintain its solvency and so protect the individual customers. When you think about it, this whole setup is a rather ingenious way of having the best of both worlds. The customer gets security from the company. The company gets security not from any individual customer, but from the averages.

God has made it so. God has ordained a world with uncertainties. But in addition he ordains regular patterns in the *averages*. We depend on averages all the time. For example, we receive enough oxygen when we breathe because of the average motion of a large number of molecules in the air. If all the oxygen molecules gathered on the opposite side of the room, we would have no oxygen. But it does not happen because God ordains a regular pattern: there are a huge number of molecules, and taken together their positions average out. They are all over the room. Likewise, the insurance company depends on God to maintain the averages. It also depends on God to maintain the uncertainties, so that people continue to feel the need for insurance.

Since we have ventured into the topic of human death, it is also well to remind ourselves that this present world is a fallen world. According to the Bible, human death is not normal, but rather a consequence of the fall of mankind into sin (Gen. 2:17; 3:19; 5:5, 8, etc.). Death is a curse. God nevertheless does control it. He even controls the patterns, that is, the regularities, as well as the uncertainties in human death. On the basis of these patterns, he opens the way for insurance companies to mitigate the grim consequences of the fall. At the same time, the uncertainties about death warn us to turn to God and to trust in Christ today, while there is still time.

TRICKS

We should note additional complexities. It is possible to have tricks that throw off the expected coherence between *a priori* and *a posteriori* probability. There can be trick coins or trick dice. By sleight of hand a trickster can swap out an ordinary coin for a coin with two heads. Or he can swap out ordinary dice for dice with faces that show only the numbers one, two, and three. There can be weighted coins and weighted dice. An expert trickster knows how to shave off a bit from the corners of a die so that the die no longer rolls in a perfectly symmetrical fashion, but is subtly biased toward coming up on one face. Tricks with playing cards can use a large number of techniques.

The possibility of such tricks shows the complexity of our environment. What looks simple and straightforward may not be so. We make a large number of assumptions. On the other hand, even in cases involving tricks there are regularities. Suppose one person is regularly winning in a card game or a dice game. Suspicions grow. People think, "He's too lucky for it to be purely by chance. There's something fishy." They look around. They discover an ace up the sleeve or a die with a lead weight hidden in one of the faces.

In this case, the suspicion can be described as the consequence of a notable difference between the *a posteriori* probability, which results in one person consistently winning, and the *a priori* probability, based on the symmetries in the cards or the dice. As the game continues, the number of trials increases. Over time, it becomes less and less probable that the difference results merely from chance. (Of course, we mean "chance" in the sense of those things that are unpredictable to human beings, not "Chance" as a substitute god.)

Because God ordains regularities along with the unpredictabilities, human beings on the basis of the difference are motivated to look for a logical explanation. There is a trick somewhere. Then they discover the ace up the sleeve. The discovery shows that all along there was an *actual* consistency between *a posteriori* results and *a priori* arrangements for the unpredictable events. The *a priori* arrangements, the ace up the sleeve, do after all harmonize with the *a posteriori* results, namely, that the person with the hidden ace is winning more often. Thus, the discovery of cheating, as well as the averages in a normal game of chance, rest on the harmony between *a priori* and *a posteriori* views of probability. This harmony depends on God, who acts consistently.

CHAPTER 17

THEISTIC FOUNDATIONS
FOR PROBABILITY

We have already seen that chance events reveal both the faithfulness of God and his creativity. Let us consider more ways in which probability reveals the character of God.

REGULARITIES

We will use the flip of a coin as our main illustration. As we have observed, the flip of a coin illustrates both regularities and uncertainties. The outcome of any one flip is uncertain. But when we consider many flips, we see regularities. The main simple regularities are the following:

1. When we flip a coin, it comes up heads half of the time and tails half of the time.
2. The probability of 1/2 for heads, plus the probability of 1/2 for tails, refer to two mutually exclusive events. It is never the case that a single flip results in an outcome of both heads and tails.
3. The outcomes of heads and tails are the only possible outcomes. So the total probability for either a head or a tail coming up is $1/2 + 1/2 = 1$.

REGULARITIES IN SPACE AND TIME

The regularities for coin flips hold for all places and for all times. In some places, such as inside stars, coins cannot exist because they would vaporize. In other places, such as outer space, beyond the gravitational attraction of the earth, a coin would not fall to the ground, and so the attempt to flip a coin would not work in the normal way. The regularities about coin flips do apply, however, to all the circumstances, anywhere in the universe, in which the appropriate conditions hold: that a coin exists there, that someone can flip it, that there is normal gravitation, and so on. The regularities also hold at all times: today, yesterday, ten years ago, or tomorrow.

These stabilities in space and in time have a close relation to terms that describe the characteristics or attributes of God. God is omnipresent (present in all places) and eternal (which implies he is there at all times). God is also immutable, that is, unchangeable. Likewise the regularities with respect to coin flips are immutable.

Are these relationships an accident? No. God has made the world and everything in it. So these regularities are a reflection of his wisdom. They also reflect God's speech (chapters 2 and 10). God's speech is divine, so it has divine attributes, including omnipresence, eternality, and immutability.[1]

IMMATERIALITY

The regularities about probability are essentially invisible. We do not literally see the regularities, but only the *effects* of the regularities on the behavior of coins. The coins are material objects, but the regularities themselves are *immaterial*. Likewise, God in his own nature is immaterial, and his speech is immaterial, but his acts produce effects within the material world.

TRUTH

The regularities about coin flips hold true. It is *true* that heads come up half of the time. The regularities include within their formulation the qualification that they are regularities concerning averages or multiple trials. But once we take this qualification into account, the formulations are indeed true. Likewise, *truth* is an attribute of God.

POWER

Scientists discover rather than invent scientific laws like Newton's laws of motion. The regularities already exist in the governance of the world, even

---

[1] The reasoning here imitates what occurs in Vern S. Poythress, *Redeeming Science: A God-Centered Approach* (Wheaton, IL: Crossway, 2006), chapter 1, which shows that scientific laws have divine attributes. The regularities about probability are a manifestation of God's law or God's speech, and so they follow the same pattern. See also ibid., chapter 14, which applies similar reasoning to truth (which originates in God).

before scientists begin to investigate and explore. The same holds true in the investigation of probability. The world of coin flips and dice rolling existed even before investigators like Cardano, Fermat, and Pascal began to formulate a theory of probability. The theory is in a sense a human product. Human beings had to think things through, watch coin flips and die rolls, and write up their arguments and conclusions. But the reality of probabilistic regularity exists in the world already. The regularities do exist. And the outcomes for coins and dice *conform* to the regularities. They obey the law.

We have to make the qualification, as usual, that the law itself is a statistical law, a law about averages, rather than a deterministic law about what *must* happen in one particular case. In addition, God's law is his personal word, not an impersonal rule. Our human sense of law is an approximation. So for us there can be surprises. But, having made those qualifications, we can see that the world around us does obey God's law. The law has *power*. It holds the events in its grip, so to speak. And there are no exceptions, because the law already has the qualifications that it applies to averages and that God may act exceptionally. If there are no exceptions, the law is all-powerful. The classical word for being all-powerful is *omnipotence*. It is an attribute of God.

TRANSCENDENCE AND IMMANENCE

The regularities about coin flips and dice rolls are both transcendent and immanent. They transcend the details of any one event, because they are general laws. At the same time, they are immanent, in the sense that they actually do apply to particular trial events that happen either in games of chance or in scientific investigation of coins and dice. They show their effects right there and then with each particular flip of a coin or roll of a die. Transcendence and immanence are characteristics of God.

REGULARITIES AS PERSONAL

By this time agnostics and atheists may be looking for a way of escape. The characteristics of the regularities in probabilities neatly match the characteristics of the God of the Bible. The most usual route for escape is to say that the regularities are just "there." It will be said that the regularities do not reveal God, but are an impersonal something—Chance is the best candidate. Chance, with a capital C to indicate its role as an ultimate explanation, is a substitute for God. But the remarkable coherence between the unpredictabilities of individual coin flips and the predictabilities about averages and patterns remain unexplained. The unpredictabilities represent chance with a small c, events that we as human beings cannot predict. Why do these unpredictabilities cohere with the predictabilities?

Moreover, the regularities about coin flips and dice are rational. We come to recognize them partly through processes of reasoning, and once we recognize them we can see that they make sense. They are reasonable. And rationality belongs to persons. The regularities are also language-like. We express and explain the regularities using language. And if our language is careful, it also includes conditions, such as specifying what a coin is, that someone must be there to flip the coin, that the flipping takes place in a gravitational field, that there is a ground or floor or something for the coin to fall on, and so on. Language of this complexity belongs to persons, not to rocks or plants or animals.[2]

When people work with probabilities and do reasoning about probabilities, they show in their actions that they are assuming in practice not only many other divine attributes that characterize the regularities, but also the rationality and language-like character of the regularities. They are assuming that the regularities display God's attributes, including his personal character as rational and capable of speaking.

THE KNOWLEDGE OF GOD AND ITS SUPPRESSION

This reliance on God is exactly what Romans 1 describes:

> For his invisible attributes, namely, his eternal power and *divine nature*, have been clearly perceived, ever since the creation of the world, in the things that have been made. So they are without excuse. For although they *knew* God, they did not honor him as God or give thanks to him, but they became futile in their thinking, and their foolish hearts were darkened. (Rom. 1:20–21)

We should also remember that in the next verses Romans 1 describes the "exchange" of God for substitutes:

---

[2] See the further discussion in ibid., chapter 1, 19–22.

Claiming to be wise, they became fools, and *exchanged* the glory of the immortal God for images resembling mortal man and birds and animals and creeping things. (Rom. 1:22–23)

In dealing with probability, the exchange typically takes the form of bringing in Chance. Chance becomes a substitute. People use talk about Chance to conceal their reliance on God and their guilt for their lack of gratitude to him.

The topic of probability therefore offers an opportunity for those who have been reconciled to God through Christ and have come to know God in an obedient rather than a rebellious way. The regularities in probability, and the creativity of God in what we cannot predict, provide occasions where we may both praise God and commend his greatness to those who are still in rebellion. We may use our opportunities to speak about God's omnipresence, eternality, immutability, immateriality, truthfulness, omnipotence, and so on. We may invite unbelievers to come to Christ to be reconciled to this God, whom they know and rely on every time they think about probability.

In addition, we may point in admiration to the ability that human beings have to understand probability. This understanding is a gift from God. God has made man in his image. As creatures made in the image of God, we have the power to think God's thoughts after him. Of course, our thoughts are not original. We are creatures, whereas God is the Creator. His thoughts are original, while ours are derivative. His thoughts are infinite, while ours are finite. But it is still true that our thoughts imitate his. When we know truth, the truth is truth that resides originally in the mind of God.

SYMMETRY AS A TESTIMONY TO GOD

We may further illustrate human abilities by considering the role of symmetry in probability. A coin is symmetrical between heads and tails. So we reasoned earlier that the probability of heads should be the same as the probability of tails. Likewise, because a cubical die is symmetrical in its six faces, the probability of the face with four dots coming up on top is the same as the probability for the face with three dots, and so on.

Our thinking about symmetry is one instance of thinking God's thoughts after him. The original symmetry lies in God. God the Father, God the Son, and God the Holy Spirit are each God. They have a common character. Jesus says, "Whoever has seen me has seen the Father" (John 14:9). The Father loves the Son and the Son loves the Father. The love has the same character in each case. The original symmetry and harmony in God is then reflected when God creates the world, and when he gives to human beings the power to craft coins that exhibit symmetry. Symmetries exist in the world, and they exist also in the human mind. We can *think* about the symmetry in the world that is exhibited in a coin or in a die. This thinking shows that symmetry exists in our minds.

Of course, God can govern the flips of coins as he wishes. But when we try to think in harmony with his character, it seems natural that the symmetry in the physical shape and weight of a coin should also be reflected in the symmetry in the number of times that heads or tails comes up. And we can think of no reason for a permanent preference for heads. God has symmetries in himself, among the persons of the Trinity. It makes sense that he would be pleased to reflect the original symmetries in himself in subordinate symmetries both in physical shapes (coins and dice) and in events (the outcomes of flipping coins or rolling dice). (See fig. 17.1)

We are creatures, so we do not know absolutely. But we can make a good guess, on the basis of God's character and his inner symmetries of love among the persons of the Trinity. Our initial guess gets confirmed again and again when we actually try it out by experimenting with many successive flips of a coin. About half come up heads. Praise the Lord!

Fig. 17.1: Archetype for Symmetries

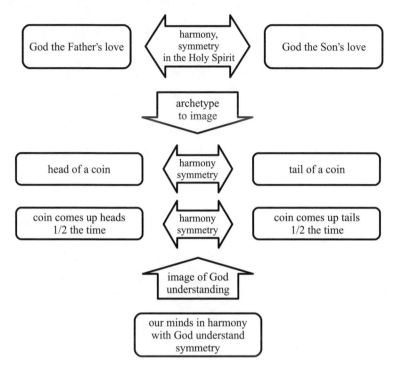

CHAPTER 18

VIEWS OF PROBABILITY

Modern philosophical discussions of the nature of probability offer several different concepts of probability. There are several main views, which are summarized by Alan Hájek as follows:

1. A quasi-logical concept [of probability], which is meant to measure objective evidential support relations. For example, "in light of the relevant seismological and geological data, it is *probable* that California will experience a major earthquake this decade".
2. The concept of an agent's degree of confidence, a graded belief. For example, "I am not sure that it will rain in Canberra this week, but it *probably* will."
3. An objective concept that applies to various systems in the world, independently of what anyone thinks. For example, "a particular radium atom will *probably* decay within 10,000 years".[1]

Within these main categories there are further variations.

Can we profit from reflections on probability written by non-Christians? Yes. Everyone who reflects on probability is made in the image of God. Moreover, God is gracious even to people who are in rebellion against him:

For he [God] makes his sun rise on the evil and on the good, and sends rain on the just and on the unjust. (Matt. 5:45)

. . . for he [God] did good by giving you rains from heaven and fruitful seasons, satisfying your hearts with food and gladness. (Acts 14:17)

---

[1] Alan Hájek, "Interpretations of Probability," *The Stanford Encyclopedia of Philosophy (Winter 2011 Edition)*, ed. Edward N. Zalta, http://plato.stanford.edu/archives/win2011/entries/probability-interpret/, §3, accessed January 18, 2012. See Maria Carla Galavotti, *Philosophical Introduction to Probability* (Stanford, CA: Center for the Study of Language and Information, 2005).

The blessings of God include intellectual blessings in the form of fruitful insights. So modern reflections offer us potential benefits.

But there are difficulties.[2] One of the main difficulties consists in the very multiplicity of concepts. At first concepts 1 and 3 may seem to be the same. But concept 1 locates the foundation for probability in "quasi-logical" relationships, and thus relates it closely to the world of ideas, while concept 3 locates the foundation in the world outside us—how radium atoms behave. Concept 1, as a "quasi-logical" concept, focuses on abstract necessities or their probabilistic analogues, while concept 2 focuses on subjective, personal evaluations and estimations, which may be based on hunches or on information that may be unique to a particular person.

Hájek helpfully summarizes the differences:

> Like the frequency interpretations, *propensity* interpretations locate probability "in the world" rather than in our heads or in logical abstractions.[3]

"Frequency interpretations" and "propensity interpretations," which locate probability "in the world," are two types of "objective concept." They are variations on concept 3 above. By contrast, the quasi-logical concept (concept 1) locates probability "in logical abstractions," and concept 2, the concept of degree of confidence or graded belief, is a subjectivistic concept that locates probability "in our heads."[4]

TYPES OF SITUATIONS INVOLVING PROBABILITY ESTIMATES

Let us illustrate the three concepts. A quasi-logical concept (concept 1) makes reasonable sense when we are focusing on situations involving evidence. The jury has to decide whether the evidence shows that the defendant is guilty. A scientist has to decide whether the evidence supports his hypothesis. The evidence from flipping a coin 1,000 times may support the hypothesis that the coin is unbiased; and then we infer that the probability

---

[2] An analogous critical analysis of difficulties in theories of statistical inference can be found in Andrew M. Hartley, *Christian and Humanistic Foundations for Statistical Inference: Religious Control of Statistical Paradigms* (Eugene, OR: Resource Publications, 2008).

[3] Hájek, "Interpretations of Probability," §3.5.

[4] D. H. Mellor's analysis distinguishes (1) "epistemic probabilities," (2) "credences," and (3) "chances" or "physical probabilities" (*Probability: A Philosophical Introduction* [London/New York: Routledge, 2005], 9–12). These are alternate labels for quasi-logical, subjective, and objective concepts of probability, respectively.

of heads is 1/2. We are engaged in reasoning based on evidence, and our reasoning may be described as "quasi-logical."

Next, consider a subjectivist approach to probability (concept 2). This kind of approach makes reasonable sense when we are dealing with a situation in which different human participants have different knowledge (see chapter 19). For example, Jill knows from her own direct observation that a die has come up with five on top. But Karen has not yet seen or heard how the die came up, so for her the subjective probability of the die coming up with five is 1/6.

Finally, an objectivist approach to probability (concept 3) makes sense when we are dealing with statistics concerning complex situations. What is the probability that a 75-year-old woman will die within the next year? We most naturally obtain an estimate based on information from the world, an objective measure based on death statistics from previous years. This kind of estimate of probability is empirical in nature. It has to do with probability "in the world."

DIFFICULTIES

But none of these approaches works in a clean way everywhere. The quasi-logical approach works well only where we have evidence in hand, or where we can imagine a situation in which new evidence would come to light. We must also have some ideas about how the evidence is relevant. In addition, we need some initial values of probability, before we get the new evidence. For example, the hypothesis that little fairies inhabit our house might seem to be confirmed when I notice that a book that I left on the couch the night before has been put on my chair. But, prior to encountering the evidence, I regard the hypothesis as extremely unlikely, so I will look for another, better hypothesis: my wife took care of the book.

Next, consider the subjectivist approach. The obvious difficulty here is that our subjective feelings about what is probable may not be reliable. Some gamblers bet on "hunches," where they have a strong feeling that they are going to win. But the hunches may be wrong. A subjectivist approach may try to evade the difficulty by talking about how we ought to act if we were thoroughly rational, rather than how we actually act. But then what is rational has to be defined, and we may find ourselves going to the probability concepts (1) or (3) to obtain a specific concept of rational behavior.

Even if we go in this direction, we need to explain how we subjectively understand the concepts of probability.

Finally, an objectivist approach to probability, based on experiments or statistics, never arrives at definitive results. With enough rolls of dice, the number of outcomes with five on top will be roughly 1/6. But the results of experiments will not necessarily be *exactly* 1/6. Suppose we roll 100 times, and come up with 19 occurrences of five on top. Does it mean that the probability of a five is 19/100? It is roughly 19/100, but we can never get an exact figure this way.

What then is the relation between the different concepts of probability? Are they just three concepts side by side, with no relation to one another? But in some situations, such as rolls of dice, all three concepts can apply. And they may result in different answers.

PERSPECTIVES ON ETHICS

We have said that the three concepts are closely related to (1) probability as a logical abstraction, (2) probability "in our heads," and (3) probability as a property of the world. What then is the relationship between logic, beliefs "in our heads," and the world? John Frame's multiperspectival approach to ethics gives a fundamental answer within a Christian framework.[5] We need first to understand Frame's three perspectives. Then we can apply them to the question of probability.

Frame distinguishes three distinct ways of approaching ethical questions. The *normative perspective* focuses on God's commandments and his instructions to us in the Bible. It focuses on *norms*. The norms tell us what actions and attitudes please God. The *existential perspective*, also called the *personal perspective*, focuses on a person's *motives*. What should I do if I am motivated by *love*? The *situational perspective* focuses on the *situation* in the world. It asks, "How may I promote the glory of God (1 Cor. 10:31), and how may I bring blessing to the people within the situation in which God has placed me?"

When we understand these three perspectives within the context of a biblical view of God and the world, they are in harmony. Each leads to the others and affirms the others. For example, if I look at my situation, God

---

[5] John M. Frame, *Perspectives on the Word of God: An Introduction to Christian Ethics* (Eugene, OR: Wipf & Stock, 1999); John M. Frame, *The Doctrine of the Christian Life* (Phillipsburg, NJ: Presbyterian & Reformed, 2008).

himself is the most important person in my situation, and so I must inquire what pleases God. That inquiry leads to the normative perspective. Conversely, if I start with the normative perspective, I find by reading the Bible that God commands me to love my neighbor and pay attention to his welfare. It also says to do all for the glory of God (1 Cor. 10:31). So it endorses the situational perspective. By commanding me to love, and by showing that God judges attitudes as well as actions, it affirms the existential perspective (motives). If we start with love as a motive, we find that love includes love to God, and hence leads to paying attention to God's norms. Thus, the existential perspective (love) affirms the normative perspective (God's standards).

If the three perspectives are in harmony, why not use just one? Yes, we can start with just one if we want. But, as we observed, one perspective leads to affirming the other two, so the perspective with which we started does not leave us where we started. It virtually forces us, if we follow it observantly, to practice the other two perspectives as well.

Moreover, because we are sinful, we can easily twist a monoperspectival approach in our own favor. For example, James 2:16 considers a situation where someone expresses goodwill:

> . . . and one of you says to them [a brother or sister in need], "Go in peace, be warmed and filled," without giving them the things needed for the body, what good is that?

The expression of goodwill may allow the comfortable person to feel good about himself. He tells himself that he has good sentiments toward the needy. He satisfies himself using the existential perspective alone. By contrast, James points to the situation and asks whether the comfortable person has done anything to change the situation where the brother or sister is in need. The situational perspective easily reveals the deficiencies in the empty expression of goodwill. But, used *properly*, the two perspectives are actually in harmony. A genuine motive of love would propel the person to action: "Little children, let us not love in word or talk but in deed and in truth" (1 John 3:18).

The three perspectives on ethics are in harmony because God ordains them all. God created the world, which is the situation. God created human beings in his image, and human beings are responsible to be holy in every aspect of their being, including their motives. Thus, God has ordained the existential perspective. God is the source of norms, because he is the standard for human action and attitudes. He makes his norms known in the Bible. Thus, God is the source of the normative perspective. The norms are also reflected existentially in our consciences (Rom. 1:32). Subjectively, we know the difference between right and wrong (though sinful people can have distorted morals). The three perspectives are in harmony because one God, who is in harmony with himself, has ordained all three.

In his perspectival approach, John Frame also observes that non-Christian approaches to ethics have difficulties. Non-Christian approaches tend to emphasize only one out of the three perspectives. So-called deontological ethics begins with norms. Existentialist ethics begins with the person. Utilitarian ethics (or more broadly, "consequential ethics") begins with the situation. But without God in the center, these systems cannot bring about a harmony between their starting point and the other approaches. Utilitarian ethics says that we ought to work for the well-being of humanity. But how do we measure such well-being in more than a simplistic or one-dimensional way, unless we have wisdom and instruction from God (norms)? And why *should* we work for the well-being of humanity? If there is no God, why should I not work merely for the well-being of myself alone? A purely utilitarian starting point lacks a way to motivate me to be unselfish. It does not satisfy the starting point of the existential perspective. Nor does it satisfy the normative perspective, because in a godless world it is not clear that there need be any genuinely ethical norms at all. People will say, "Let us eat and drink, for tomorrow we die."[6]

Existentialist ethics ends up saying that we must create our own life and thus our own standards for behavior. But our self-created standards have no real normativity. Deontological ethics wants to start with norms, but without a robust revelation from God, the norms end up either being empty or being nonnormative (the existentialist can always ask, "Why *should* I follow your proposed norm?").

PERSPECTIVES ON PROBABILITY

Now we may apply these perspectives to probability. Concept 1, the quasilogical concept of probability, is intended to be normative. It searches for

---

[6] First Corinthians 15:32 offers this saying as a quotation from Isaiah 22:13, which in turn quotes what godless Israelites were saying. The Bible is not approving this proverb, but is showing us the character of godless despair.

the foundations of probability in logical abstractions or normative principles for weighing evidence. It thus offers us a *normative* perspective on probability. Concept 2 focuses on "an agent's degree of confidence, a graded belief." This concept is subjective, and gives us an *existential* perspective on probability. Concept 3 focuses on the world. It gives us a *situational* perspective on probability.

Within a Christian view of the world, these three are intrinsically in harmony, for the same reason that the perspectives on ethics are in harmony. God ordained all three—the norms, the persons, and the world. He ordained the regularities that we find in mathematics of probabilities, which are one focus of the normative perspective. God made us in his image, so that we can subjectively understand, according to the existential perspective. God also ordained the regularities in the world of events, which are the focus of the situational perspective. We understand both the regularities that he ordains (normative) and the world that he has made (situational). But our understanding is always partial. So there will be various cases when people make bad guesses. The three perspectives harmonize in the mind of God. But their harmony within us as finite, sinful persons is a work in progress, so to speak.

As with ethics, so here: a non-Christian approach produces difficulties, because it does not acknowledge that God is the one who brings ultimate unity to the three perspectives. A non-Christian approach to the existential perspective tends to make human persons an *ultimate* source, rather than a proximate source, for ideas about probability. It does not consider God's understanding of probability. It confines itself to human views, thereby practicing a kind of practical atheism. It treats man as if he were God. This move is idolatrous; it is wrong. In addition, it will not work, because our subjective notions do not *always* match either the inherent logic of principles or the progress of chance events in the world (for example, see appendices C and F). Using human persons as a starting point cannot give us the harmony between the three perspectives in the way that God gives harmony.

A non-Christian approach can then start with the world instead of starting with the subjectivity of persons. Such is the "objective concept" of probability, concept 3. But what is this so-called objective probability, which is in the world independent of all human beings? This approach is in danger of leaving God out of its account. God knows all future events, so in a sense there is no "objective" probability at all. Probability arises first of all because of God's creativity, and second because of the limitations of human knowledge. If a concept of "objective" probability ignores God, it will end up being based on an assumption of ultimate chance—what we have called Chance with a capital C, Chance as a substitute for God.

In philosophical discussions, concept 3 can be subdivided into "frequency interpretations" and "propensity interpretations" of probability. Frequency interpretations say that probability is the frequency of an outcome as measured by a trial. But this approach is unsatisfactory because the outcome from 1,000 coin flips need not be exactly 500. It will vary. Suppose there are 517 occurrences of heads. Shall we then *define* the probability of heads as 517/1,000? And what do we do when a second trial produces 494 heads? No permanently fixed probability can ever be assigned.

The usual way of fixing this situation is to say that probability is the limit frequency, as the number of outcomes increases indefinitely. But this idea for fixing probability has to go beyond the world. In the real world, we cannot extend the number of outcomes to infinity. The finite length of our lives does not permit it. The fix goes beyond the world in two ways. First, it makes a transition from an actual trial to imagined or hypothetical trials of longer and longer length. This act of imagination uses human subjectivity. Second, it invokes a normative idea of a limit. How do we know that there will be a limit? Both the human subjectivity and the idea of a limit come from God—but a non-Christian account does not acknowledge it.

A non-Christian approach to frequency uses the situational perspective to focus on the world of events. Insights result. But the situational approach is being treated as if it were the unique origin of the whole interlocking system of probabilistic thinking. Such an approach again amounts to idolatry, this time replacing God with the world of events. And again it will not work, because it fails to bring about appropriate harmony between the world of events and our subjective and quasi-logical notions. Or if it appears to bring harmony, it does so by bringing in subjective and quasi-logical notions in the process of defining frequency. And then it has still not answered the question of why there is harmony in the first place.

A TRUE FOUNDATION

If we are followers of Christ, we have a clear explanation for the origin of probability. God made the world. He made it in such a way that the world contains both regularities and unpredictabilities. We who are made in the image of God can understand both his plan and the world, by thinking God's thoughts after him. God shows his faithfulness and stability on the one hand, and his creativity on the other hand. Our subjective sense of probability has harmonious correlations with both the world and the "logic" of truths about the world. Yet neither we nor the world is the origin of these relationships, and so we must be prepared for surprises (and more displays of creativity on the part of God). (See fig. 18.1.)

Fig. 18.1: Views of Probability

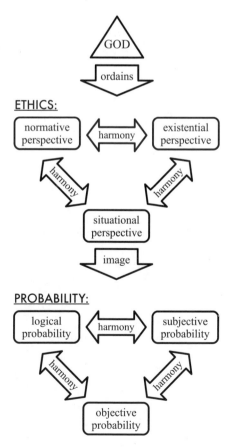

CHAPTER 19

SUBJECTIVITY AND PROBABILITY

Probability has to reckon with human subjectivity, because it depends on how much people know.

VARIATIONS IN AVAILABLE INFORMATION

Suppose Jill flips a coin, and the result is tails. Jill sees the result but temporarily hides the information from Karen. From Jill's point of view, before she flipped the coin, the probability of tails was 1/2. After she flipped the coin and saw the result, the probability of tails was 1. For Karen, however, the probability of tails is still 1/2.

We can set up a more complex situation where information is partially revealed. Jill rolls a die, and it comes up 5. She then tells Karen that the result is odd. Before the roll, the probability of 5 is 1/6. After the roll, Jill knows that the result is 5; so *for her* the probability of 5 is now 1 (it is certain). But Karen only knows that the result is 1 or 3 or 5. There is no reason why one of these should be more likely than another, so *for Karen* the probability of 5 is 1/3.

Suppose now that Jill promised Karen that, if the die came up a 3, Jill would reveal the result to Karen. If, on the other hand, it came up any other number, Jill would only reveal whether the result was odd or even. After rolling the die, Jill then reveals to Karen that the result is odd. If Jill is trustworthy, Karen can now infer that the result must be either 1 or 5. The probability that the die shows a result of 5 is 1/2.

We can see from these simple cases that probability depends on the available information. This information varies from person to person. It also varies with time, since both Jill and Karen obtain more information after the die has actually been rolled.

We have analogous experiences in more complex situations. For example, Mary tells Karen that she is looking forward to the party tonight, and she will definitely be there. When Karen arrives at the party, Mary is not there yet. Bill asks Karen whether Mary is coming, and Karen assures him that she is. If Karen were asked to give a numerical estimate, she might guess that there is a 0.96 probability that Mary will come.

However, Jill, who is also at the party, has just received news that Mary was in a serious auto accident on the way to the party, and had to be taken to the hospital. In Jill's estimate, the probability that Mary will come to the party is .0005 (still not zero, because it is *conceivable* that she might be released from the hospital or by special arrangement might be brought in on a stretcher). Jill and Karen have very different probability estimates. Both are reasonable estimates, based on the information that they have received. If either of them receives further information, their estimate may change.

GOD'S KNOWLEDGE AND PROBABILITY

What about God's viewpoint? God knows all outcomes even before they happen. He controls them. So there is no uncertainty from God's point of view. The probability of Mary's coming to the party is 0. The probability of 5 coming up on the die that Jill has rolled is 1.

But that is not the whole story. God's creativity comes into play with chance events. God *could have done otherwise*, that is, if his plans had been otherwise. We are not God, so we must be aware of our human limitations when we think about God's knowledge. Yet it does seem to be the case that we can make a distinction with respect to God's knowledge. God not only knows what *will* happen, but what *could* happen had he planned otherwise.

First Samuel 23 offers an interesting case. David has saved the city of Keilah from the Philistines, and he and his men are temporarily staying in Keilah. He inquires of God as to whether Saul will come to Keilah in pursuit of him, in order to try to kill him. God answers "yes": "He [Saul] will come down" (1 Sam. 23:11). David asks whether the citizens of Keilah will hand David and his men over to Saul rather than protect him. Again God says "yes": "They will surrender you" (v. 12). Given these predictions from

God, David sees that he cannot remain in Keilah. He departs with his men (v. 13). When Saul finds out that David has left Keilah, he calls off his plans. He never goes to Keilah, and of course the citizens of Keilah never have to deal with the issue of whether they will surrender David and his men.

The passage has focused on two significant events, Saul's coming to Keilah and the people of Keilah surrendering David to Saul. The sequel indicates that neither of these events ever took place. But they could have taken place. They are possible events. David talks meaningfully about them. And, more significantly still, God talks about them. He demonstrates his knowledge of what Saul would do if David had remained in Keilah. And he demonstrates his knowledge of what the people of Keilah would do if Saul had come. God's knowledge extends to possible events, hypothetical events that could take place but as a matter of fact do not. The *Westminster Confession of Faith* includes an affirmation of God's knowledge of possibilities:

> Although God knows whatsoever may or can come to pass upon *all supposed conditions*, yet hath He not decreed any thing because He foresaw it as future, or as that which would come to pass upon such conditions.[1]

God's knowledge includes possibilities that never actually come to pass. He also understands the situation of human beings who live with incomplete knowledge. He knows how much and in what respect each human being knows what he knows. He has designed the world so that we can think in terms of probabilities. These probabilities express truths about the limited character of our knowledge, and truths about the possibilities that *might* become actual but some of which never will become actual. All this richness exists in the world because God has planned it to be so.

CONDITIONAL PROBABILITY

One area of particular interest is *conditional probability*. *Conditional probability* describes situations in which we, with our limited knowledge, ask about probabilities that depend on conditions. "If event *A* takes place, what is the probability that event *B* will take place?" We can see a background for such thinking in the questions that David poses to God. "Will the men of Keilah surrender me and my men into the hand of Saul?" (1 Sam. 23:12).

---

[1] *Westminster Confession of Faith* (1646), 3.2. The attached "Scripture proofs" include 1 Samuel 23:11–12.

David does not say so explicitly, but it is obvious that this question presupposes a situation in which Saul has come up to Keilah and surrounded it. If we make the presupposition explicit, it takes the form of a *condition*. We might say, "Let us suppose as a condition that Saul comes up to Keilah and demands that Keilah surrender David. *If* this condition holds, will the men of Keilah surrender David?"

The condition that Saul comes up to Keilah depends on still another implicit condition: that David remains in Keilah. Saul's coming up to Keilah is motivated only if David is there. As it actually turned out, David departed from Keilah, and Saul "gave up the expedition" (v. 13). He never went up to Keilah.

So we have two conditions. First, if David were to remain in Keilah, would Saul come up? Second, if David were to remain in Keilah and Saul were to come up, would Keilah surrender David? God answers both of David's questions. Since both depend on conditions, God's response is to be understood in the light of these conditions. He is saying, in effect, "If A, then B; and if B, then C." But he does not say whether or not the condition A holds. David departs from Keilah, so the starting condition does not actually hold, and the whole discussion is hypothetical. It is hypothetical, but not meaningless. God is Lord of possibilities, even possibilities that never happen to be actualized.

God's lordship provides space for conditional probability. Here is how conditional probability works. Jill rolls a die. Karen can see that the die is symmetrical and has six faces. She concludes that the probability of the die coming up 5 is 1/6. If, however, Jill tells her that the result is odd, the probability changes. The information that the result is odd is an additional *condition*. If the result is odd, what is the new probability? The new probability is called a conditional probability because it depends on the special condition.

Conditional probability depends not only on God's lordship over chance and over possibilities, but also on the multiplicity of personal perspectives. We can appreciate the difference between the perspectives of Karen and Jill. Or we can perform all of our thinking within Karen's perspective, because Karen can still imagine what it would be like if she had the extra knowledge that Jill has. Or she can project herself into the future, as it were, and imagine herself rather than Jill having the knowledge.

The plurality of possible perspectives on knowledge goes back to God.

God is one God, and so there is unity in him, and unity in the world that he has made. God is also three persons. So there are three personal perspectives on knowledge.[2] God is the original pattern, the origin of all perspectives. Human beings are made in God's image, and so they can appreciate the view of another person. Conditional probability relies on two viewpoints, the original viewpoint and a viewpoint on the basis of the condition. Karen thinks, "If I were Jill, and had more knowledge, what would probabilities look like from her point of view?"

CALCULATING CONDITIONAL PROBABILITY

Let us see how to reckon with conditional probability. We consider again the situation where Jill rolls a die, and it comes up 5. Jill then reveals to Karen that the result is odd.

Before Jill rolled the die, there were six possible outcomes. The probability of the result being 5 was 1 out of 6, or 1/6. What is the probability that the result would be odd? There are three cases of an odd outcome, namely 1, 3, and 5. These three cases are out of a total of 6 possible cases. The probability of odd is obtained by dividing the number of favorable cases (3) by the total number of cases (6). The probability is 3/6, which is the same as 1/2. Or we can obtain the same result by adding up the probability of the three distinct events, 1, 3, and 5. The probability of getting 1 is 1/6. Likewise, the probability of getting 3 is 1/6, and the probability of getting 5 is 1/6. Since these three outcomes are mutually exclusive, the probability of getting either 1 or 3 or 5 is 1/6 + 1/6 + 1/6 = 3/6 = 1/2.

Now look at things from Karen's point of view. Jill has told her that the result is odd. Given this information (a condition), what is the probability that the outcome is 5? There are three possible odd outcomes, namely 1, 3, and 5. So from Karen's point of view, the probability of getting 5 is 1 out of 3, or 1/3. This probability is a *conditional* probability, since it is dependent on the condition, known to Karen, that the outcome is odd.

We can now observe that there are two ways of obtaining the probability of the die coming up with 5 on top. The first way is to calculate it directly: there is one successful outcome out of a total of six possible outcomes, for a probability of 1/6. The other way is to do it in two stages. First, we observe

---

[2] Vern S. Poythress, *Symphonic Theology: The Validity of Multiple Perspectives in Theology* (Grand Rapids, MI: Zondervan, 1987; reprint, Phillipsburg, NJ: Presbyterian & Reformed, 2001), 47–51.

that in order for the die to come up 5, it must come up odd. There are three ways to obtain this outcome. Given that it comes up odd, there is only one way out of three for it to come up 5. We move from a total of six outcomes at the beginning, to three outcomes that are odd, to one outcome with 5 on top. Getting 5 is one outcome out of 3 (the odd outcomes) out of 6. The probability of getting 5 is the probability of getting 5 out of the three odd outcomes, times the probability of getting an odd outcome, out of the 6 total possibilities. We can represent the reasoning compactly as follows:

> 1 outcome out of 3, once we have narrowed down to 3 outcomes out of 6.

By dividing by six, we can represent the same process in fractions or probabilities:

> 1/6 [1 outcome out of 6 where we get 5 on top] = 1/3 [1 out of 3 odd outcomes] × 3/6 [3 odd outcomes out of 6].
> Or: 1/6 = 1/3 × 3/6.

We can introduce a special notation to keep track of this reasoning. We use of the letter P to stand for probability. P(die-comes-up-5) stands for the probability that the die will come up with 5 on top. P(die-comes-up-5) = 1/6. In general, for an event A, $P(A)$ denotes the probability that the event A will take place. P(die-comes-up-odd) stands for the probability that the die comes up odd. So P(die-comes-up-odd) = 1/2. We represent *conditional* probability using a vertical bar "|". P(die-comes-up-5 | die-comes-up-odd) is the conditional probability that the die comes up with 5 on top, given that we know that it has come up odd. The vertical bar | is shorthand for the expression "on the condition that" or "given the knowledge that." Using our notation about probabilities, the result about the outcome with 5 on top is written as

$$P(\text{die-5}) = P(\text{die-5} \mid \text{die-odd}) \times P(\text{die-odd}).$$
$$1/6 = 1/3 \times 3/6$$

Consider a second example. Suppose we have two dice, each with six faces. Let us suppose that one die is white and the other red, so that we can distinguish them from one another. We consider the possible outcomes when we roll both of them. The white die may come up with any of six numbers as outcomes. For each one of these results, the red die may come up with any of six outcomes. White coming up 1 and red coming up 1 count together as one outcome. White coming up 1 and red coming up 2 count as a second outcome. And so on. Because of the multiple possible outcomes for the red die, the total number of possible outcomes for both dice taken together includes 6 distinct outcomes (for the red die) for *each* of the 6 outcomes for the white die alone. The total number of possible outcomes is $6 + 6 + 6 + 6 + 6 + 6 = 6 \times 6 = 36$. Here is a list:

1, 1	1, 2	1, 3	1, 4	1, 5	1, 6
2, 1	2, 2	2, 3	2, 4	2, 5	2, 6
3, 1	3, 2	3, 3	3, 4	3, 5	3, 6
4, 1	4, 2	4, 3	4, 4	4, 5	4, 6
5, 1	5, 2	5, 3	5, 4	5, 5	5, 6
6, 1	6, 2	6, 3	6, 4	6, 5	6, 6

Now, how many of these outcomes lead to a total of 5 for the sum of the two dice? And why should we care? In one dice game, if a player rolls 5 with a pair of dice, he has to roll 5 a second time (before he rolls a seven) in order to win. So the player may want to know how likely that is. And if we are studying the wisdom of God in the way in governs chance events, maybe we will want to know too! There are 4 outcomes in all where the sum is 5: $1 + 4$ (the white die comes up 1, while the red comes up 4), $2 + 3$, $3 + 2$, and $4 + 1$. So what is the probability of rolling a 5? Out of a total of 36 outcomes, all of which can be assumed to be equally likely, only 4 outcomes result in a total of 5. The total probability for getting a sum of 5 is 4 out of 36, or $4/36 = 1/9$.

Suppose now that we roll the two dice, but do not observe the result. Jill tells us that the result is a total of 5. Given this extra information or condition, what is the probability that the white die has come up 2?

Using Jill's extra information, we know that there are only four ways of obtaining a total of 5. Each of these is equally probable. So the probability of getting any one of them is 1 out of 4, or 1/4. Only one out of these four outcomes has the white die coming up 2. So the probability that the white die has come up 2 is 1/4.

We can perform similar reasoning in which we begin by focusing on the number of outcomes rather than the probabilities. We have said that there are 36 possible outcomes. All are equally probable. How many outcomes result in the white die coming up 2 and the sum of the two dice amounting to 5? Obviously there is only one way to do it, namely, by having the white die come up 2 and the red die come up 3. There is only one outcome that will match both conditions.

We could reach the same outcome by two steps instead of one. First we narrow down to the outcomes that give a sum of 5. Then we narrow down from there to the outcomes that *also* have the white die come up 2.

If we select the outcome with a white 2 and sum of 5 in one step, we have 1 outcome out of 36 that meets these two conditions. If we do it in two steps, we have 4 outcomes out of 36 that have a sum of 5, and then out of these 4 outcomes we have 1 outcome with the white die coming up 2.

The relevant probabilities correspond to these facts. The probability of white 2 and a sum of 5 is 1/36, corresponding to 1 outcome out of a total of 36 possible outcomes. The probability of obtaining a sum of 5 is 1/9, corresponding to 4 outcomes out of 36. The probability of a white 2, *given that* the sum is 5, is 1 outcome out of 4, or 1/4. This last probability is a *conditional probability*, because it depends on the *condition* that we know that the sum of the two dice is 5. The one desired outcome (white 2 and a sum of 5) is 1 out of 4, and these 4 outcomes are 4 possible outcomes out of a total of 36.

We can use our notation for probability. Let P(sum-of-5) be the probability that the sum will be 5. Let P(white-2 and sum-of-5) be the probability that the white die will come up 2 and the sum will be 5. Let P(white-2 | sum-of-5) be the conditional probability that we get a white 2 once we already know that the sum has come up 5.

Our reasoning about narrowing down to the final result in two stages leads to the equation

$$P(\text{white-2 and sum-of-5}) = P(\text{sum-of-5}) \times P(\text{white-2} \mid \text{sum-of-5}).$$
$$1/36 \quad = \quad 1/9 \quad \times \quad 1/4$$

The right-hand side of the equation represents the two stages. In the first stage, we narrow down to the outcomes with a sum of 5. The probability is P(sum-of-5). In the second stage, represented by P(white-2 | sum-of-5), we narrow down further, given the assumption (condition) that we already know that we have a sum of 5.

We can generalize this principle. Suppose that instead of 36 possible outcomes we have a total of T possible outcomes for some trial. Among these outcomes, suppose there are k outcomes that make two conditions, A and B, both come true. Then the probability of A and B both coming true is k out of T outcomes, or k/T. Let P(A and B) denote the probability that both A and B occur. Then P(A and B) $= k/T$. Suppose now that there are m outcomes that make B come true. The probability of B coming true is m outcomes out of T, or m/T. We write P(B) $= m/T$. The conditional probability of A and B, given that B, corresponds to k outcomes out of m, for a probability of k/m. P($A \mid B$) denotes the conditional probability that A occurs, given that we know that B occurs. P($A \mid B$) $= k/m$.

Then

$$k/T = (m/T) \times (k/m)$$

by normal arithmetic. Using our definitions,

$$P(A \text{ and } B) = P(B) \times P(A \mid B).$$

If the event B is possible, P(B) is greater than zero. So we can divide both sides by P(B), obtaining

$$P(A \mid B) = P(A \text{ and } B)/P(B)$$

This equality can be used as a definition of the conditional probability P($A \mid B$) if we like. (Customarily, if P(B) $= 0$, the conditional probability P($A \mid B$) is left undefined.)

This equation works with the earlier example. Consider the case where Jill knows that the die came up 5, while Karen knows only that it has come up with an odd number. If A stands for the die coming up 5, and B stands for coming up an odd number,

$$P(\text{5-up} \mid \text{odd}) = P(\text{5-up and odd})/P(\text{odd})$$

Now P(5-up | odd) $= 1/3$; P(5-up and odd) $=$ P(5-up) $= 1/6$; and P(odd) $= 1/2$. Substituting in these values, we obtain

$$1/3 = (1/6)/(1/2),$$

which checks out.

Conditional probabilities reveal another pattern of harmonies that God has ordained for the world. They can be another stimulus to praise him.

CHAPTER 20

ENTANGLEMENT OF PROBABILITIES

We have seen that probabilities can be affected by what someone already knows. Jill knows that the die has come up 5, so that for her the probability of a 5 is 1—it is certain. Karen knows only that the die has come up odd. So for her the probability of a 5 is 1/3. Laura, let us say, has no specific information about the die. So for her the probability of a 5 is 1/6. We have to pay attention to what information is available to a particular person.

COMPLEX INFLUENCES

Complex events in everyday life frequently involve much more information and many more possible influences than the case of a roll of a die. Large amounts of information may be potentially relevant. We mentioned earlier the question of whether a 75-year-old woman will die within one year. The actuaries can look up the probability in a collection of statistics about death rates. But the statistics give us only an average rate, based on a large number of individuals. Each individual is different.

Has the woman ever smoked? Does she smoke right now? Do her parents or other blood relatives have a history of heart disease or colon cancer? Is she overweight? What is her diet like? Junk food or health food? Does she exercise regularly? Does she have a history of auto accidents, which might make it more likely that she would die in an auto accident? Is she depressed? Is she taking care of herself? What do her doctor's records say about her current state of health?

The questions go on and on. Each answer would give us more information about the woman, and each bit of information has the potential to change our probability estimate about the likelihood of her dying. We have statistics that address some of the questions and give us an idea about how much effect some one factor has on the final estimate of probability. But can we calculate the *joint* effect of several factors together, or all factors taken together? If we mix in enough factors, this one woman may be the only woman in the world who meets all the criteria. And then we have a sample of one, and we cannot get a good statistical average.

The complexities that belong to any one factor, like a family history of heart disease, may force us to admit that we can give only a rough estimate. When we have many factors, and the factors interact, the challenges multiply. For example, does smoking contribute to heart disease, so that smoking and a family history of heart disease might make a particularly dangerous combination? When operating together, they might raise the probability of death more strongly than if we just add one effect on top of the other, while ignoring interaction.

It should be clear that many questions about which we have a natural human interest are also complex questions, involving many possible causal factors. We may see that lots of information is pertinent, but we may be unable to assess just how much a particular piece of information should change our initial probability estimate.

SIMPLE CASES

We can make the most confident progress when we deal with simple cases. For example, when we deal with a single roll of a die, we know there are only six possible outcomes, and from symmetry we can infer that these six outcomes are equally probable. We can also deal in a precise way with cases where one or more people have extra information about the outcome (Jill versus Karen versus Laura).

Now consider a case where we roll two dice rather than one. We can do it either by rolling the same die a second time, or by rolling two distinct dice at the same time. Do these two cases differ in their outcomes?

Here we confront another kind of regularity. God has designed the world so that regularities in probabilities occur in both time and space. A regularity occurs in time, in the sense that a trial roll at one time is just as likely to come up with a 5 as a trial roll at a different time. The probability remains the same over time, and this "sameness" is a regularity. A regularity also occurs in space, because two different dice at two different spatial locations have the same probability of coming up 5. This "sameness" in space is another regularity.

In these cases we need a proviso: "other things being equal." At the margins of our experience we can always imagine strange cases, where the die is weighted, or a trick die substituted in, or a magnet is used to manipulate a die that has some magnetic material within it. We cannot completely specify all possibilities for how there might be strange deviations. We rely on a broad sense of regularity. Underneath, we rely on God. And probability does work for us in ordinary cases. God is faithful to himself, and he is faithful to the world that he has designed and created.

INDEPENDENCE

We can rely on another regularity, called *independence* of events or *independence* of probabilities. *Independence* is a key idea in the theory of probability, but it takes some explaining. Suppose we have two dice, one white and one red. The probability that the white die will come up 5 is 1/6. The probability that the red die will come up 5 is also 1/6. These truths follow from symmetry and also from the regularities in space and time.

Now picture a situation in which we roll the white die, and it comes up 5. Then we proceed to roll the red die. What is now the probability that it will come up 5, given the extra information that we have, namely, the information that the white die has already come up 5?

The actual answer is that the red die still has a 1/6 probability of coming up 5. Knowing the outcome from the white die does not affect the red die. Its probabilities are still the same as they were before. The technical term for this situation is probabilistic *independence*. We say that the outcome for the red die is *independent* of the outcome for the white die. This kind of independence does not occur in our examples about the 75-year-old woman who smokes or exercises regularly. The probability that she will die in the next year is influenced by such extra information. It is not *independent* of the information. Some kinds of knowledge influence probability estimates, but other kinds of knowledge *do not*. When one kind of knowledge does not have an influence, we describe the situation as a situation of *probabilistic independence*.

The roll of one white die does not affect the outcome of the roll of a red die. The two are independent. Similarly, a previous roll of a white die does not affect the outcome of the next roll of the *same* die. This independence is an independence in time.

Some people's intuitions fail them when they think about situations like these. For example, they may imagine that since the white die has already come up 5, a second roll of the same die is *less* likely to come up 5. They may try to bolster their reasoning by pointing out that the average for a large number of die rolls must work out so that the outcome of 5 is no more frequent than any other outcome. So surely the next roll is a little *less* likely to come up a 5, in order to "balance" the long-run frequencies of all six outcomes. By similar reasoning, if a single die has come up 5 six times in a row, it is quite a bit less likely to come up 5 again, because it has to balance out the total number of 5s with the totals for the other possible outcomes.

Some people's intuitions may actually go in the opposite direction. They may think that, after several occurrences of an outcome of 5, the die is *more* likely to come up 5 because maybe there is a tendency to stick to a pattern that is already in place.

There are indeed situations in ordinary life that show patterns like these. Suppose you go to a Little League game knowing nothing about either team. You watch the pitcher, and the first eight pitches you see are all strikes. Is the next pitch likely to be a strike? Yes. There is a good chance that you are watching a very accurate pitcher, and that he has decided to try to throw a strike every time. You learn from watching that there is a pattern to his pitches. The probability of his throwing a strike is very high, especially when compared to another pitcher with poor accuracy.

Now let us go back to the situation with dice. We have to see that the two dice are more like two pitchers than one. Just because one pitcher is accurate, it does not make another pitcher more accurate. The same is true for the situation where we repeatedly roll a single die. We throw the white die a second time, a third time, and so on. Is it more likely to come up 5? What if it comes up 5 three times in a row? Is it likely to come up 5 on the fourth throw? The answer is no. The fourth throw still has a probability of 1/6 of coming up 5. If it comes up 5 ten times in a row, or a hundred times in a row, the probability of coming up 5 on the next roll is still 1/6. That is what we mean by probabilistic independence.

But we must insert a qualification. The probabilities we are talking about for dice are *a priori* probabilities. We knew what these probabilities were before we ever starting rolling the dice. But suppose we start for the first time with rolling a die, and it does come up 5 a full 10 times in a row, right after we start. What then? That is a very unusual result, so unusual that we begin to suspect that there is something fishy. Someone has tampered with the die. It looks symmetrical, but maybe it is not. Ah, it feels funny. The face opposite to the 5 seems to be very heavy. What is happening here is that in our assessment of the die we are being influenced by *a posteriori* probabilities. The actual results of conducting trials, that is, conducting rolls, are so unusual that we look around for some explanation for why the results, that is, the *a posteriori* samples, differ strongly from the *a priori* predictions.

Gamblers sometimes get trapped by their feelings or hunches about probabilities. They *feel* that a particular die or a roulette wheel or other object has mysteriously gotten "stuck" on some pattern, and therefore it is very likely that the pattern will continue. Or, conversely, they notice that 5 has not come up for a long time on the die, so, they feel, it is "time" for it to come up, and the probability of it coming up on the very next roll is higher than it would otherwise be. Are they right? The answer is no. The patterns that the gamblers think that they see are all temporary, ephemeral. Despite the gamblers' feelings, the outcome of the next roll of the die is just as unpredictable as the very first roll. The probability of coming up 5 is 1/6. This probability is *independent* of all the previous rolls, as far back as we go.

How do we know that is the case? We are finite; we do not know absolutely. But those who have studied events like repeated coin flips and repeated dice rolls and repeated drawing of cards from well shuffled decks discern a pattern of independence in all these types of events. The pattern is ordained by God in his faithfulness and creativity and love.

We can, in part, understand something of the rationale and the wisdom in this pattern. Each roll of a die is distinct. And each is going to involve minute differences in the initial orientation of the die, and how it first strikes the ground, and so on. Such differences cannot be controlled by human beings. So the spatial symmetry of the die's faces do suggest, by means of *a priori* reasoning, that the six distinct outcomes should be equally likely. And since each roll of each die is different in the details of how it starts, there will be no intrinsic correlation between two distinct rolls or two distinct dice. The lack of intrinsic correlation means independence.

This independence contrasts with the intrinsic correlations that we sense do exist in cases where we consider, for example, the relation of smoking or family history to the likelihood of death. Things that happen in the woman's body earlier in time influence the state of her health. By contrast, the history of a die does not influence the next roll, because the roll starts fresh with slightly different orientation, slightly different rate of spin, and so on.

THE BLESSINGS OF INDEPENDENCE

God has ordained this type of independence of events for reasons that we do not fully understand, but we can appreciate them in part. First, independence of events makes it possible for us to enjoy calculating probabilities with more precision in these cases. We can admire the intricacies of the theory that deals with independent events. Second, the limitations on our knowledge testify to the superiority of God's knowledge and power, and should lead us to praise.

Third, probabilistic independence is a kind of extreme case that exemplifies a more general pattern about the nature of the world. There are distinct creatures, and each creature has a kind of integrity to its own existence. In particular, human beings are distinct from one another, and each person has his own moral responsibility. His attitudes and behavior are not determined by the attitudes and behavior of any other person. He is, in a sense, "independent." But he is not isolated. There are indeed influences. Parents influence children, teachers influence students, and so on. So the "independence" of each individual is a kind of relative independence. By contrast, each roll of a die is in a sense *absolutely* independent of each other roll. There is no causal influence. The outcome of each roll is in this sense *isolated* from the outcome of every other roll. It is completely unpredictable, even if we have massive information about the outcomes of many previous rolls.

Scientists in physical science use an analog to this form of independence, namely, physical isolation. For many experimental tests, a scientist tries to set up a small physical system that is not influenced in any decisive way by physical causes or interference from the environment. The physical system is *isolated*. The system may consist of a single atom or a single molecule or a pair of molecules or a compact solid object. If the scientist suspects that the system will be affected by light, he does the experiment within a darkened room or a darkened chamber. If he suspects that the system will be affected by vibration, he takes care to isolate the system from vibration.

When the scientist succeeds, his experimental results show only what is going on within the small system. They are not probabilistically influenced by outside light or outside vibration or anything else in the larger environment. Physical isolation produces probabilistic isolation or rather probabilistic independence in the experimental results. Only in this way is it feasible to have confidence that the results that the scientist obtains are results from the atom that he is testing, and not from the tides or the odors in the air. Experimental science would be impossible without probabilistic independence. We should thank God that he has designed into the universe many forms of probabilistic independence, and that scientists can, with careful thought and preparation of their experiments, achieve enough isolation so that they get good results rather than meaningless garbage.

CHAPTER 21

PROBABILISTIC INDEPENDENCE

Since independence of events is so important, and such a blessing in the world that God made, we may examine it more closely. Our examination can continue to increase our appreciation for God's wisdom. In particular, we can examine the relation between events in the world on the one hand and their numerical probabilities on the other. If two events are independent, does it imply anything about their probabilities? In fact, the numbers, that is the probabilities, are in harmony with the world. And that harmony is due to God's wisdom. Let us see how.

What does it mean for two events to be independent? Intuitively, it means that neither event influences the other. Can we translate this absence of influence into a statement about the probabilities of the events?

A PROPERTY OF PROBABILITIES

Consider a simple situation, namely, two flips of a coin. There are a total of two outcomes for the first flip, and two outcomes for the second flip. If we take the two flips together, there are a total of $2 \times 2 = 4$ possible outcomes:

HH (a head followed by a head)
HT (a head followed by a tail)
TH (a tail followed by a head)
TT (a tail followed by a tail)

If we consider one flip of the coin all by itself, the probability of a head is 1/2, and the probability of a tail is 1/2. Now suppose that the first coin has come up heads. To say that the second flip is independent of the first means that knowing that the first has come up heads gives us no extra clue as to what will happen with the second flip. Hence, the probability of the second flip coming up heads is still 1/2, and the probability of it coming up tails is still 1/2.

Both of these probabilities for the second flip are *conditional* probabilities. What we are saying is that, given the condition that the first flip has come up heads, the conditional probability that the second will come up heads is 1/2. The same holds for the second flip coming up tails.

We can express this result mathematically, once we have a symbol to represent each result. Let P(1H) be the probability of the first flip coming up heads. Likewise, P(1T) will be the probability of the first flip coming up tails. P(2H) will be the probability of the second flip coming up heads, and P(2T) for the second flip coming up tails. Then we also have combinations: P(1H & 2H) will denote the probability that both flips will come up heads; P(1H & 2T) will denote the probability that we will get a head followed by a tail; P(1T & 2H) is the probability that a tail will be followed by a head; and P(1T & 2T) the probability of two tails.

Independence of the two events, we have said, means that the conditional probability of a second flip of heads, P(2H | 1H), is the same as the probability P(2H) of a second flip of heads when we have no condition. The knowledge of the condition 1H makes no difference. From a previous chapter, we know in general that the conditional probability P(A | B) of an event A given the occurrence of event B satisfies the equation

$$P(A \mid B) \times P(B) = P(A \text{ and } B)$$

If B is the occurrence of heads on the first flip, and A the occurrence of heads on the second flip,

$$P(2H \mid 1H) \times P(1H) = P(1H \& 2H)$$

If P(2H | 1H) = P(2H), which is the condition for independence, then

$$P(2H) \times P(1H) = P(1H \& 2H)$$

The probability of two heads, that is, P(1H & 2H), is simply the probability of the first flip of heads (P(1H)) multiplied by the probability of the second flip of heads (P(2H)).

P(1H & 2H) = (1/2) × (1/2) = 1/4.

Similar reasoning holds for the case where we roll a die twice. The outcome of the second roll is independent of the outcome of the first roll. What then is the probability that the first roll will come up 5 and the second will come up 4? By the general principle for conditional probabilities,

P(1st-5 & 2d-4) = P(2d-4 | 1st-5) × P(1st-5)

By independence, P(2d-4 | 1st-5) = P(2d-4). Substituting into the equation just above,

P(1st-5 & 2d-4) = P(2d-4) × P(1st-5).

Since the probability for any one face coming up is 1/6,

P(1st-5 & 2d-4) = (1/6) × (1/6) = 1/36.

INDEPENDENCE EXPRESSED NUMERICALLY

The result can be generalized. If two events *A* and *B* are independent,

P(*A* & *B*) = P(*A*) × P(*B*)

That is, the probability P(*A* & *B*) of both events *A* and *B* occurring is the product of the probability P(*A*) of *A* and the probability P(*B*) of *B*. This numerical relationship is often used as the *definition* of independence, because the numerical condition is logically equivalent to the idea that the probability of the second event *B* is uninfluenced by any knowledge of whether event *A* has occurred. Events *A* and *B* are probabilistically independent if and only if

P(*A* & *B*) = P(*A*) × P(*B*)

This result can be established in the same way as with the special examples that we have already given. By the rule for conditional probability,

P(*A* & *B*) = P(*A* | *B*) × P(*B*).

If *A* and *B* are independent, P(*A* | *B*) = P(*A*). Substituting,

P(*A* & *B*) = P(*A*) × P(*B*),

which is the result desired.

We can observe a coherent relationships between mathematics on the one hand and physical probabilities on the other hand. On the one side we have a relationship of multiplication in mathematics. On the other side we have a physical situation, in which the two events A and B do not influence each other. Satisfying the mathematical condition of multiplication implies physical independence, and conversely, physical independence implies the multiplicative relationship on probabilities. We have here a marvelous coherence between mathematics and physical events. It is one of many such coherences. God is author of both the mathematics and the world of events. His wisdom and his self-consistency offer the foundation for coherence between the two realms. So we should use the contemplation of probabilistic coherence as an occasion to praise God.

We could also show that when events A and B are independent, A is also independent of the complementary event not-B, the event where B does not occur.

MANY EVENTS

We can contemplate a whole series of coin flips or die rolls. Suppose we flip a coin 10 times, and record the result each time. Will this record enable us to make a better prediction about the outcome of the 11th flip? The answer is no. The 11th flip is probabilistically independent of all the previous flips. It is independent of any one flip when taken by itself. The outcome of the third flip gives us no information about the outcome of the 11th flip. But the independence of the 11th flip is of a stronger kind, since even the total record from all previous flips taken together gives us no helpful information about the 11th flip. That is the same as saying that the outcome of the 11th flip is independent of each of the combinations for previous flips. It is independent of the probability of each of the following:

HHHHHHHHHH,
HHHHHHHHHT,
HHHHHHHHTH,
HHHHHHHHTT,
HHHHHHHTHH,
HHHHHHHTHT,
HHHHHHHTTH,
HHHHHHHTTT,

HHHHHHHTHHH,
HHHHHHHTHHT,
etc.

That is to say, the probability of any one outcome for the 11th roll of a die is independent of *each* of the events that consist in a record from all 10 previous rolls.

As the number of repetitions of coin flips or die rolls increases, the total number of possible outcomes for all of the previous rolls taken together increases rapidly. It quickly becomes hopeless to perform a meticulous check of probabilistic independence. Instead, students of probability simply assume that independence holds true in cases like these. They can see that the physical setup for the events suggests there is no causal influence, and previous experience with physical setups has confirmed independence when we have been able to check it.

The assumption of independence relies on God. God has established regularities in the world. And these regularities include regularities in the midst of unpredictabilities. Any one coin flip is unpredictable. But the connection of probabilities among successive coin flips is in a sense predictable. We have confidence, based on the faithfulness, wisdom, and creativity of God, that the pattern of successive coin flips will show probabilistic independence. And this independence holds true no matter how long a record or how many coin flips we accumulate. No such accumulation, no matter how long, gives us any ability to predict the next outcome any better.

This kind of independence is quite remarkable, when you think about it. It is remarkable enough that God has made a world in which some events are independent of one another. It is still more remarkable that there should be indefinitely extending sequences of events, all of which are independent of the entire preceding sequence. We can never thoroughly test this property, since for long sequences the number of possible outcomes quickly exceeds the time it would take to do a test. We *believe* that independence extends out beyond the comparatively small region where we can do a few tests. In so doing, we are relying on the faithfulness of God.

We rely on him whether or not we consciously acknowledge him. By contrast, look at the kind of thinking that arises if a person tries to rely on Chance as the substitute god. If Chance is in control, it is an unpredictable control. Unlike God, who is faithful and wise, Chance as a substitute is a god about whom a person can say nothing for certain. A person may think, "Anything can happen." If truly anything can happen, we have no basis for predicting regularities in the midst of unpredictabilities. We would be looking, so to speak, at unpredictabilities all the way down, if we were to arrive at a region where Chance took over.

If Chance means *pure*, irrational unpredictability, we have no foundation for postulating probabilistic *regularities*. These regularities include the regularities with respect to conditional probabilities and probabilistic independence. If we really believed in Chance, we could not count on anything. The theoretical mathematics for probability theory can still exist, because it can simply postulate the property of independence at the level of its axiomatic assumptions. But we lose the grounds for thinking that the mathematics has applications in the real world.

No one consistently abandons confidence in regularities. We all rely on regularities in the midst of unpredictabilities. It is natural to us because we are made in God's image, and it is natural to think God's thoughts after him. Admittedly, when we are in rebellion against God, the relation of our thinking to God's is partially disrupted. But we may still retain some common sense, and this too depends on God. God is merciful even to those in rebellion against him.

CHAPTER 22

INDEPENDENCE AND HUMAN NATURE

The independence of events involving coin flips, dice, and similar chance events has practical implications. Independence of events means that accumulating experience with coins or keeping a record of past outcomes does not help at all. No matter how much information we accumulate from the past, the next event, the next flip of the coin, is just as unpredictable as it was without the information from the past.

GAMBLERS VERSUS CASINOS

This principle applies to gamblers in casinos. It tells us why gamblers cannot win in the long run (see appendix A). Gamblers often hope to win because they think they have a "system," using either explicit record keeping or intuition. For instance, if the roulette wheel has come up with an even number seven times in a row, the gambler may tell himself that "it is time" for odd. He thinks that odd has now become more likely than even for the next spin of the wheel. But he is wrong. The outcome of the next spin is probabilistically independent of all the previous spins, no matter how far the record-keeping goes back. A similar principle holds for slot machines (if they are not "rigged"). The next play on the machine is probabilistically independent of all the previous outcomes.

What difference does this make? It makes a difference to casinos. If probabilistic independence did *not* hold true, it would mean that there was some correlation, however complex, between the previous series of outcomes and the next outcome. By developing the right scheme—

a "system"—a gambler could give himself an advantage. If he could predict an outcome with certainty, he would have a big advantage. He would have a way of betting without any risk, and he could make a lot of money quickly. But a gambling system would work even if it gave the gambler only a slight advantage. Over the long run he could win more than he lost in individual bets.

As an example, consider a roulette wheel. A European roulette wheel has 37 pockets, labeled with the numbers 0–36. (The pocket numbered 0 is in effect the 37th pocket.) In the USA, many of the wheels have a double zero 00 as well. We will take as our example a European roulette wheel, which has a zero but no double zero. While the wheel is spinning, a small ball is let loose above the wheel, and the ball eventually settles into one of the 37 pockets. The pocket into which the ball settles is the outcome of one particular "turn" of the wheel. There are 37 possible outcomes, one for each of the pockets 1–36, and an additional, 37th outcome, having the ball land in the zero pocket.

Manufacturers of roulette wheels take great care to produce exact symmetry in their wheels. Because of the symmetry, each of the outcomes is equally probable. The probability of any one outcome is 1 out of a total of 37, or 1/37.

If a gambler bets on a number and it does not come up, he loses the entire bet. If it does come up, the "house" (the casino) pays 35 times the amount of his bet. If he tries 37 successive bets of $1, he will on the average win once, and get $35 extra. The other 36 times he will lose, losing $1 each time. So he has a net loss of $1. That averages out to a net loss of 1/37 of a dollar, or a little under 3 cents, for every time he bets.

Now suppose that he has a "system" that enables him to choose a number that is more likely to come up. Instead of a probability of 1/37, let us say that, in at least a few situations, he can use his system to win with a probability of 1/4. If he is wise, he will first watch the outcomes without betting, and then will bet only when his system gives him an advantage. With this strategy, for every four bets he makes he will win one bet on the average. He will gain $35. The other three times he will lose $1. His net gain is $32, or $8 per bet. After one day at the roulette table, he will be hundreds or thousands of dollars richer, depending on how often the special situations come up that give him his special advantage. Once he sees that his system is working, he can safely increase his bets. Instead of betting $1 per turn, he can bet $10 or $100 or $1,000 per turn (provided he has enough spare cash so that he can afford to lose a few times before his first win).

The casino will soon notice his success. Winning in this way is so unusual that the casino manager might suspect that the gambler has formed a secret partnership with the employee managing the roulette table, and that together they have found some secret way of manipulating the outcome of the wheel. If the manager can find no explanation of this kind, he will nevertheless ban the gambler from the roulette table beginning on the next day. He cannot afford to do otherwise. If he were to let the gambler continue, he would continue losing money to the one gambler. But in addition, other gamblers would soon notice the "good luck" and begin to imitate his bets, thereby "piling on" and winning money themselves.

We can imagine such a sequence of events. Some gamblers dream of it happening to them. But in real life it never happens. A gambling system may *seem* to work for a few minutes. But then its temporary gains are wiped out as the number of trials increases. The inability of gamblers to find a winning system confirms that in fact the outcomes are probabilistically independent.[1] A gambler cannot beat the house.

Thus the existence of casinos is an impressive confirmation of the regularities that God has put in place with respect to chance events. These regularities can be depended on, and in fact casinos do depend on them day by day, every day, to stay in business.

Is gambling morally wrong? Many students of the Bible have focused on the eighth commandment, "You shall not steal" (Ex. 20:15). They have argued that taking someone else's money without a compensatory exchange of goods (selling food or clothing, for example) is a case of theft. They may also argue that a person who loses his money to gambling is not acting responsibly with respect to what God has entrusted to him. These arguments are weighty, but we will not enter into their details. At the end of any moral analysis, there remains a significant question: does God allow immoral human activity? The answer is that he does. The immoral actions of Herod and Pontius Pilate during the crucifixion of Christ are one key example. God exercises his control over the events in this world, but his

---

[1] Technically, there are minor exceptions in the case of some card games, because the probabilities may depend on the cards previously played. See appendix A.

control does not imply his approval, nor does it diminish the moral responsibility of human beings who are following their own way.

God expresses his lordship in more than one way. God is Lord in ethical standards, so that we can consider whether gambling is right or wrong. God is also Lord of events, including chance events. This second kind of lordship is what we have been considering in this book. This kind of lordship extends even to events where God *disapproves* of the motives of human actors, such as casinos and gamblers. God's lordship is still manifested in the regularities exhibited in chance events. The outcomes of the roulette wheel are still probabilistically independent. God sustains the regularities even when human beings are using those very regularities as a platform for morally reprehensible actions.

Human gamblers may think that they can come up with a system to help predict the next outcome on the roulette wheel. But human beings only have enough time and energy to try a limited number of schemes. What about computers? Computers can be programmed to digest data from records of thousands or hundreds of thousands of past outcomes, looking for complicated patterns. Can a computer beat the casino using some complex calculation? As we might expect, the answer is still no. Probabilistic independence means that there is no correlation with the past. By trying out a huge number of possible patterns, a computer might perhaps find one pattern that looks promising. But when the pattern is tried out, it fails. Once it fails, we know that it was just by chance that it happened to match the record from the past. The alleged pattern provides no insight into the future.

RANDOM SEQUENCES

So far we have focused on the question of whether we can *detect* patterns in a sequence of coin flips or roulette wheel outcomes. We can also ask how to *generate* such a sequence. How can we produce a sequence of outcomes that a gambler can never win against? As we have observed, coin flips, roulette wheels, and dice produce such sequences. They are called *random sequences*. Roughly speaking, a *random sequence* is an indefinitely long sequence of outcomes, such that it has no inherent predictability, even of the slightest kind. The probability of heads on the next flip is exactly 1/2, no matter what is the sequence of previous outcomes. By contrast, a sequence of outcomes is nonrandom if we can predict the next outcome based on information from all the previous outcomes. We do not require that the first few outcomes be predictable, but only that eventually, given a long enough sequence of previous outcomes, we should be able to predict the next one. Moreover, we do not require that our prediction be certain, but only that it give us *some* advantage.

For example, if we can guess the outcome of a coin flip exactly half of the time, our probability of winning is 1/2 or 0.5, which is exactly the *a priori* probability of the coin coming up heads (or tails). We have no advantage. If, on the other hand, we have a system that enables us to increase the success of our guesses to 0.51, we have a slight advantage. This increase in accuracy can take place only if the sequence is nonrandom. Or suppose that we find a way to decrease the accuracy of our guesses to 0.49. That too is nonrandom. By making our guess exactly the opposite of what it would have been, we can be successful 0.51 of the time, again achieving a slight advantage.

For a random sequence, there is no scheme by which we may achieve even a slight advantage of this kind. The gambler cannot improve his chances. The same is true even if we use a computer to help us.

GENERATING RANDOM SEQUENCES

Coin flips and roulette wheels generate random sequences. But ordinarily computers do not. Computers are designed to make exact calculations and not to make mistakes, even in the course of trillions of individual operations. There is no randomness in their calculations. But computer programmers have nevertheless been able to write programs that generate random number sequences. Or rather, the sequences appear for all ordinary purposes to be random. There is no discernible pattern. Actually, the sequences are *pseudorandom*. The computer program goes through a large number of operations, which can be likened to shuffling cards using a large number different patterns, one for each successive shuffle. Any one shuffle has a determinate outcome (unlike a shuffle with human hands). But after a large number of shuffles, all the obvious patterns in the original sequence of cards are destroyed, and the cards appear to be in random order.

In addition, random number programs in computers typically start the process using a "seed," a single starting number. If the same number is used every time, exactly the same sequence is produced as output. But by using as the seed the value from the computer's clock, which is always changing, the program is enabled to generate a new pseudorandom sequence every time it is used. The sequences appear to be completely unrelated to one another, as well as being unpredictable within any one sequence.

For some specialized applications, however, these pseudorandom sequences are not good enough, because theoretically the whole sequence is calculable once we know both the seed number and the program used to generate the sequence. To get a more "solid" version of randomness, some computers are linked to sensors that detect random physical events, such as the radioactive decay of a single atom[2] or small thermal variations. Theoretically, the computer could use the input from coin flips or dice, but it is easier to use other physical sources.

Even without input from unpredictable physical events, computers can do a very good job generating a pseudorandom sequence. A human being cannot succeed in guessing the outcomes. If the outcomes are 0 and 1 with a 1/2 chance of each, a human being will end up in the long run being right half of the time—neither more nor less on the average.

Suppose now that we switch the roles of the human being and the computer. The human being is supposed to produce a sequence of 0 and 1 (or H and T, standing for heads and tails). The computer is supposed to guess the next outcome on the basis of the record of all the preceding outcomes. If the human being is allowed to flip a coin each time, or roll dice, or use some other physical source for producing a random sequence, he will generate a truly random sequence, and the computer has no way of gaining an advantage.

But suppose that we forbid the human being from using coins or dice. We might guess that the situation is fundamentally the same; but it is not. A suitably programmed computer can always beat the human being. Why?

Human beings are incapable of producing random sequences just by using their minds. Without realizing it, they begin to prefer certain patterns. Maybe one person tends to oscillate between 0 and 1. He produces more cases of the sequence 01 and 10 than 00 and 11. After the computer is given the opportunity to see enough previous outcomes, it detects this preference, and then makes each guess the opposite from the previous one. Or perhaps

---

[2] The decay of a *single* atom is unpredictable ("random"), but the *average* rate of decay can be measured accurately by watching a large number of atoms. See appendix J for an analysis of the relationship between single events and averages.

the human being realizes that he is preferring the sequences 01 and 10, so he overcompensates by putting in more instances of 00 and 11 than he should by pure chance. Maybe he is able to put in all four possibilities, 00, 01, 10, and 11, with a probability of 1/4, but he still has more instances of 001 than 000, or more instances of 0001 than 0000, or maybe his preference goes the other way. With a long enough record of outcomes, a computer begins to detect these preferences and is able to predict the next outcome with better than 0.5 rate of success. Pure randomness is very difficult for a human being, because it requires him to avoid simultaneously all detectable preferences for patterns of all possible complexity. In practice, it cannot be done, though some human beings may do better than others.

This situation of pairing human beings against computers shows that a random sequence is really an extraordinary, wonderful kind of phenomenon. We as human beings cannot achieve it unaided. Nor can a computer achieve it, though a program to generate pseudorandom numbers can imitate it. The only way for us to get genuine random sequences is by getting information from physical processes like coin flips or dice.

THE ROLE OF GOD

Physical processes are going on around us all the time. Quantum mechanics reveals that at the atomic level there are continual sequences of random events. As far as we can see, these are truly random, unlike the pseudorandom sequences generated by computers or the attempts at randomness from human minds. Physical processes continually succeed in tasks that exceed the capabilities of both human beings and the most powerful computers. Such a thing is a genuine marvel.

We say that the physical processes succeed. But are they just going by themselves? Where do they get this superhuman ability? Our earlier reflections on Scripture remind us that physical processes are not independent of God. God is the one who produces randomness. And his doing so is one remarkable display of his greatness. In this matter, he does what we cannot do.

People who do not want to acknowledge God have difficulty explaining randomness. Consider again the flip of a coin as an example. Why should it be the case that no possible pattern in previous flips allows any advantage in predictability for the next flip? The outcome of the next flip is unpredictable. That means that, as far as we know, either outcome is compatible with known physical laws. That is, an outcome of heads conforms to law, and an outcome of tails also conforms to law. It follows that an outcome of heads followed by a second outcome of heads conforms to law. We can infer that it is lawful for the next 100 outcomes all to be heads, and then 100 tails, and then 100 heads. People who will not acknowledge God cannot explain why, in addition to the physical laws, we rightly expect no future series of outcomes to be any more probable than another. The record of the past gives us no guarantee, because the principle of randomness says that the future is not predictable from the past. The fact that we cannot *predict* any particular outcome has no power to force the outcome to be what it is.

The ultimate explanation goes back to God's control. God, who is all wise, produces what we experience as randomness, and this randomness is far above our ability to produce.

RELIANCE ON RANDOMNESS

Coin flips may seem to be a minor affair in life. But they are only one example of randomness. The second law of thermodynamics depends on randomness. The second law is a statistical law, which says that *on the average* a closed physical system will travel toward maximal "entropy," where entropy is a technical way of measuring randomness. The second law is valid only because God faithfully governs randomness as one aspect of his governance of the world. The second law is behind the workings of combustion, chemical reactions, weather, and many complex systems.

Many statistical studies depend on randomness. Statistics may be compiled by taking what is called a *random sample* from a larger "population" of cases. It may be a sample of 1,000 people out of a population of 100 million. Or it may be a sample of cells from the total number of cells in a person's blood stream, or a sample of soil out of a field—there are many situations.

For many purposes it is important that the sample be representative. The 1,000 people who are polled in a statistical sample should not be hand-picked all to be male, or all to be exactly 20 years old, or all to be graduates of Harvard University. To get a representative sample, a researcher can use special techniques to eliminate bias and to make sure that any one of the 100 million people is equally likely to be picked to be part of the sample.

The expression "equally likely" goes back to the idea of randomness, and the result is often obtained by using a random number generator to pick from an initial list that is comprised of 100 million individuals. Or it may be obtained by letting some physical process generate randomness. Because blood circulates in a complex way through the body, a blood sample drawn from a single vein at a single time can for most purposes be considered to contain a random sample of the red blood cells that circulate throughout the body.

In many areas we rely, without realizing it, on the faithfulness of God in giving us randomness.

CHAPTER 23

IS GOD PROBABLE?

Some people have endeavored to apply the language of probability to God. They might say that "God probably exists" or "God probably does not exist." Usually they do not offer us a specific numerical value, such as saying that the probability of God's existence is 0.3. If no numerical value is offered, the word *probable* is being used in a looser sense, to indicate at least that one option is more likely than the other. What should we think about such claims?

THE DIFFICULTY OF GLOBAL CLAIMS

Such claims are odd for several reasons. First, in any *global* claim, a claim about the nature of reality as a whole, it is difficult to know the meaning of probability. We can contrast global claims with local claims. In a local claim we make some probability estimate about a particular event located at a particular time and place. We say, for example, that the probability of a die coming up with a 5 on top is 1/6. Or we say that coming up with a 5 is not probable—that is, it is less probable than the alternative, coming up with something that is not 5.

We can test a local claim by comparing it with claims about nearby times and places. We may roll the die a second and a third time. If we like, we roll it 10,000 times. Or we roll 100 dice simultaneously, and see how many come up with a 5 on top.

By contrast, we cannot perform multiple experiments on reality as a whole. We have only one universe. We cannot inspect two universes, much less 10,000, in order to see in which ones God exists.

IS THE UNIVERSE PROBABLE?

An analogous difficulty occurs when cosmologists discuss whether there are multiple universes, and what is the probability that a universe with characteristics like ours should exist. A probability estimate makes sense only if we have some means, either *a priori* or *a posteriori*, for providing a foundation for it. For a case of *a posteriori* probability, we need a sample consisting of multiple cases. When we are discussing the global question of the universe as a whole, that means we need a sample of multiple universes, hopefully a large sample. How do we get the sample? For all we know, other universes may exist, but we cannot observe them. So in fact we have only a sample consisting of one. With a sample of one that meets the criteria we have in mind, the *a posteriori* probability is defined as the number of cases that meet the criteria, divided by the total number of cases. This recipe gives us a probability of $1/1 = 1$. The result is not very interesting, because it is automatic. In effect, it says what we already knew: we are where we are. *The* universe, the only one we know, does exist, and its existence is certain—given the knowledge that we already have.

What about *a priori* probability? The situation here also has difficulties. To get an *a priori* probability, we should first enumerate all the possible outcomes, like the situation in which we enumerate all possible outcomes for a roll of a die. That is, we enumerate all the possible universes. And then we also look for a symmetry that would allow us to say that each of the cases can be expected to be equally probable. Each of six outcomes for rolling a die is equally probable because of the symmetrical shape and weight of the die. How do we see symmetries between multiple universes?

These difficulties have not prevented some cosmologists from trying to calculate probabilities for universes. But to do it they have to have equations that describe the common behavior of all possible cases—all possible universes. The equations still allow choices—perhaps choices for some fundamental physical constants, or choices for the amount of matter and energy. The cosmologists also have to obtain, separate from the equations, some symmetry criteria that allow them to specify what universes or ranges of universes are equally probable.

Cosmologists do not yet know what the equations may be. Some think that string theory or M-theory is a good candidate. Others think that loop quantum gravity might do it. As of 2012, these are still open questions. But now suppose that cosmologists *do* come up with a system of fundamental equations for physics, and do get decisive experimental confirmation. What then? All we know is that the equations in question work for *this universe*. We have only one case. It is a bold and questionable venture to use one case as a basis for pronouncing what *must* be the case for billions of other possible instances. It is as if one made confident pronouncements about all meteorites after having examined one.

Of course in the case of the universe, we have only one, and we can never have any more. The boldness can proceed undisturbed, because it can never be contradicted. But the limitations of our position (one universe) do not by themselves generate a solid basis for boldness. Why should the mere absence of an alternative give us positive grounds for believing that we can get solid insights by trying to exceed our built-in limitations (i.e., the limitations of having only one universe to observe)?

But in another sense we do have an alternative: we can admit that we do not know. But that is not very exciting. Mathematical cosmologists may still, if they like, do the mathematical calculations about what the probabilities would be, given such-and-such specific assumptions about sample universes. They just have to tell us in addition that it is all pretty much an abstract game, because no one knows what are the correct assumptions for other universes:

> Nothing is wrong with scientifically based philosophical speculation, which is what multiverse proposals are. But we should name it for what it is.[1]

The difficulties increase if we admit that God created the universe rather than postulating that impersonal equations plus Chance, the substitute god, did the trick by themselves. God can do as he pleases. How do we calculate the probability for what choice he will make? We do not know. We should admit our limitations.

IS GOD PROBABLE?

What about the biggest question of all: does God exist? What is the probability that he exists?

---

[1] George F. R. Ellis, "Does the Multiverse Really Exist?" *Scientific American* 305/2 (August 2011): 43. Note also: "The key step in justifying a multiverse is extrapolation from the known to the unknown, from the testable to the untestable. You get different answers depending on what you choose to extrapolate" (ibid.).

This question is another *global* question, and has the difficulties that we have already discussed. It has an additional difficulty connected with the nature of God. God is a God who can and does create the universe. Maybe, unknown to us, he has created more than one universe. No matter how many he has created, he himself is more ultimate than any of them. That is part of the meaning of his being God.

If God does exist, he exists as the One who is ultimate and absolute. He exists in a relationship of Creator to creature with respect to any and every universe that does or could exist. Hence, it contradicts the nature of God to say that he could exist with respect to a possible universe A but not exist with respect to a possible universe B. If he exists at all, he exists with respect to them all. From a probabilistic point of view, if he exists, the probability of his existence, averaged over all possible universes, is 1: he certainly exists. On the other hand, if he does not exist, he exists with respect to no universe, and the probability of his existence is 0. (We are here talking about actual existence, not whether one or another person *thinks* he exists.)

But we have an even more serious difficulty, which in fact undermines the reasoning with respect to the possibility of God's nonexistence. God is the foundation for probability. He has ordained both regularities and unpredictabilities in the world. He has also ordained the creation of human beings, who are made in his image. We are created in such a way that we can think God's thoughts after him—albeit on the level of a creature, by analogy with our Creator. We can think thoughts about regularities and unpredictabilities, because God has thought them first. We calculate probabilities *based on* the assumption of these regularities and unpredictabilities. Without God's work of creation and sustenance, we have nothing to talk about and no assurance of regularities from which to begin. And of course we ourselves cannot begin anyway, because first we have to be brought into existence by God.

Moreover, according to Romans 1:21 we know God inescapably. We know that he displays his divine nature in the nature of probability. We know that he exists. The probability is 1. But even this statement is paradoxical, because we know it before we even begin our probabilistic reasoning. If we ask whether "God probably exists," we are already at odds with the reality of our own previous knowledge.

But Romans 1 also indicates that when we are in rebellion against God we suppress the knowledge that we have. It may indeed *seem* to us, as we engage in naive conscious introspection, that we do not know whether God exists. We may even go further and try to estimate how probable it is, just as we estimate probabilities for other events for which we do not have firm knowledge.

SUBJECTIVITY IN ESTIMATING GOD'S EXISTENCE

In this area of subjectivity, it does make sense to talk about probabilities. We may remember the situation in which Jill knows that a die has come up 5, while Karen knows only that it has come up with an odd number. The probability differs from person to person, depending on his or her state of knowledge.

Similarly, suppose God has acted to save Jill from her rebellion against him, and she has been freed from her desire to suppress the knowledge of him. Jill knows God. The probability for her is 1—though it is still odd to speak about a probability for God, who sustains the very structures that permit our thinking about probability.

Karen, on the other hand, remains in a state where she suppresses the knowledge of God. It *seems to her* that the existence of God is doubtful. It is probable, or it is improbable. It is not certain. She may waver. After being overwhelmed by the beauty of a sunset or an outpouring of human love, or thinking about the intricate design of her own hand, she may feel that she can say that the probability of God's existence is 0.9. After experiencing a horrible tragedy, she may revise her estimate and say that the probability of God's existence is only 0.1. Such language makes sense, because Karen is talking in terms of subjective perception on the basis of those pieces of knowledge of which she is most aware and by which she is most swayed at the moment.

On the other hand, there is still a massive oddity. Karen is all the while depending on God. His faithfulness, his creativity, his love, his wisdom, his knowledge are "clearly perceived" (Rom. 1:20) and must be confidently relied on in order for Karen to know about probability at all, and for her to engage in any kind of estimate, either with respect to the roll of a die or with respect to the big issue of the existence of God. There is a deep tension between Karen's covert reliance on God and her overt doubts. Such is the nature of unbelieving, rebellious humanity.

It is not a comfortable situation. Romans 1 also reminds us that "they are without excuse" (v. 20). Unbelievers cannot excuse rebellion and their claim not to know, because they show that they rely on God in the very assumptions that they make about regularities and unpredictabilities and probabilities in the process of undertaking to doubt him.

Thus Christian believers, who have by God's grace come to know the truth, should avoid joining unbelievers in talking about the probability of God's existence. We can understand the meaning of what people like Karen are saying. But we know that they are not aware of the whole story. They have suppressed decisive truths. Probability testifies clearly to God, and they know it.

PART IV

PROBABILITY AND MATHEMATICS

CHAPTER 24

PICTURES OF PROBABILITY

We can represent properties of probability spatially. A spatial picture can make things easier to grasp. In addition, once we have a spatial picture, we can appreciate a harmony between space and probability, a harmony that God has put in place. But it will take some time to get there. Readers who do not care for the detail and just want to see the conclusions may of course just read the concluding summary at the end of this chapter. The same is true for the remaining chapters of this book.

REPRESENTING THE ROLL OF A DIE

The roll of a die can have six possible outcomes. We can represent the outcomes spatially by drawing a separate region of space for each outcome. (See fig. 24.1.)

Fig. 24.1: Six Regions

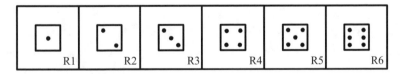

We can label the regions so that we can distinguish them. Let region R1 represent the outcome in which the face with one dot comes up on top; let region R2 represent the outcome where the face with two dots comes up; and so on.

We now assign a probability to each region. Because of the symmetry of the die, each region should have the same probability as the others, namely

1/6. The probability of 1/6 for region R1 is the probability that the die will come up with one dot on top. Or equivalently, we can think of the probability of 1/6 as the probability that region R1 will be chosen. We write P(1 up) = P(R1) = 1/6 for the probability of region R1. Likewise for the other regions, P(2 up) = P(R2) = P(R3) = P(R4) = P(R5) = P(R6) = 1/6. (See fig. 24.2.)

Fig. 24.2: Six Regions with P

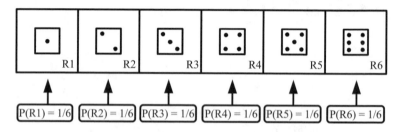

We can use the additive property to obtain the probability for a composite region, consisting of one or more of the smaller regions. For example, the composite region consisting in the three rectangles R1, R2, and R3 has an associated probability

P(R1 united to R2 united to R3) = P(R1) + P(R2) + P(R3)
= 1/6 + 1/6 + 1/6 = 3/6 = 1/2.

Hence, the probability that the die will come up with one of the numbers 1–3 is 1/2. In general, the probability for a composite region is the sum of the probabilities of each of the smaller regions that it contains.

SETS

The regular way of describing a region composed of smaller regions is to use the special sign ∪, which designates set union. The region that includes R1, R2, and R3 is designated R1 ∪ R2 ∪ R3. So P(R1 ∪ R2 ∪ R3) = P(R1) + P(R2) + P(R3) = 1/6 + 1/6 + 1/6 = 1/2. In general, for any regions A and B, the expression $A \cup B$ designates the region including everything in region A and also including everything in region B.

What is the probability that the die will come up with an even number on top? The even numbers correspond to the regions R2, R4, and R6. An even result corresponds to the set union of these three regions; that is,

R2 ∪ R4 ∪ R6.

The probability is P(R2 ∪ R4 ∪ R6) = P(R2) + P(R4) + P(R6) = 1/6 + 1/6 + 1/6 = 1/2. The probability of the occurrence of an even number is represented by the region in fig. 24.3 that is shaded by lines going diagonally from the upper right to the lower left.

Fig. 24.3: Six Regions with P Even

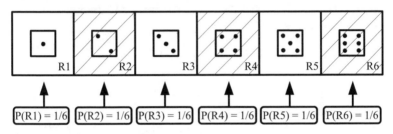

What is the probability that the outcome of the die roll will be *either* 1–3 or even? The probability is the probability for the union of all these regions:

P((R1 ∪ R2 ∪ R3) ∪ (R2 ∪ R4 ∪ R6)) = P(R1 ∪ R2 ∪ R3 ∪ R4 ∪ R6)
= P(R1) + P(R2) + P(R3) + P(R4) + P(R6)
= 1/6 + 1/6 + 1/6 + 1/6 + 1/6 = 5/6.

The two regions (R1 ∪ R2 ∪ R3) and (R2 ∪ R4 ∪ R6) overlap in R2. (The former of the two regions is shaded by diagonal lines going from upper left to lower right in fig. 24.4, below, while the latter of the two regions was shaded in the opposite direction in 24.3, above.)

Fig. 24.4: Six Regions with P Even and 1–3

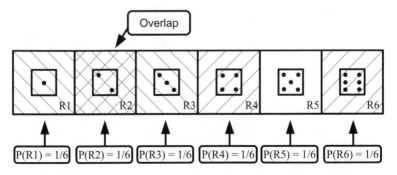

In calculating the total probability, we must not count R5, which belongs to neither of the two shaded regions. In addition, we must not count R2 twice. So the total probability of 5/6 is less than the sum of the two probabilities P(R1 ∪ R2 ∪ R3) and P(R2 ∪ R4 ∪ R6). What is the probability that the outcome of the die roll will be in the range 1–3 and *also* will be even? There is only one region that meets both criteria, namely R2. So the probability is P(R2) = 1/6. This region R2 can be described as the *intersection* of the region 1–3 with the region with 2, 4, and 6. The standard symbol for intersection is an inverted U shape: ∩.

R2 = (R1 ∪ R2 ∪ R3) ∩ (R2 ∪ R4 ∪ R6).

In general for any regions *A* and *B*, the intersection *A* ∩ *B* designates the region consisting in everything that is inside *A* and also inside *B*.

Suppose we denote the entirety of the region R1 ∪ R2 ∪ R3 as *A* (1–3 dots turn up), and the entirety of the region R2 ∪ R4 ∪ R6 as *B* (the whole region where an even number turns up). The regions *A* and *B* have an overlap consisting in their intersection *A* ∩ *B*. If we depict *A* and *B* as circles rather than rectangular regions, we obtain fig. 24.5.

Fig. 24.5: A Intersection B

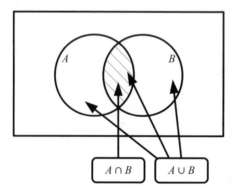

A ∩ *B* (which is R2) is the region contained in both *A* and *B*. The region *A* ∪ *B* (which contains all of *A* and all of *B*) is composed of three smaller areas: the part of *A* outside *B* (unshaded in fig. 24.5), the intersection *A* ∩ *B*, and the part of *B* outside *A* (also unshaded). The part of *A* outside *B* is the part of R1 ∪ R2 ∪ R3 that is outside R2 ∪ R4 ∪ R6, which is R1 ∪ R3. P(R1 ∪ R3) = 1/6

+ 1/6 = 1/3. The part of *B* outside *A* is R4 ∪ R6. P(R4 ∪ R6) = 1/6 + 1/6 = 1/3. The remaining part composing *A* ∪ *B* is *A* ∩ *B* or R2, which has probability P(*A* ∩ *B*) = P(R2) = 1/6. Since these three regions are have no overlap, the total probability of *A* ∪ *B* is the sum of the probabilities of each of the three regions:

P(*A* ∪ *B*) = P(R1 ∪ R3) + P(R4 ∪ R6) + P(R2)
= 1/3 + 1/3 + 1/6 = 5/6.

Two regions with no overlap are called *disjoint*. Their intersection is empty. (See fig. 24.6.)

Fig. 24.6: Nonintersecting A and B

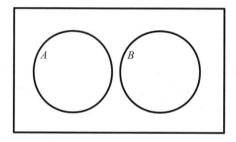

The empty region is designated ∅. The probability of the empty region must be 0, because it represents a situation that cannot occur. P(∅) = 0.

The principle of additivity says that when two regions are disjoint, their probabilities add:

P(*A* ∪ *B*) = P(*A*) + P(*B*).

The result easily generalizes. For any number *n* of disjoint regions A_1, A_2, A_3, ... , A_n,

P(A_1 ∪ A_2 ∪ ... ∪ A_n) = P(A_1) + P(A_2) + ... + P(A_n).

For the original situation with regions R1, R2, R3, R4, R5, and R6,

P(R1 ∪ R2 ∪ ... ∪ R6) = P(R1) + P(R2) + ... + P(R6)
= 1/6 + 1/6 + 1/6 + 1/6 + 1/6 + 1/6 = 1.

The complement of *A*, which is designated A^c, is the whole area *outside* *A* but inside the enclosing rectangle, a rectangle that represents all possible outcomes (see fig. 24.7).

Fig. 24.7: Complement of A

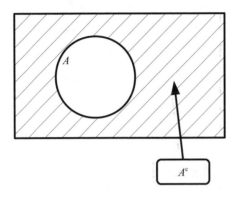

In the diagram for $A \cup B$, given in fig. 24.5, the part of A outside of B is $A \cap B^c$. Similarly, the part of B outside of A is $B \cap A^c$. In an intersection, the two areas being intersected can be written in either order: $B \cap A^c = A^c \cap B$.

In general, for any region A, the region together with its complement A^c make up the entire region of possible outcomes. So

$$P(A) + P(A^c) = 1.$$

This formula can be used to calculate either $P(A)$ or $P(A^c)$, once the other is known:

$$P(A) = 1 - P(A^c)$$
$$P(A^c) = 1 - P(A)$$

For example, what is the probability that the die will not come up with a four on top? Rather than count each of the other outcomes, we can first ask what is the probability that the die *will* come up with four on top. That is the probability $P(R4) = 1/6$. So the probability that the die will not come up with four on top is the probability of the complement:

$$P(\text{not four}) = P((R4)^c) = 1 - P(R4) = 1 - 1/6 = 5/6.$$

All of these properties are consequences of two principles. (1) The principle of additivity says that, if two distinct events cannot occur at the same time, the probability that at least one of two events will happen is the sum of the probabilities of the two events. (2) The total probability for all possible outcomes is 1.

Both of these principles have their foundations in God. Consider the first principle. As we saw earlier, the existence of distinct events has its foundation in the separations that God has ordained through his word. The separations within this world have their ultimate foundation in the distinction among the persons of the Trinity.

The second principle is that the total probability is one. This principle is true because of the way in which we decided at the beginning to define probabilities as fractions or percentages. Moreover, we have the ability to conceive of the total number of outcomes as a single whole, because God has given us this thinking ability. We see the total as a whole, as a unity. And this unity is composed of the diversity of distinct individual outcomes. The unity and diversity in outcomes rest, as usual, on the original pattern of unity and diversity in God. God has caused the creation to reflect his glory and wisdom.

SPATIAL ANALOGY

We have now seen that we can represent probabilities using spatial pictures. If we like, we can go a step further and draw the spatial pictures in such a way that the amount of area in each region is proportional to the probability of the event represented by that region. For example, for the regions R1, R2, R3, R4, R5, and R6, the associated probability is 1/6 in each case. So we make all six regions the same size. On the other hand, if we draw a picture of only two regions, R4 and its complement $(R4)^c$, the probabilities for the two regions are not the same. $P(R4) = 1/6$ and $P((R4)^c) = 5/6$. We should therefore draw the region $(R4)^c$ so that its area is five times the area of R4.

We can represent the probabilities spatially because of the coherence or analogy between space and probability. Into this picture also comes the coherence or analogy between space and numbers and between probability and numbers. God has comprehensively ordained all the properties of space, number, and probability. The coherence depends on God. It therefore has its ultimate foundation in the inner coherence of God himself. God is one, and the persons of the Trinity are in harmony with one another. In particular, the harmony between space and number goes back to God. He has created this world by his word, and his word specifies the harmony between space and number.

CHAPTER 25

MATHEMATICAL POSTULATES FOR PROBABILITY

Our examples of probability have used unpredictable events in the real world, events like the flip of a coin or the roll of a die. These probabilities have mathematical properties. God has ordained harmony between the physical events and corresponding properties in mathematics.

FORMING A MATHEMATICAL THEORY

The correspondence between events and numbers has enabled thinking to develop about the mathematical side of probability. As a result, we can look at mathematical properties of probability that characterize events, without specifying just what events we have in mind. We can use as an example the flipping of a coin. Each flip has a probability of 1/2 of coming up heads. We can get the same result with any number of coins of different sizes and weights, as long as all of them are "fair" (unbiased). But we can imagine other kinds of events where there are two outcomes, each with a probability of 1/2. We can roll a die, and call the result "heads" if the roll comes up with an odd number, "tails" if the roll comes up with an even number. The two are equally probable. Or consider a deck of 52 playing cards. Exactly half of the cards (26) belong to a black suit (spades or clubs). If the deck is shuffled and we draw a single card, the probability that we draw a black suit is 26/52 or 1/2.

The common properties shown in coin flips, die rolls, and other unpredictable events can be summed up in a single kind of numerical reckoning with the probabilities of the events. The mathematical theory of probability is designed to accomplish this task in a general way, without ever specifying *which* events we have in mind. At the beginning we choose the starting mathematical assumptions about a number of probabilistic "events," where the events are abstractions. The assumptions are our *postulates*. Several postulates together make up a *theory*—in this case the theory of probability. We can then make deductions, even without first associating these abstract events with any specific events in the physical world.

AN ADVANTAGE TO POSTULATES

By using postulates we can achieve generality. If the postulates hold for any particular physical phenomena, we can immediately conclude that all the deductions from the postulates also hold. For this reason, the mathematical treatment can take place once and for all. Then the results can be applied to many physical situations: coin flips, die rolls, playing cards drawn from a pack, spins of a roulette wheel, lotteries, and still other chance events. In fact, the results hold for still other fields of study that do not involve chance, such as the measurement of spatial areas. The previous chapter showed how reasoning about probabilities can be correlated with reasoning about spatial areas.

The application of mathematical probability to many distinct phenomena is one instance of the principle of the one and the many. A general mathematical result about mathematical probability is a single result. It shows unity. It also has applications to many physical situations. The many situations show the diversity. The many situations go together with the one general result. At the same time, the general result is motivated by the long-range purpose of applications to the many physical situations. Human beings understand the meaning of the general result by referring to particular illustrations that apply it. Conversely, the particular illustrations gain meaning through being seen as embodiments of one general principle. The relations between the one and the many go back, as usual, to a foundation in God, who is the original one God in three persons.

For example, suppose we know that we have a situation where one of two mutually exclusive events A or B can take place, and where the probability of the event A is 1/2. Then the probability of the other event B is also 1/2 (because the total probability for both together must be 1). The general principle says that the probabilities must add to 1: 1/2 + 1/2 = 1. This general principle applies to the flip of the coin, which can come up heads or tails. It also applies to the roll of a die, which can come up odd (1, 3, or 5) or even (2, 4, or 6). And it applies to many other physical situations in the world. God ordains the consistency between the general principle, the one, and the particular applications, the many.

BASIC CONSTITUENTS FOR A MATHEMATICAL MODEL

The transition from physical situations to a mathematical treatment takes place by producing a kind of mathematical model for the physical situations. The model strips out all the particulars about coins, dice, cards, and slot machines. Instead, we start with an abstract set S, the set (collection) of all possible outcomes for a trial of some kind.[1] For example, for a die roll, the outcomes are 1 through 6, so the set S has members 1, 2, 3, 4, 5, and 6. The usual notation for writing the members of a set S is to enclose a list of members in braces:

$S = \{1, 2, 3, 4, 5, 6\}$

For a coin flip, with outcomes H (heads) and T (tails),

$S = \{H, T\}$.

The trial on which we are focusing can be a simple trial, such as a single flip of a coin, or a whole sequence, such as three successive flips of a coin. If our trial consists in three successive flips, then the set S of possible outcomes is

$S = \{HHH, HHT, HTH, HTT, THH, THT, TTH, TTT\}$.

In most simple cases of probability, there will be only a finite number of possible outcomes. But we can also consider the case where there are infinitely many outcomes. If the possible outcomes can be put into one-to-one correspondence with the positive integers, the set of outcomes is said to be *countably infinite*. (Even though someone can never finish counting the outcomes, any particular outcome will be counted if he persists long enough in the counting process.) If the outcome can be any real number within a certain range, the set of outcomes is *uncountable*.

---

[1] Textbooks sometimes use other letters besides S to designate the set of possible outcomes.

In all these cases the set S of all possible outcomes is called the *sample space*. The designation *sample space* means that each member of the set S is a "sample," that is, one possible outcome among many. The set S as a whole is the "space," that is, the realm in which these outcomes are collected together. The set S is analogous to the outside enclosing rectangle in the spatial diagrams of probability that we constructed in the previous chapter.

In addition to a sample space, we must have what has been called a *probability law* or *probability measure*, which specifies the probability that a given outcome will occur. In previous chapters, we have used the symbol P( ) as the symbol for this probability law. In the spatial diagrams in the previous chapter, we have included added information underneath the spatial regions to indicate what probabilities are assigned to each region.

For a coin flip with an unbiased coin, the sample space is $S = \{H, T\}$. The probability law is given by $P(H) = 1/2$ and $P(T) = 1/2$. For an unbiased die with six faces 1–6, $S = \{1, 2, 3, 4, 5, 6\}$ and the probability for each of the elements in S is $1/6$. $P(1) = P(2) = P(3) = P(4) = P(5) = P(6) = 1/6$. In the case with a finite sample space S, P is a function that assigns a numerical value to each outcome, that is, each member of S. The assignment given by P need not be the same value for each of the members of S. In principle, we allow for cases where higher or lower probabilities are assigned to the various members of S. If, for example, a particular die is known to be biased toward coming up with four on top, we may have $P(4) = 0.25$, $P(1) = P(2) = P(3) = P(5) = P(6) = 0.15$.

It is customary to have the probability law P also assign probabilities to *subsets* of S. A *subset* of S is a set of elements all of which are members of S. For example, if $S = \{1, 2, 3, 4, 5, 6\}$, then $\{1, 2, 3\}$ and $\{2, 4, 6\}$ are both subsets of S. Let $A = \{1, 2, 3\}$ and $B = \{2, 4, 6\}$. Then the following are also subsets of S:

$A \cap B = \{2\}$,
$A \cup B = \{1,2,3,4,6\}$,
$A^c = \{4, 5, 6\}$,
$B^c = \{1, 3, 5\}$.

S itself is a subset of S. So is the empty set $\varnothing$ (the set with no members). For a subset with one member, such as the subset $\{2\}$, P assigns to the subset the same probability as it assigns to the member 2 itself: $P(\{2\}) = P(2)$. In the technical language for the mathematical theory of probability, the subsets are called *events*. Events are sets like *A*, *B*, and A^c that may include as members more than one outcome. A set with one member, such as {2} is also an event. Even the empty set ∅ is an event in this technical sense, though it is an "event" that can never occur.

POSTULATES

Now that we have a sample space *S* and a probability law P, we must add *postulates*, fixed assumptions about the behavior of P. The three fundamental postulates are as follows:[2]

1. (called the postulate of *nonnegativity*). For any subset *A* of *S*, P(*A*) ≥ 0.

   In the nature of the case, probability is never negative. A zero probability means that the outcomes described by the subset *A* will never occur. The probability cannot be lower than a case that never occurs. This postulate is obvious for cases of physical probability. We must nevertheless write it out explicitly, because the postulates are intended to make deduction possible, without further reference to physical situations.

2. (the postulate of *additivity*). Let *A* and *B* be any two subsets of *S*. If *A* and *B* are disjoint, that is, if they have no elements in common (i.e., *A* ∩ *B* = ∅, the empty set), then P(*A* ∪ *B*) = P(*A*) + P(*B*).

   We have already considered this principle of additivity in a practical context in previous chapters (see especially chapter 24).

3. (the postulate of *normalization*). The probability assigned to the sample space as a whole is 1: P(*S*) = 1.

   This third postulate for the probability law P corresponds to the fact that in any physical situation, the total probability for all the possible outcomes is 1.

By repeated application of the postulate of additivity, we may see that for any number *n* of disjoint subsets A_1, A_2, A_3, ... , A_n, the following equality holds:

$$P(A_1 \cup A_2 \cup A_3 \cup \ldots \cup A_n) = P(A_1) + P(A_2) + P(A_3) + \ldots + P(A_n).$$

---

[2] Dimitri P. Bertsekas and John N. Tsitsiklis, *Introduction to Probability* (Belmont, MA: Athena Scientific, 2002), 9.

If the sample space S is infinite,[3] postulate 2 still applies. But we must also add to postulate 2 an analogue for a countably infinite number of subsets. For any countably infinite number of disjoint subsets A_1, A_2, ... ,

$$P(A_1 \cup A_2 \cup \dots) = P(A_1) + P(A_2) + \dots.$$

SOME BASIC DEDUCTIONS

Using these three postulates, but with no direct appeal to situations with physical probability, we may now deduce some basic conclusions with respect to probability.

First, there is a rule for calculating the probability of the complement of a subset A.

Theorem 1: $P(A^c) = 1 - P(A)$ and $P(A) = 1 - P(A^c)$.

The proof is given in appendix H. Intuitively the result makes sense, because A and A^c, the complement of A, together make up the total space, which has a probability of 1. (See fig. 25.1.)

Fig. 25.1: Complement of A and PA

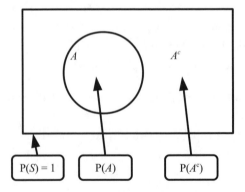

Next, we have a theorem stating that the probability increases with the size of the set.

Theorem 2: If A is a subset of B, $P(A) \leq P(B)$.

---

[3] With uncountable infinite sample spaces S, there are still further complications, because probabilities will typically be assigned only to measurable subsets of S.

The proof is given in appendix H. This result makes sense, because postulate 1 indicates that probability is always nonnegative. Together with the postulate of additivity, it means that increases the size of the set cannot decrease the probability.

We also have a general rule for calculating the probability associated with a set union $A \cup B$.

Theorem 3: For any two subsets A and B of S,

$$P(A \cup B) = P(A) + P(B) - P(A \cap B).$$

The proof is given in appendix H.

When A and B have an intersection $A \cap B$, the probabilities from this region of overlap are counted once within $P(A)$, and then a second time within $P(B)$. It therefore makes sense that we can calculate the actual value of $P(A \cup B)$ by first adding $P(A)$ and $P(B)$, thereby counting $A \cap B$ twice, and then subtracting away one of the two counts by subtracting $P(A \cap B)$.

As an illustration, consider the example of the previous chapter, $A =$ R1 $\cup$ R2 $\cup$ R3 (1–3 dots turn up) and $B =$ R2 $\cup$ R4 $\cup$ R6 (an even number of dots turn up). $P(A \cup B) = P($R1 $\cup$ R2 $\cup$ R3 $\cup$ R4 $\cup$ R6$) = 5/6$; $= P(A) =$ P(R1 $\cup$ R2 $\cup$ R3) $= 3/6$; $P(B) = P($R2 $\cup$ R4 $\cup$ R6$) = 3/6$; $P(A \cap B) = P($R2$) =$ 1/6. $5/6 = 3/6 + 3/6 - 1/6$, which checks out. The point of the theorem is that this relationship among probabilities holds not merely in the case of throwing a die, but in any case for which the three fundamental postulates hold.

Here is a theorem about probabilistic independence:

Theorem 4: If events A and B are independent (i.e., if $P(A \cap B) = P(A) \times$ $P(B)$), then (1) A and B^c are independent, (2) A^c and B are independent, and (3) A^c and B^c are independent.

As with the other theorems, the conclusions can be shown to follow using only the three postulates, and no other information.

MULTIPLE PERSPECTIVES ON PROBABILITY

The postulates that we have introduced are built on the two basic constituents, the sample space S and the probability law P. We can, if we wish, also use other perspectives on probability. The most obvious route is to begin with ideas of probability for actual physical events. But there are also alternative perspectives compatible with formal postulates. For example, rather than beginning with a set *S*, we can begin with spatial representations, where distinct areas within a larger spatial region *S* represent distinct events (see chapter 24).

We can also use an approach where we start with the *logic* of probability. The set intersection *A* ∩ *B* corresponds to the probability that event *A* and event *B* will *both* occur. The key word is the word *and*. It represents a logical operation of *conjunction*. Logic considers simple propositions such as "*A* will occur" and "*B* will occur." It also considers the logical *conjunction* in which we link together two such propositions into a compound proposition: "*A* will occur and *B* will occur." Set intersection clearly corresponds closely to logical conjunction of the corresponding propositions. Likewise, set union *A* ∪ *B* corresponds closely to logical *disjunction*, expressed by the word *or*. *A* ∪ *B* corresponds to the compound proposition, "*A* will occur or *B* will occur." The complement set A^c corresponds to the logical operation of negation. The probability of A^c is the probability that *A* will not occur, and it corresponds to the proposition "It is not the case that *A* will occur," which contains the operation of logical negation in the expression "It is not the case that … ."

Ordinary propositional logic deals with propositions that have fixed truth value. We can say that a true proposition has the "truth value" 1. We mean that it is certainly true. A false proposition has the truth value 0. It is certainly not true. Probability deals with propositions for which (typically) we do not yet know the truth value. So we attach to each proposition, not the value 1 for truth and the value 0 for falsehood, but an intermediate value, P(*a*), the probability that the proposition *a* is true (or will be true). In general $0 \leq P(a) \leq 1$. Thus, we can construct the entire model for mathematical probability within the context of logic. Instead of the sample space *S* we will have a list of elementary propositions *a*, *b*, *c*, … . Instead of the probability law P assigning values to subsets of *S*, we have a probability law P assigning values to propositions. The three postulates get converted into postulates about this probability law P. In particular, the postulate of additivity goes as follows:

2. (additivity). Let *a* and *b* be propositions with which is associated a probability law P. If (*a* and *b*) is definitely false, i.e., if P(*a* and *b*) = 0, then

$$P(a \text{ or } b) = P(a) + P(b).$$

With these changes, the model for probability becomes a model based on logic. We can also produce models based on lattices or Boolean algebra.[4]

COHERENCE COMING FROM GOD

God has ordained the distinctive character of each of these areas of study. They cohere with one another because of the unity of God, the unity of his wisdom, and the unity of his plan for the world. We may praise the Lord for the different ways in which we may consider the nature of probability.

---

[4] See Vern S. Poythress, *Logic: A God-Centered Approach to the Foundation of Western Thought* (Wheaton, IL: Crossway, 2013), especially chapters 33–38.

CHAPTER 26

THEISTIC FOUNDATIONS FOR SOME PROPERTIES OF PROBABILITY

Let us reflect further on some underlying assumptions used in reckoning with probabilities.

SYMMETRIES

We have already observed that our reckoning with *a priori* probabilities depends on symmetries. The coin is symmetrical between heads and tails. The die is symmetrical with respect to its six faces. Symmetries within this world have their ultimate root in the plan of God. And God's plan reflects the ultimate symmetries within God himself: the persons of the Trinity have the same character, and each shows the character of the others (chapter 17). God's basic symmetry within himself is the foundation for our confidence as creatures that probabilities about events in this world will be in harmony with symmetries in this world. God has made the world in a way that reflects his character.

ADDING EXCLUSIVE PROBABILITIES

Second, reasoning about probabilities includes the assumption that when two or more events are mutually exclusive, the probability of at least one of the events happening is the sum of the probabilities of the individual events.

We have already used this principle a number of times. If the probability of heads is h, and the probability of tails is t, the probability that the coin will come up *either* a head or a tail is $h + t$, the sum of the two. In this case, the total probability $h + t$ is 1, since it is certain (probability of 1) that one of the two outcomes will take place.

Why do the probabilities add? The relation between mathematical addition and this property of probability is a beautiful harmony. God has ordained it. Can we dig deeper into it?

With a die, there are six possible outcomes. We can represent these six outcomes by addition:

$$1 + 1 + 1 + 1 + 1 + 1 = 6$$

This addition of six ones to make up a total of six outcomes is our first perspective.

But we can look at the same reality in another way. Suppose that the total "pie" of all outcomes together is represented by 1 instead of 6. Then each of the individual outcomes represents 1/6 of the pie. This way of thinking in terms of a total pie is a second perspective on the same reality of six possible outcomes.

The second perspective is related to the first through a simple proportionality. In the first perspective we have a total of six outcomes, represented by the number six. In the second perspective, the totality of outcomes is represented by the number one. The proportionality is the proportionality of six to one. We can represent the perspectives side by side in a table (table 26.1).

Table 26.1: Two Perspectives on Outcomes

perspective #1	perspective #2
total: 6	total: 1
one outcome: 1	one outcome: 1/6
1	1/6
1	1/6
1	1/6
1	1/6
1	1/6

We can also represent the same proportionality spatially (see fig. 26.1).

Fig. 26.1: Proportion 6 to 1 in Space

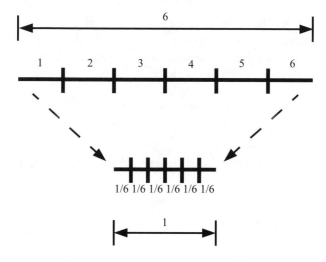

We can represent the same proportionality directly in numbers by starting with the equation:

$$1 + 1 + 1 + 1 + 1 + 1 = 6$$

Then we divide both sides by six:

$$(1 + 1 + 1 + 1 + 1 + 1)/6 = 6/6$$

The division by 6 on the left-hand side can be "distributed" through the individual terms, so that we get:

$$1/6 + 1/6 + 1/6 + 1/6 + 1/6 + 1/6 = 6/6 = 1$$

These proportionalities are harmonies in (1) physical outcomes; (2) geometric representations; and (3) numerical relationships. Such harmonies have their origin in God's word, which specifies them. The original harmony is in God himself. And it is regularly mirrored in proportionalities in the created world.[1]

The additive character of the outcomes also has its foundation in God's specification through his word. In Genesis 1 we can see that God introduces distinctions and separations:

---

[1] Vern S. Poythress, *Redeeming Science: A God-Centered Approach* (Wheaton, IL: Crossway, 2006), chapters 20–22.

And God *separated* the light from the darkness. (Gen. 1:4)

And God said, "Let there be an expanse in the midst of the waters, and let it *separate* the waters from the waters." And God made the expanse and *separated* the waters that were under the expanse from the waters that were above the expanse. (vv. 6–7)

We can infer that all the separations and distinctions in the world are a product of God's word. The separating power of his word has its foundation in the plurality of persons in the Trinity. Each is distinct from the others.

So God's word, we conclude, separates the distinct faces of a die, and separates the distinct outcomes, 1, 2, 3, 4, 5, and 6. The separation means that they do not overlap, and when one outcome occurs the others do not occur. The total number of outcomes can be added:

$$1 + 1 + 1 + 1 + 1 + 1 = 6$$

By using the proportionality of six to one, we can then see that the corresponding fractions add:

$$1/6 + 1/6 + 1/6 + 1/6 + 1/6 + 1/6 = 6/6 = 1$$

By using the symmetry of the faces, we can see that the probabilities associated with each fraction should be the same. So 1/6 represents not only a fraction of the pie of total outcomes but the probability of one of the outcomes. All of these ways of reasoning about outcomes and probabilities hang together because God's inward coherence is expressed and reflected in the coherence of his word governing outcomes and probabilities.

MULTIPLICATIVE HARMONY

Another wonderful harmony concerning probabilities arises in connection with probabilities of independent events. As we indicated in chapter 21, if events A and B are probabilistically independent of one another, the probability that A and B will both occur ($P(A \,\&\, B)$) is the product of the probabilities of the two events taken separately ($P(A)$ and $P(B)$). Thus:

$$P(A \,\&\, B) = P(A) \times P(B)$$

Why should this be the case?

The result can be seen as another case involving simple proportionalities. Let us consider an example. Suppose that the event *A* is the outcome where a die roll comes up with four on top. Let the event *B* be the outcome where a coin comes up heads. Intuitively these two events are independent of one another, since neither influences the other. P(*A*), the probability of event *A*, is 1/6. P(*B*), the probability of event *B*, is 1/2. According to the formula P(*A* & *B*) = P(*A*) × P(*B*), the probability of the die coming up four and the coin coming up heads is

P(*A* & *B*) = (1/6) × (1/2) = 1/12.

Suppose that we represent the total space for all the events by a circular "pie." The event *B* takes up half the pie, since it has a probability of 1/2. (See fig. 26.2)

Fig. 26.2: A Half Pie

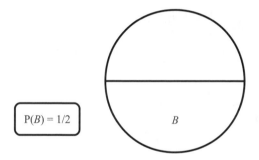

The event *A* has a probability of 1/6, out of the total probability of 1. We can think of this as a proportionality, a ratio of one to six, which holds not only for the event *A* but also for the situation when the event *A* is *combined* with another event, like the event *B*, which is independent of it. Specifying that *A* will occur within the situation in which we already know that *B* will occur divides the *B* part of the pie into six smaller pieces. 1/2 divided by 6 is 1/12. (See fig. 26.3.)

We can represent the same result geometrically. Let *B* be represented by half of a line that is one unit long. Draw a second line which is also 1/2 of a unit long. Using the proportionality of six to one, map out a part (called *c*) of this second line that will be projected from *B*, with a length only 1/6 of the length of *B*. This part *c* will be only 1/6 × 1/2 unit long, or 1/12. (See fig. 26.4.)

Fig. 26.3: A Half Pie into Sixths

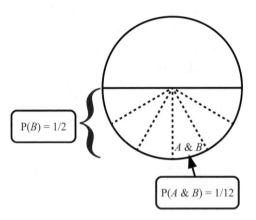

Fig. 26.4: Proportion of 1 to 1/6 in Space

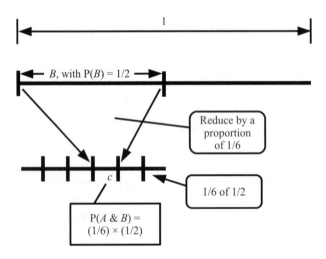

The part *c* represents the occurrence of *A* within the small space of 1/2 unit where *B* occurs. That is, the length 1/12 (part *c*) is the probability of *A* and *B* both occurring.

We can also represent the multiplicative property in another diagrammatic way. We plot the probability of *A* in one direction and the probability of *B* in another direction. Within a vertical line segment of length 1, represent the event *A* by a shorter segment whose length is P(*A*), the probability of *A*. In our case, the length is 1/6. On a horizontal line segment of length 1, represent the event *B* by a shorter segment whose length is P(*B*), the probability of *B*. In our case, P(*B*) = 1/2. The rectangle mapped out by these two segments represents the area where both *A* and *B* occur. The area is P(*A*) × P(*B*). (See fig. 26.5.)

Fig. 26.5: Events A and B in Two Dimensions

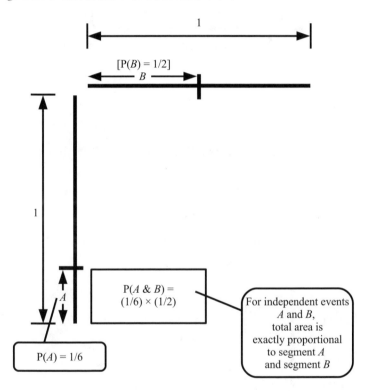

These proportionalities are all a product of God's word, which expresses the original harmony in God.

The procedure that we have used is a general one. It will work for any independent events *A* and *B*. For any such events, we can represent the proportionalities geometrically. (See fig. 26.6.)

Equivalently, the relationships can be represented in a diagram with two dimensions, one for event *A* and the other for event *B*. (See fig. 26.7.)

Fig. 26.6: Proportion with A in Space

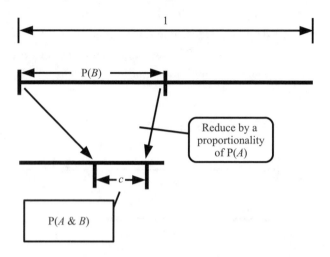

Fig. 26.7: Events A and B in Two Dimensions (the General Case)

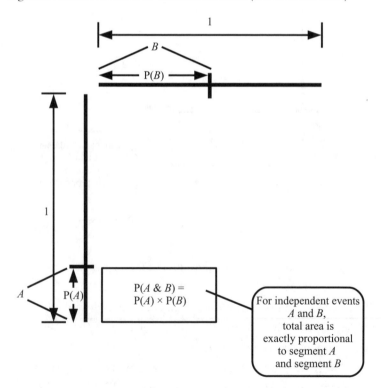

SYMMETRY AND INDEPENDENCE

We can also see a relationship between the theme of symmetry and probabilistic independence. As an example, consider again the event A where a die comes up with four on top, and an event B where a coin comes up heads. The probability of A is uninfluenced by whether B occurs or does not occur. That is, the probability of A is unchanged under a "symmetry" in which we exchange event B for not-B. In terms of conditional probabilities, this symmetry means that $P(A \mid B) = P(A \mid \text{not-}B)$.

If the probability of A is unchanged under the symmetry, we can infer that $P(A) = P(A \mid B) = P(A \mid \text{not-}B)$. By the definition of conditional probability, $P(A \ \& \ B) = P(A \mid B) \times P(B)$. Substituting $P(A)$ for $P(A \mid B)$, we find that $P(A \ \& \ B) = P(A) \times P(B)$, which is the traditional definition of probabilistic independence of A and B.

Similarly, the probability of B is unchanged under a "symmetry" in which we exchange A for not-A. The property of probabilistic independence of A and B can be derived from this symmetry as well. (The steps are the same, except for substituting A for B and B for A in all the equations.)

MULTIPLE PROPERTIES

In sum, the fundamental properties of probabilities have their roots in the harmony of God's trinitarian nature. Symmetry in probability has roots in symmetry among the persons of the Trinity. Additivity in probability for mutually exclusive events has roots in the distinctiveness of persons in the Trinity and in the harmony of proportionality, which goes back to the harmony in God. The archetypal "proportionality" lies in the Son, who is "the exact imprint of his [God's] nature" (Heb. 1:3). Multiplicativity in probability for independent events depends on proportionality, which is rooted in God. Multiplicativity can also be seen as an implication of a symmetry between B and not-B. This symmetry again has roots in the symmetry among the persons of the Trinity. The symmetry between the Father and the Son is simultaneously the archetypal proportionality between the Father and the Son.

CHAPTER 27

LIMITATIONS IN HUMAN THINKING ABOUT EVENTS AND PROBABILITIES

Because God has ordained separations and distinctions within the world, we can distinguish one event from another. For example, we know what we mean when we ask whether the event A occurs in which a die comes up with one of the numbers 1–3 on top. In many cases, we can directly observe whether the particular event A occurs. And we can distinguish the event A from an event B, in which a die comes up with an even number on top. Events of this kind have a close relation to propositions in the realm of logic. Event A is related to the proposition "One of the numbers 1–3 came up on top." If the event A occurs, the proposition is true, and if it does not occur, the proposition is false. Likewise the event B is related to the proposition "The die came up with an even number on top."

PROPOSITIONS IN LOGIC

Are propositions like these perfectly clear? And are the corresponding events perfectly defined? A careful analysis of the foundations of logic shows that the idea of an isolated proposition with a perfectly determinate meaning is an idealization.[1] The historical developments in classical logic represent certain features of the self-consistency of God, but they also simplify. The limitations in logic carry over into limitations about our knowledge of events.

---

[1] Vern S. Poythress, *Logic: A God-Centered Approach to the Foundation of Western Thought* (Wheaton, IL: Crossway, 2013), especially chapters 17–23.

The idea of an isolated event whose occurrence or nonoccurrence is perfectly defined, independent of personal perception, is also an idealization.

For example, there may be difficult cases. We roll a die, and instead of coming to rest on a flat floor, it rolls up against a wall and remains propped up on one side. No one face of the die is clearly the face that is "up." But maybe the faces with 1 and 2 dots are the ones closest to facing upward. So does the position of the die confirm that event A has indeed occurred? Or do we consider a die propped against a wall as a "nonevent," for our purposes, and re-roll it to obtain a legitimate outcome? Who decides?

What if we roll the die on an uneven surface? Suppose it comes to rest in such a way that the faces with 1 and 2 dots are closest to facing upward. In addition, the face with 2 dots is more nearly upward than the face with 1 dot. Does this result count as an instance where the outcome is 2 facing up? Or does it count as a "nonevent" since the face with 2 did not face *exactly* upward? What if the die comes up 2, but then slides off the edge of the table and lands on the floor with 1 facing upward? The boundaries between the occurrence of event A and its nonoccurrence are not perfectly defined—at least in the typical case where we are not being pedantically precise about just what constitutes a proper roll of the die.

The meaning of an event or a proposition also depends on context. We say that event A occurs if the die comes up on any of the faces with 1, 2, or 3 dots. But which die are we talking about? To deal with a specific, unique, unrepeatable event, we have to specify a specific die. We also have to specify a specific time. There has to be a specific person (or mechanical device) who will start the die rolling. And some specific person has to observe the outcome of the roll. All this specificity typically belongs to the context. We may try to use words to pin down a specific time and place. But sometimes we just use the fact that we ourselves are in a specific place at a specific time. So Sharon might say, "Please roll this die." The context takes care of the details about which die and which time and which person. If there are several people present, Sharon may hold out the die to the one to whom she is speaking, and her gesture is the part of the context that indicates who the chosen person will be.

In many ways, the idea of a decontextually, perfectly precise event is analogous to the idea of a decontextualized, perfectly precise proposition. Both are idealizations. In contrast to the idealizations, propositional statements in real language depend on analogy (in their use of meanings), the interlocking of unity and diversity, relative but not perfect stability of meaning, the interlocking of form and meaning, the use of context, the participation of persons who interpret meaning, and religious commitments. The same limitations hold for idealized events. Let us consider some of these limitations.

1. ANALOGY IN EVENTS

Events are described by analogy with other events with which we are familiar in ordinary life. Moreover, our knowledge of events is an imitation or created reflection of God's knowledge. As human beings, we are made in the image of God, so our thinking in analogous to God's. But we are not God, so the analogy is not pure identity. A mathematical model for an event inevitably simplifies. Within the model there is no direct reference to God and how he is the source for truth. Nor is there a direct reference to analogies that help to identify the event for what it is.

2. UNITY AND DIVERSITY IN EVENTS

If we identify a particular event, such as a roll of a die, we accomplish the identification of the event by treating it as a member of a class of events. In this case the class in question consists in all rolls of the same die, which in turn is a subclass of the class of all rolls of all dice. The unity of the class interlocks with the diversity of the instances of the class. The unity of one particular die roll that we identify interlocks with the diversity of the other rolls that are like it. So any one event does not exist in isolation. The interlocking of unity and diversity has its foundation in the ultimate unity and diversity in God, as we have observed earlier (chapter 11).

3. STABILITY OF MEANING

When we specify a particular roll of a die, we do not specify it in every detail. The exact boundaries for what count as a roll remain vague. We have touched on this issue in mentioning the situation where the die rolls up against a wall and remains propped up there, with no face being the one face clearly facing up. A mathematical model necessarily idealizes an event by treating the event as if it were defined precisely.

4. FORM AND MEANING OF EVENTS

When we use language to set forth a proposition or to describe an event, the language has both form and meaning, and the two interlock. The sound and grammar of a sentence interlock with its meaning. We idealize if we try to think in terms of pure meaning that would be isolated from form or that would need no form. Likewise, when we deal with an event like a die roll, form and meaning go together. We can consider the form to be the physical aspects of what goes into the process of rolling. The meaning is the interpretation of the result, such as when we observe, "The die has come up with four on top." We then fit this meaning into a larger context of human purposes. We rolled the die as part of a game, or part of an experiment in probability, or part of an illustration of the physics of a die, viewed as a rigid body. The roll has significance.

The mathematical model focuses on only one aspect of the meaning, namely, the interpreted outcome, that the die has come up with four on top. It simplifies by "stripping out" the larger context and its human significance. But it still has meaning: "the die has come up 4." Or perhaps the meaning is even more abstract: "event *A*" has happened. In addition to meaning, the model has its own *forms*, namely, in its use of written symbols and the arithmetic calculations with symbols. So we do not have meaning in pure isolation. But the model's focus on a narrow meaning can tempt people not to notice the dependence on form.

5. THE CONTEXT OF EVENTS

We identify an event such as a roll of a die through context: which die, at which time, rolled by which person, for which purpose? The mathematical model with its narrow focus strips away a large amount of this context.

6. THE INVOLVEMENT OF PERSONS IN EVENTS

People may suppose that a mathematical model is "objective." It is made so that it will function in the same way for whatever person uses it. The model thereby leaves out the persons who are inevitably involved when people experience chance events or attempt to analyze chance events. The mathematical model still involves personal intentions underneath the surface. The model is constructed by persons, and the persons who do the constructing have definite intentions, even if their intentions are partly to exclude influence of personal intention! The person who uses the model has intentions in using it, and the person understands relationships between the model and the real-world events that it might imitate. Thus the model *excludes* intentions from its inner working, but nevertheless includes intentions on the part of the persons who use it. It is not self-functioning or self-interpreting, and this limitation is part of what it means for it to be a model.

If we use a mathematical model for a single event (a roll of a die) or for a sequence of events (multiple rolls), we as persons are involved in the use of the model. We have to judge *which* model to use. For example, we can use a model that assumes that the die is unbiased, and that the probability of any one face coming up is 1/6. Or, if we know that the die is biased, we can represent the bias by assigning distinct probabilities for each face. Or, if we do not know for sure, we can designate the probabilities by symbols, p_1, p_2, p_3, p_4, p_5, p_6, without specifying beforehand what numerical values the symbols stand for.

We can also decide whether the *sample space* will consist in all possible outcomes for one roll, or for a sequence of eight rolls, or for an indefinitely long sequence. We also have to judge whether our model actually provides a good match for what is happening in the world. A simple model for describing dice rolls may be useful. But what about a simple model for representing the probability of war breaking out between two countries? Any simple model for war is likely to be *oversimple*, since so many factors might influence the rise of war.

What about probabilistic models for economics or for social interaction? Keen observers of human interaction know that human beings are exceedingly complex, and that any mathematical model can capture only a few features of human action. Yet we are tempted to pretend otherwise. The impressive success from using probability in simple cases, and the prestige of exact and indubitable results in mathematics, can tempt people to overestimate the value of using models, and to underestimate what is left out. The attitude can become, "What my model does not capture must not be important." Importance gets defined by the models themselves, and human beings no longer stand back and judge adequacy using robust human judgment. We abdicate personal responsibility and give ourselves to the direction of our models. We become virtual slaves to the models that we ourselves have constructed.

Is the danger of overreliance on models merely theoretical? We have only to look at the widespread appeal to statistics on poverty, educational success, sexual behavior, family life, spending, employment, and so on. Statistics often serve as a main reason for advocating various social and political programs, or inviting people to join in some trend. We are in danger of substituting statistics for genuine moral judgment. And the appeal is all the more powerful because it seems "objective." Direct appeal to moral judgments often leads to disputes, while statistics are (allegedly) indisputable. The biggest difficulty is that statistics in themselves do not announce any moral standard. Moral assumptions are concealed rather than debated. And much depends on which statistics one cites, and what interpretation one gives to their significance within the larger context of social life.[2]

7. RELIGIOUS COMMITMENTS IN RELATION TO EVENTS

People have religious commitments, either to serve God or to rebel against him. These commitments are there under the surface, whether or not people are conscious of them. Commitments influence the motives in using or not using mathematical models. Commitments also influence the way people interpret the significance of probability and models for probability. We have already touched on such commitments in previous chapters, especially chapters 11–12, where we indicated how events reveal the character of God. A mathematical model does not include within its inner structure a direct representation of the religious commitments of the persons. It includes only a stripped-down analog to probabilities for physical events. Religious commitments belong to the context that includes the persons—not only the persons who participate in events, but the persons who analyze the events using mathematical models or other forms of analysis.

Mathematical models of physical events have a powerful appeal, because of their effectiveness and because of the impressive harmony between the mathematics and the physical events. Both the effectiveness and the harmony depend on God. We should be motivated to praise God in the midst of multiple displays of his goodness and wisdom. Do we? Or

---

[2] On the limitations of scientific sociology, see Vern S. Poythress, *Redeeming Sociology: A God-Centered Approach* (Wheaton, IL: Crossway, 2011), appendices B and C.

do we treat chance events and probability as if mathematical models were religiously neutral?

IMPLICATIONS OF LIMITATIONS

When we build models of the world involving probability, it is always *we* who build the models. We always use simplifying assumptions. And we simplify in a number of ways when we use propositions about events to represent the world. It is wise to recognize such simplifications, and to understand that we should reckon with larger contexts. We start in a rich situation in which God calls us to know him and to grow in his wisdom. That responsibility lies in the background when we make ourselves probabilistic models and use propositional descriptions of events. We evade rather than escape responsibility if we ignore God.

CHAPTER 28

CONCLUSION

Regularities and unpredictable events go together.

Every day in our lives, we live in the midst of regularities on which we depend. The sun rises. Our hearts beat. We breathe air. The cells in our body maintain defenses against infection. Our stomachs and intestines digest food. Our phones function. We are relying on God, who governs the world by his faithfulness, in accordance with his wisdom. His goodness is revealed in what he has made:

> for he [God] did good by giving you rains from heaven and fruitful seasons, satisfying your hearts with food and gladness. (Acts 14:17)

Every day of our lives we live in the midst of unpredictable events. Every day is new. Every day is uncertain. Every day we ourselves do something a little different, and we sometimes surprise ourselves by what we do. We ourselves, as individuals, are somewhat unpredictable. And prosperity or disaster around us is also unpredictable.

God is creative. His mercies are "new every morning" (Lam. 3:23). If we have received reconciliation and forgiveness from God, through the work of Christ the Lord, we may rejoice in God's works and praise him day by day.

Not least among these praises, we may praise God for the unpredictable events. If we have come to know God as our heavenly Father, we can rest secure about what is unpredictable, because it is not a surprise to him. He plans it. He rules it. He brings it about. "And we know that for those who love God *all things* work together for good, for those who are called according to his purpose" (Rom. 8:28).

A look into the subject of chance and probability should increase our praise. In the subject of probability, God brings together regularity and unpredictability in a marvelous way. He brings together his faithfulness and his creativity.

It is important for us to see God's hand in chance and probability, because it deepens our respect for him and our worship. It is also important because chance and probability play a key role in our lives through their influence on science. Virtually all of modern science rests on ideas about chance and probability. And these ideas inescapably reveal God.

Materialistic philosophy in our day tries to use scientific progress as a lever to claim that we are self-sufficient, or that the material world is self-sufficient. But it is suppressing the truth. We are relying on God. The scientists themselves are relying on him, though they may make for themselves substitute accounts. They may postulate impersonal law and impersonal chance (Chance!) in order to avoid this God on whom they nevertheless rely.

Let us not make the same mistake. Let us not listen to materialist propaganda. Let us listen rather to the God who made us and who owns us, who speaks to us in the Bible. He tells us about ourselves, our world, and those events that we cannot predict. Let us love him and serve him, the One who is faithful and creative.

REDEMPTION AS SURPRISING

We have to admit that we have not served God as we ought to. We have rebelled. We have proved ungrateful. We have complained. But God has not left us in our misery and guilt. He has displayed his faithfulness and his creativity by sending a remedy. God himself has become man in Jesus Christ.

Consider an example. Mark 2:1–12 records that Jesus healed a paralytic. He also forgave the sins of the paralytic, thereby indicating that the physical healing symbolized its deeper counterpart, spiritual healing. This healing of the paralytic was a one-time, surprising event. From a human point of view, it was unpredictable. It was surprising because the healing itself was miraculous, and the crowd reacted accordingly: "they were all amazed and glorified God, saying, 'We never saw anything like this!'" It was also surprising because Jesus did not accomplish the healing in the obvious way. When the paralytic was lowered down into his presence, Jesus surprised everyone because he did not heal the man right away. He said first, "Your sins are forgiven" (v. 5). He indicated that there was a paralysis deeper than physical, the paralysis of sin. And he came to address it, to heal it. Only God has authority to forgive sins (v. 7). Jesus was God in the flesh, and this fact was even more surprising than his pronouncement of forgiveness.

God's forgiveness has to be compatible with his justice and holiness. Sin is not to be brushed off or overlooked. It is offensive. God's wrath is against sin. Jesus offered forgiveness to the paralytic because he was the Messiah, sent by God to accomplish atonement through his death on the cross. The surprising healing of the paralytic pointed forward to the surprising work of Jesus in his crucifixion. The cross, as God's central display of love for us who are rebels (Rom. 5:6–8), is the maximal surprise in all of history. Through it comes our forgiveness, our healing. We get mercy that we did not deserve. Christ took on himself punishment that he did not deserve. The result demonstrates God's justice (Rom. 3:25–26).

After Jesus had died and was buried, he rose from the dead. That too was surprising to his disciples. They did not expect it (Luke 24:11, 21, 25; John 20:25). But this surprising event provides the foundation for a regularity, a general principle of salvation:

> If you confess with your mouth that Jesus is Lord and believe in your heart that God raised him from the dead, you will be saved. (Rom. 10:9)

God is continually faithful to his promise to save those who trust in Christ. His faithfulness forms the foundation for our trust and assurance. His faithfulness harmonizes with his creativity, displayed in the surprise of redemption. He healed the paralytic, once. He will heal you and me, each one of us, when we come to Christ in faith. He brings his creativity to bear on each of us who come. He will heal you surprisingly, in a way that addresses you in your uniqueness and the unique shape of your sins and struggles, because he has promised to do so in his faithfulness.

Faithfulness and creativity, regularity and surprise, cohere in Christ's work. From the center point of Christ, we can grow in understanding that faithfulness and creativity cohere in God's particular care for each one of us, and they cohere in his governance of the whole world. They cohere in chance events and in the calculations of probability. Praise the Lord!

APPENDICES

WHY GAMBLING SYSTEMS FAIL

Do gambling systems exist that allow a gambler consistently to win at casino gambling? Some gamblers think that they have found a system that can win. We will consider some systems.

CARD-COUNTING AT BLACKJACK

One gambling system, a system of card-counting for winning at blackjack, has effectiveness. It utilizes the fact that an observant player can keep track of which cards have already been played from the deck of cards that is used by the dealer in the game. Keeping track enables the card counter to infer which cards are still left, and to figure out whether the cards still left in the deck at a particular time favor a win for the dealer or a win for a player. The player then bets larger amounts only when his card counting shows that the remaining cards favor a player's winning.

This kind of system can actually work, but it is complex. It depends on the fact that the process of dealing some cards from a deck directly affects which cards are left. Therefore, the cards that appear from the early part of a deck affect the probability of winning during the use of the later part of the deck.

Even when card counting shows that a player has an advantage, the amount of advantage is very small. It takes many bets over a long period of time to profit significantly from the advantage.

In addition, in our day casinos are well aware of the possibilities for using such a system. Some casinos have changed the rules for betting or for payoff in blackjack, or they use more decks and switch decks in and out, so that it becomes difficult or impossible to use card counting systems. Casinos can also train their blackjack dealers or other staff members to watch out for the distinctive pattern of betting that characterizes a card-counting system. If they see this pattern, they "ban" the player from the blackjack tables. Information can also be passed on to other casinos in the area, so a player trying to win in Las Vegas or in Monte Carlo will find himself banned from all the casinos in the area before he wins very much.

WHAT ABOUT OTHER FORMS OF BETTING?

No successful system of gambling can exist when later events are unaffected by earlier events. In the language of probability, the later events are *probabilistically independent* of the earlier events (chapter 21). In such a case, no human being can achieve an advantage based on information from the earlier outcomes. Such independence is normally the case with dice, slot machines, roulette wheels, and lotteries. Most "systems" invented by naive gamblers fail because they try—always unsuccessfully—to circumvent this independence of events.

BETTING "EVEN MONEY"

Let us consider an example. A European roulette wheel is a round wheel with 37 evenly placed depressions or pockets, labeled with 37 numbers, the numbers 0 to 36. A small ball is let loose into the spinning wheel, and the ball eventually settles in one of the pockets. A gambler can place various kinds of bets. He can bet on a single number such as the number 16. He loses his bet unless the number 16 comes up. Since the outcome of 16 is unlikely, the payoff is correspondingly greater—typically, he will be paid 35 times his original bet if the number 16 comes up.

A gambler can also bet "odd" or "even." For a bet of "odd," he wins if an odd number comes up, and loses if an even number comes up. Since an outcome of an odd number happens about half of the time, the payoff for winning is only one-to-one. For a $1 bet, the payment for winning is only $1. (That is, when he wins, the player keeps the original bet of $1 and receives in addition another $1 as the payoff.) Let us calculate the probability of winning. There are 18 odd numbers on the wheel: 1, 3, 5, 7, 9, 11,

13, 15, 17, 19, 21, 23, 25, 27, 29, 31, 33, and 35. There are 18 positive even numbers: 2, 4, 6, 8, 10, 12, 14, 16, 18, 20, 22, 24, 26, 28, 30, 32, 34, and 36. There is also a zero (0). The presence of the zero is what gives the casino its small advantage. Since there are 37 total possibilities, each of which is equally likely, the probability of an odd number is 18/37, and the probability of losing is 19/37. If a gambler bets 37 times, on the average he will win 18 times and lose 19 times. He will gain $18 from the 18 wins, and lose $19 from the 19 times when he loses. He has a net loss of $1, spread over the 37 outcomes. The average loss per bet is 1/37 of a dollar, a little less than 3 cents. It is not much, per bet, but it mounts up over time. It is enough to keep the casino making a profit.

Suppose the gambler bets on even. He loses if an odd number comes up, which happens in 18 cases. He wins if a positive even number comes up, for 18 cases. He also loses if zero comes up. Once again, the presence of a loss in the case of zero gives the casino a slight advantage in the long run. If a gambler bets 37 times on even, on the average he will win 18 times and lose 19 times, for a net loss of $1, spread over the 37 bets. The average loss per bet is 1/37 of a dollar.

If the number zero were eliminated from the roulette wheel, the gambler would win on the average 18 out of 36 times, or 1/2 of the time. He would also lose 1/2 of the time. There would be neither a net gain nor a net loss over time. On the average, he would break even. But of course if the gambler bets on even every time, and the wheel turns up several evens in a row, the gambler temporarily experiences a winning "streak." He is several dollars ahead. But that result is *temporary*. In the long run, as we have said, the results neither favor the gambler nor count against him. He may have a winning streak. But he is just as likely to hit a losing streak of several losses in row, in which case he is temporarily in a situation of net loss.

Suppose now that the gambler puts in place a "system" to try to exploit the long-range evenness of the results. The gambler decides on a policy or a system in which he does not bet at all, except immediately after a string of at least six successive occurrences of odd numbers on the roulette wheel. Whenever odd has occurred six times in a row, the gambler bets on even for the next spin of the wheel. He reasons that, since the number of occurrences of odd has to become similar to the number of occurrences of even in the long run, an outcome of even becomes more probable after a string of occurrences of odd.

But the reasoning is incorrect. It is so common a mistake in reasoning that it has received its own name, the *gambler's fallacy* or the *Monte Carlo fallacy*. Why is the reasoning mistaken? The occurrence of odd or even on the next spin is probabilistically independent not only of the previous spin, but of the entire record of all previous spins. Even if an odd number has come up on six successive previous spins, the probability of odd on the next spin is still 1/2. So the gambler's strategy will not win him anything, on the average.

The designation *Monte Carlo fallacy* derives from a famous event on August 18, 1913, at the casino in Monte Carlo. Darrell Huff describes it:

> . . . black came up a record twenty-six times in succession [on a rou-
> lette wheel]. . . . What actually happened was a near-panicky rush to
> bet on red, beginning about the time black had come up a phenomenal
> fifteen times. In application of the maturity doctrine [the fallacious as-
> sumption that the time for red had "matured" because of the previous
> blacks], players doubled and tripled their stakes, this doctrine leading
> them to believe after black came up the twentieth time that there was
> not a chance in a million of another repeat. In the end the unusual run
> enriched the Casino by some millions of francs.[1]

On a roulette wheel, 18 of the numbers are red and 18 are black. Black will come up about half of the time, just as an even number will come up about half of the time. But the wheel does not remember previous occurrences of black, no matter how long a run of occurrences it may have been. The chance of black coming up the next time is still about 1/2.

THE CASINO'S ADVANTAGE

On an actual roulette wheel, we have to include in our reckoning the possi-
bility of zero as an outcome. Zero is neither red nor black. When we include zero, there are 18 possible outcomes in which the gambler wins by betting on black, and 19 outcomes in which he loses. On the average, he will win about 18 times and lose about 19 times in every 37 tries, for an average of one more loss than the number of wins. He loses (on the average) $1 for

---

[1] Darrell Huff, *How to Take a Chance*, illustrated by Irving Geis (New York: W. W. Norton, 1959), 28–29.

every 37 tries. Once again, it works out to an average loss of 1/37 of a dollar per try.

This average loss holds for gamblers who follow a "system" by watching for a long run of occurrences of odd numbers, or a long run of occurrences of black. They do not fare any better than anyone else who simply bets on odd or even at random.

American casinos often have roulette wheels with a double zero (00) as well as a zero (0). A bet on odd or on even loses if either zero or double zero comes up. With this arrangement, the percentages are slanted further in the direction of the casino's advantage. The result for a single spin of the roulette wheel can be any of 38 different outcomes: any of the numbers 1–36, or 0, or 00. The chance of winning on a single bet is now 18/38, instead of 18/37. Out of a total of 38 possible outcomes, 18 are favorable or winning outcomes, while 20 are losing outcomes. If a gambler bets 38 times, he will on the average lose about two times more than he wins. That is, he will lose $2 on the average. That works out to 2/38 of a dollar per bet (again, on the average). If we convert 2/38 to decimal form, it is 0.052631579. We can round off this decimal to 0.053. He loses $0.053 or a little more than five cents per bet. By contrast, a European roulette wheel results in a loss of 1/37 = 0.027027027 of a dollar, which rounds out to 2.7 cents per bet. The difference between the two may not look like much, but over time it adds up. And in terms of percentages, 5.3 cents is almost twice 2.7 cents per bet. A gambler will go through his money nearly twice as fast at an American casino that uses a double zero.

DOUBLE OR NOTHING

Now consider another system that gamblers have tried. The gambler comes to the gambling table with an initial "stake," a quantity of money that he is willing to risk in the game. He begins by betting $1 on odd. If he wins the bet, he has gained $1. If he loses, he doubles his money on the next bet: he bets $2 on odd. If he wins this second bet, after losing the first $1 on the first bet, he is $1 better off than when he started. So far so good.

Suppose, however, that after losing the first bet of $1 he also loses his second bet of $2. He doubles the money again on the third bet, and bets $4 on odd. He has now lost a first bet of $1 and a second of $2, for a total of $3. If he wins with his bet of $4, he is $1 ahead of his original position.

Suppose, however, that he loses his third bet, which was a bet for $4. He has now lost a total amount of $1 + $2 + $4 = $7. He doubles his money for the fourth bet, making the fourth bet $8. If he wins, he is now $1 richer than when he started. By making the bet a full $8, he is able to recover all the money that he already lost in the previous three bets, and in addition win an extra $1.

Suppose he loses the fourth bet of $8. He has now lost a total amount of $1 + $2 + $4 + $8 = $15. He doubles again, to $16. If he wins, he recovers everything he lost, plus one more dollar. He is once again $1 ahead.

It might appear that through this strategy the gambler can always come out $1 ahead of his initial position. After he is $1 ahead, he can repeat the process and end up $2 ahead. And then $3 ahead. So he can gain however much money he desires by simply persevering long enough in the process. It might appear that he has a surefire recipe for success.

Are there flaws in this reasoning? There are. First, we confront a practical difficulty because casinos usually have "betting limits." For instance, they may allow gamblers to wager up to $2,000 on a single outcome of a roulette wheel—but not more. Or maybe they set the limit higher, at $10,000 or $50,000. But there is a limit. So the casino will not permit a gambler to continue in his strategy if he loses too many times in a row and ends up doubling his bet again and again.

We also confront a difficulty on the side of the gambler. The gambler must start with an initial stake, a quantity of money that he is willing to risk. If, theoretically, he had an infinite amount of money, and an infinite amount of time in which to make bets, and the casino had no betting limits—all of which, by the way, are unrealistic assumptions—he could always win $1 more. But $1 added to infinity is still infinity. It makes no real difference. If he really did start with an infinite amount of money, he would also have no motivation to engage in gambling, because he would have at the start all the money he would ever need.

Suppose, on the contrary, that the gambler has a realistic stake. Suppose he starts with $1,024. We have picked this number rather than an even $1,000 because 1,024 is 2 multiplied by itself 10 times, $2 \times 2 \times 2 \times 2 \times 2 \times 2 \times 2 \times 2 \times 2 \times 2$. A calculation will show that a stake of this size allows a gambler to bet up to ten successive times, losing each time, and doubling the next time, until the tenth time. If he loses nine times in a row, he has lost

1 + 2 + 4 + 8 + 16 + 32 + 64 + 128 + 256 = 511. He bets 512 for the next bet, and if he wins, he recovers all his previous losses (511) and gains one dollar. On the other hand, if he loses this final tenth bet, he has lost a total of 511 + 512 = 1,023, and has only $1 left out of his initial stake of $1,024. He can no longer continue the strategy of doubling.

The person who likes this strategy can still argue in its favor. He can say, for example, that surely the chance of losing ten times in a row, with no win at all, is very small. Hence, the gambler is virtually certain to win $1 in the process. At some point, short of the situation in which he has to double repeatedly for a total of ten tries, he will win once. Then he ends up $1 ahead. So he is virtually certain to win $1, and he can go ahead with confidence.

Yes, it is almost certain that he will win $1. But if he does not win, he loses, not $1, but a total of $1,023 as a result of the successive losses from ten successive bets. Is it really worth his while risking the full amount of $1,023 for a measly $1? The chance of his winning $1 is as high as it is only because he is willing to risk a correspondingly big amount of money.

Let us estimate how much the gambler will gain or lose on the average. Suppose he is betting on the result of a roulette wheel where the number zero has been removed or is ignored, so that his chances of winning on any one spin of the wheel are exactly 1/2. On the first bet, he bets $1 on odd. His chances of winning are 1/2. His chances of losing are also 1/2. If he loses, he proceeds to bet $2 for a second spin. This case must then be split into two, depending on whether he wins or loses the second bet. The chances of his winning on this second try are 1/2.

Now consider the sequence again from the beginning. What is the chance that the succession of events will take place in which (1) he loses the first time and (2) in addition wins the second time? Since the two phases are independent of one another, the chance that both will happen in succession is the product of the chance of a loss the first time and a win the second time, that is, the product of 1/2 × 1/2, or 1/4. The chance of winning on the first bet, as we observed, is 1/2. The chance of losing the first bet and then winning the second is 1/4. The total chance of winning on *either* the first bet, or on the second when it follows a loss on the first, is 1/2 + 1/4 = 3/4. The chance of losing on the second bet is also 1/2. The chance of losing on the second bet *after also* losing on the first bet is the product of 1/2 and 1/2, or 1/4. We can lay out all the possibilities in a table (see table A.1).

Table A.1: Chances for Two Successive Bets

First bet alone	Sequence of events	Probability of the first event	Probability of the second event	Probability for both events happening in succession
win on first bet:	win, then win	1/2	1/2	1/4
	win, then lose	1/2	1/2	1/4
lose on first bet	lose, then win	1/2	1/2	1/4
	lose, then lose	1/2	1/2	1/4

If this second bet is lost, the gambler undertakes a third bet for $4. Since the probability of losing twice in a row is 1/4, the probability that he will have to make this third bet is 1/4. Given that he places the bet (conditional probability), his probability of winning is 1/2. When we consider the entire sequence of bets, there is a probability of $1/4 \times 1/2 = 1/8$ that he will lose twice and then win on the third bet. There is also a probability of $1/4 \times 1/2 = 1/8$ that he will lose twice and then lose a third time when he makes his third bet. The total chances of winning using up to three bets is now 1/2 (if he wins immediately on the first bet) + 1/4 (if he wins on the second bet after losing on the first) + 1/8 (if he wins only on the third bet). The total is $1/2 + 1/4 + 1/8 = 7/8$, while the chance of losing all three bets is a mere 1/8.

By this time, it is easy to see a pattern. The probability of losing all three initial bets, as we have observed, is 1/8. For this 1/8 case, the gambler places a fourth bet, which he wins 1/2 of the time. Including this case in the total, he now wins in cases $1/2 + 1/4 + 1/8 + 1/16 = 15/16$. He loses in the one other case, for a probability of losing that is $1/8 \times 1/2 = 1/16$.

When we include reckoning with the possibility of a fifth bet, his total probability of winning is 31/32, and his probability of losing all five bets in a row is only 1/32. When we include the possibility of a sixth bet, his probability of winning is 63/64, and his probability of losing is 1/64. With a possible seventh bet, his probability of winning is 127/128, and his probability of losing 1/128. Clearly the probability of losing is getting quite minuscule. With an eighth bet, his probability of winning is 255/256, and his probability of losing 1/256. With a ninth bet, his probability of winning is 511/512, and his probability of losing 1/512. Finally, when we include the possibility of a tenth bet as well, his total probability of winning is 1,023/1,024, and his probability of losing is a mere 1/1,024.

This result may now look very "safe." His chances of winning are indeed very good. Out of a total of 1,024 possible cases, he will win on the average 1,023 of them. In each of these cases he will win a net amount of $1. So, if we imagine him repeating this strategy again and again, he will win on the average about $1,023 dollars. But what about the remaining one case? In the remaining case, the case that is 1 out of 1,024, he will lose all ten bets in succession. Because he is doubling his bet each time, he will have lost a total of $1 + 2 + 4 + 8 + 16 + 32 + 64 + 128 + 256 + 512 = 1,023$. When we consider all 1,024 possibilities, his net gain from 1,023 of them is 1,023, and his net loss from the remaining case is also 1,023. He has no net gain. On the average, the scheme does not give him any advantage.

The scheme superficially *looks as though* it gives him an advantage because it does give him an advantage *in the great majority of cases*. But the gain he gets from these cases is always small ($1). The catastrophic case, the one case in 1,024, wipes out all the advantage of all the other cases, because in this one case he suffers a loss that is as big as all the gains from all the other cases put together.

If we are rooting for the gambler to find some way of winning consistently, we may feel disappointed. But we can look at the situation another way. It is wonderful how God rules the world. It is wonderful that he so governs the spinning of roulette wheels that whichever strategy the gambler chooses, the result comes out the same: no advantage. The calculations about the probabilities of losing a seventh or an eighth or a tenth time in row all work out. There is marvelous harmony about it. God planned it. God governs it all, at every casino in the world. God expects us to depend on him and not on man-made systems.

USING A LARGER STAKE

"Well," says the hopeful gambler, "all I need is a larger initial stake." Let him have an initial stake of about one million dollars, or more precisely $1,024 \times 1,024 = 1,048,576$ dollars (2 multiplied by itself 20 times). This larger stake will allow him to double his bet not merely ten times in a row (that is, nine doublings after the first bet of $1), but twenty times in a row. Surely then he will be able to gain $1 by betting $1 and then doubling if necessary.

Will his new strategy work? No. The same reasoning applies to a large stake, just as we applied it to the stake of $1,024. With the larger stake of

$1,048,576, we can see that, in over a million cases, the gambler will indeed gain $1 using his scheme. To be precise, he will gain $1 in 1,048,575 cases. But in the one additional case, he will lose his bet 20 times in a row, and will lose a total of $1,048,575. He has no net advantage. On a practical level, he is better off keeping his million, because gaining $1 means very little in comparison to the slim prospect of losing the entire million.

Will a stake of 1,024 × 1,024 × 1,024 = $1,073,741,824 help? The gambler now has over a billion dollars. In 1,073,741,823 cases, he will be able to win an additional dollar. Not much. In the additional one unusual case, he will lose thirty times in a row and lose a total of $1,073,741,823 dollars. There is no net gain.

"Well," proposes the still-hopeful gambler, "all I have to do is to exercise restraint. I will use my strategy only a few times, so as not to let the unusual case of catastrophic loss catch up with me." The trouble with this idea is that no human being knows exactly *when* the unusual catastrophic loss will occur. With a stake of a billion dollars, the gambler might indeed succeed with his stratagem for half a billion tries. He might even succeed for more than a billion. Or he might lose on the first try. The chance of losing on the first try is 1 in 1,073,741,824. But it wipes out the alleged advantages in all the other 1,073,741,823 outcomes. If he wins on the first try, he still has the same chance of losing catastrophically on the second try. However many tries he makes, he has no net advantage.

CASINO ODDS

When a gambler plays at a real roulette wheel in a casino, he has the odds slightly against him because of the presence of the additional pocket for zero. (For the moment we will ignore the American case with a double zero, but clearly this situation would further lower his chances.) His chance of winning on any one bet that he places on odd or even is not exactly $1/2 = 0.5$, but only $18/37 = 0.486486486 \ldots$. His chances of losing such a bet are $19/37 = 0.513513513 \ldots$. His chance of losing twice in a row is the product of the chance of losing the first time $(19/37)$ and the chance of losing the second time $(19/37$ again). So the chance of losing both times is $(19/37) \times (19/37)$, or 0.26369613. We have reported this result with many decimal places, but we are really only interested in the general trends, so we can round off these numbers. We can say that the chance of losing both times is roughly 0.264. (In order to avoid rounding errors, which can become bigger when we perform several successive calculations, the best practice is to do the initial calculations using many decimal places of accuracy, but then report the results in a rounded form. That is what we will do.)

In this case, the gambler's chance of losing twice is 0.264, or slightly more than 0.250, or 1/4, which is his chance of losing if there is no zero pocket. His chance of losing three times in a row is $(19/37) \times (19/37) \times (19/37) = 0.135$. By the same kind of reasoning, his chance of losing a full ten times in a row is 19/37 multiplied by itself for 10 occurrences, or $(19/37)^{10} = 0.001275$. In this case, he loses a total of $1,023. In all the other cases, he gains $1. The other cases have a total probability of $1 - 0.001275 = 0.9987$. His result is a loss of $1,023 in 0.001275 of the time, for a total average loss of $1,023 \times 0.001275$. His result is a gain of $1 in 0.9987 of the time, for an average gain of 1×0.9987. Subtracting the amount of loss from the amount of gain, we obtain a net negative number, –0.3056. The fact that the number is negative indicates that the net effect is a loss of 0.3056 rather than a positive gain. That is, on the average he will lose about $.3056, or 31 cents, for every time he follows the proposed strategy of doubling again and again until he wins. True, in 99.87% of the cases he will succeed in winning $1. But the one case where he loses ten times in a row is so devastating that it results in a net balance that is negative.

A similar calculation shows that the gambler achieves no advantage by further increasing his initial stake. In fact, the situation becomes worse. Suppose the gambler starts with an initial stake of $1,048,576. He has positioned himself so that he can double his bet up to 20 times. With this situation, his chance of losing his bet a full 20 times in a row is $(19/37)^{20}$, that is, 19/37 multiplied by itself for a full 20 occurrences. It comes out to 0.0000016257. That is, there is only about 1.6 chance in a million that he will lose catastrophically. But it is enough to wipe out his expected gains from all the other outcomes. He will win $1 in all the other cases, and these cases together have a probability of $1 - 0.0000016 = 0.9999984$. The average net result of employing his strategy is $1 \times 0.9999984 = \$0.9999984$ average gain for the cases where he is successful and $1,048,575 \times 0.0000016 = \$1.705$ average loss in the catastrophic case. The net result per try is $0.9999984 - 1.705 = -0.705$. On the average, he loses a little over 70 cents every time he uses his stratagem.

If his stake is over a billion dollars, $1,073,741,824, the chance of losing 30 times in a row is $(19/37)^{30} = 0.00000000207$. It is very small. But in this one case he loses a big amount, $1,073,741,823. The net loss per try is $1,073,741,823 \times 0.00000000207 - (1 - 0.00000000207) = 1.226$, or more than $1.20 per try.

COMPARING THE OPTIONS

The losses are of course worse with an American roulette wheel with a double zero, because the probability of winning on any one bet is slightly less, and this slight difference adds up, the more times one bets and the larger the bets are. Table A.2 shows the approximate average loss for each time that the gambler carries through to completion his planned strategy of doubling until he wins.

Table A.2: Average Losses through Doubling Bets

Initial stake:	European roulette (with zero):	American roulette (with zero and double zero):
$1,024	$.31 loss per try	$.67 loss per try
$1,048,576	$.70 loss	$1.79 loss
$1,073,741,824	$1.23 loss	$3.66 loss

In the worse cases, the gambler is actually losing on the average *more* than his initial bet of $1 for every time he uses his strategy. How can this be the case?

Suppose that the gambler has an initial stake of $1,048,576 and is playing on an American roulette wheel with a double zero. The table indicates that he suffers an average loss of $1.79 per try. Let us watch how it works out in practice. The gambler uses his strategy only three times. The first time, he wins his initial bet of $1. He is now $1 ahead. The second time, he loses the first bet and the second, but wins on the third time. He has a net gain of $1. He is now $2 ahead. The third time, he wins his initial bet of $1 and is now $3 ahead. Everything appears to be going according to plan. He is steadily adding to his earnings. All is well—apparently. As long as he does not hit the catastrophic case, he gains $1 for every time he carries through his plan. But he is heading for disaster *in the long run*.

The situation is similar to what we have already seen. The probability of catastrophic disaster has to be included in the calculation of averages. And when we do the calculation, the disaster is likely enough that it not only wipes out all the average gains from normal, noncatastrophic tries, but results in so much loss that it overwhelms these gains and results in a *net* average loss of a full $1.79. This is the average loss *per try*.

The gambler cannot improve the situation by stopping after only three tries and sending someone else in as a substitute. The probabilities are the same for the substitute. The dreaded catastrophe can strike anytime, not just later on (after several thousand tries). No one knows when.

The casinos will stay in business, and will smile at the gambler's naivete. They will, of course, also protect themselves by putting in place a betting limit, to avoid even the slim possibility that they themselves might suffer catastrophic loss through an unusual run of payoffs.

PRACTICAL LIMITS

It is worthwhile for us to reflect briefly on the practical limits related to gambling systems. Suppose that a prospective gambler has devised a gambling system which seems to him virtually to guarantee a win. Suppose also that he has managed to persuade a billionaire to finance him with a million dollars and give his system a chance. This supposition is already unlikely, because billionaires are not usually gullible people. They will not easily believe a gambler's claim to have found a foolproof scheme. If a billionaire *is* gullible, he will soon lose a large amount of his billion to swindlers and con men. Moreover, people do not usually become billionaires through "get rich quick" schemes, so they are not attracted to gamblers' proposals.

But let us ignore this first unlikelihood, and think what will happen. The gambler may have a scheme in which he proposes to wait for a rare event such as the occurrence of 20 successive instances of odd coming up on a roulette wheel. On the next spin, he will then bet a large amount, maybe the whole one million dollars. Should a casino allow it? Let us suppose that the casino is using a European roulette wheel with a zero but no double zero. Unlike the gambler, the casino knows that the probability of a win on the next spin of the roulette wheel is unaffected by the previous run of 20 instances of odd coming up. The casino knows that its probability of winning a million dollars is 19/37, and its probability of losing is 18/37. On the average, it will gain 1/37 of a million dollars, or about \$27,000, if it allows the bet. Should it go ahead?

The key issue is whether the casino can afford to wait for what we have called "the long run." Can it afford to deal with the real possibility that in the short run it will have an unfavorable run, maybe for five, six, or more losses of a million dollars? The casino may be rich, but maybe not that rich. It runs the risk of going into bankruptcy, in which it will not make any more money forever. So the casino must not become too greedy by wanting to get rich quick with large bets. It too must avoid a "get rich quick" scheme. To avoid the risk, it sets a betting limit, perhaps of \$10,000. To gain one million dollars, the gambler then has to have a long run of favorable outcomes. There must be 100 more cases when he wins than when he loses.

Let us say that the gambler engages in 150 bets of \$10,000, in the hopes that at least 125 of them will be favorable. The other 25 may be unfavorable, but he will still come out ahead in $125 - 25 = 100$ more cases than the cases when he loses. So he will come out a total of $100 \times \$10,000 = \$1,000,000$ ahead. Using the mathematical theory of probability, we can calculate that the probability of exactly 125 wins is $(18/37)^{125} \times (19/37)^{25} \times {}_{150}C_{125}$, where ${}_{150}C_{125}$ is the number of possible combinations of 150 things taken 125 at a time (see appendix E). ${}_{150}C_{125}$ is $150!/(125!25!)$.[2] The result comes out to about 8.7×10^{-19}. There is less than one chance in 10^{18}, or a billion billion, that he will succeed. The chance that he will get 126 wins is even less (1.6×10^{-19}). Suppose he allows himself 1,000 bets, of which 550 will be favorable; his chances are 8×10^{-6}, or 8 in a million. This is better. But of course the more bets he makes, the more opportunity there is for the casino's advantage (due to the zero on the roulette wheel) to make a notable difference. With 10,000 bets, of which 5,050 are favorable, his chances of success are still 8 in a million. With 100,000 bets, his chances are 2×10^{-20}, or 2 out of 100 billion billion. The casino need not worry.

Suppose the gambler adopts the strategy of doubling his bet when he loses. This strategy causes even fewer worries for the casino. If the gambler initially bets \$1, he will at best gain \$1. He bets large amounts, like \$1,024, only when he has already lost previous bets in the amounts \$1, \$2, \$4, \$8, \$16, etc., that is, when he has already lost \$1,023. The casino has the money

---

[2] The use of the exclamation mark (!) is a special mathematical notation, explained in appendix E.

from these previous losses, so it can afford to pay the full payoff of $1,024 in case the gambler wins his bet of $1,024.

There is still a problem for the casino—that the gambler may go on winning a small amount of $1 for a long time before he encounters catastrophic loss. All this time, the casino is gradually losing money. Can the casino afford to wait until the catastrophe hits?

Partly, it depends on whether the casino is making money from *other* gamblers. If it is, it may be able to wait a long time for a loss from this one gambler. So what about the other gamblers? The same reasoning applies to them as to the first one. The greater the number of gamblers, the more their individual gains and losses will average out. The casino takes many bets from many different gamblers, and gradually the instances when zero comes up will give the casino a steady stream of income.

But suppose, for the sake of the argument, that the casino deals only with the single gambler who has the strategy of doubling his bet. How long will it be before the gambler hits a catastrophe? That depends on how likely the catastrophe is. And the likelihood depends on how many times the gambler is allowed to double his bet. So a betting limit is still useful to protect the casino from mounting up a big total loss.

Suppose the betting limit is $10,000. Suppose also that the gambler follows a strategy where his initial bet is always $1. If he loses multiple times in a row, he keeps doubling until he wins. With a stake of $1,024, he can afford to double up to nine times (for a total of ten bets, counting the initial bet of $1). The last of his doubled bets will be $512. If he is allowed to bet up to $10,000, he can double four more times, with bets of $1,024, $2,048, $4,096, and $8,192. The casino ends up with a big win, amounting to $16,383, if it wins all these successive bets. Otherwise, it loses $1. How long must the casino wait for a win? If it has to wait too long, it runs a significant danger. With even odds, the probability of losing 14 times in a row is one out of 2^{14}, or one out of 16,384. If we reckon with the zero on the roulette wheel, the probability of losing 14 times in a row is $(19/37)^{14}$, or 8.9×10^{-5}. It is 9 times out of 100,000.

If the roulette wheel gets spun again every 30 seconds, it is spun 120 times an hour. About half of the time, the spin will take place after the gambler has lost the previous bet, so only half of these spins will correspond to new attempts when the gambler starts with his initial bet of $1. That means that the gambler can use his strategy about 60 times an hour. If he is there for a 12-hour day, it means 720 tries per day. In one week, he will do 7×720 or about 5,000 tries, and in one month, 20,000 tries. By that time, he will probably have lost catastrophically about two times. If the casino is willing to wait for a month, it can be reasonably confident that it will come out ahead. If, on the other hand, it wants more reliable short-term gains, it can always decrease the betting limit. With a betting limit of $1,024, the casino may see a favorable payoff after about 2,000 tries,[3] or three days. But of course the casino's gain will not be as big, because the bets will be smaller. The casino sets its betting limits in such a way that it can increase its profits without increasing its risk to a dangerous level.

The gambler on his side faces his own challenges. With an initial bet of $1, he can win at most $1 for every time he uses his strategy. If he stays with his strategy for a 12-hour day, he can win only $720 from 720 tries per day. That is not much. The gambler can try to increase the quantity of his winnings by increasing his initial bet. He can bet $5 or $10 or $20 as a starting bet. With a starting bet of $20 each time, he can win $720 \times 20 = \$14,400$ per day, a tidy sum. But of course he has to risk losing a greater amount if he loses. And the betting limit will catch up with him. With a betting limit of $10,240, he can double his initial bet only 9 times, with a final bet of $10,240. The chance of catastrophe is the probability of losing 10 bets in a row, both the initial bet and the nine times afterward when the doubling takes place. This probability is $(19/37)^{10}$, or about 0.0013, or 1.3 out of 1,000, or 1 out of 800. He will probably lose within a little more than a day. If he tries an initial bet of $100, and the betting limit is $10,000, he can only double 6 times, up to a maximum of $6,400. The chance of catastrophe is $(19/37)^7$, or 0.0094. This probability is about 1 out of 100. He will probably lose within two hours. He does not have a good strategy.

As usual, the regularities that God has ordained for probabilities operate to show the futility of alleged gambling systems. In addition, God has moral requirements that address gambling. We consider these in the next appendix.

---

[3] The number of tries comes out to about 2,000 rather than 1,000 because a betting limit of 1,024 means that the gambler reaches his limit only after 11 successive bets, the first of which is $1 and the last of which is $1,024. The probability of losing 11 successive bets is roughly 1/2,048 (ignoring the presence of the zero pocket). The gambler's total loss from his successive bets in this catastrophic situation is $2,047.

THE REAL PROBLEM WITH GAMBLING

The preceding appendix has analyzed a number of gambling systems by which gamblers hope to "beat the odds" and make a killing. We could consider still more systems. In each case, careful calculations of the probabilities show that the gambler will not win in the long run. In fact, in casino games the probabilities are always stacked against the customer, so that in the long run the casino consistently takes in money from every form of gambling that it offers on its premises.

The calculation of probabilities is a form of mathematics—specifically, the mathematical theory of probability. So it has jokingly been said that gambling is a form of tax on nonmathematicians. The mathematicians know better, because they can do the calculations. More accurately, it could be said that gambling is a tax on people who do not know probability theory.

KNOWLEDGE NOT ENOUGH

But the real problem with gambling does not consist merely in ignorance. It is possible to know the theory and still be tempted to gamble. The temptation arises partly because sin in essence is irrational. It is rebellion against God. According to Romans 1:18–25, all human beings already know God inescapably. It does not make sense to engage in rebellion.

TEMPTATION

But we can see some specific forms of temptations in gambling. The mathematical theory of probability must start with some assumptions about the nature of events—for instance, that some events are probabilistically independent of one another. The outcomes of successive flips of a coin, or the outcomes of successive spins of a roulette wheel, are probabilistically independent. If they were not, it might be possible to find a winning system by observing a pattern in a large enough number of previous outcomes.

Gamblers may or may not be aware of the technical concept of probabilistic independence. Whatever awareness they have, in practice they want to believe that the events *do* contain some secret patterns. They want to believe, partly because if it were true, they might achieve marvelous success. It is as if they invest hope in a utopian story of winning, and they behave as if they partly believe it. Their own desires urge them to believe in it, even if part of their mind tells them otherwise.

So why should we believe or not believe that the spins of a roulette wheel are probabilistically independent of one another? What establishes such independence? In reality, it is God who ordains all probabilities. Our convictions about probability must ultimately go back to God. And so they depend on what *kind* of God we believe in. The issue of Romans 1:18–25, where people substitute an idol or a counterfeit for the true God, rises to the surface.

THE GODS OF GAMBLERS

Gamblers who hope to beat the odds do not really accept the God of the Bible. He does not match their desires for the way that they want the world to be and what they hope the world will be, for the sake of achieving prosperity in their lives. Their desires are twisted, as are the desires of all sinful people. Gamblers may look foolish to those of us who see through the foolishness of gambling. But we all fall captive, each in our own way, to substitutes and idols of one kind or another, because desire resides within us to make ourselves gods. Gamblers just have one particular form of the desire, where their desire to be rich and to boast in their luck is a desire that makes them serve false gods. They serve the god of self. At the same time they make Lady Luck into a goddess to serve, in order to serve the deeper god of self.

Gamblers have false gods. They have such false gods because they fail in knowing God and in experiencing fellowship with God. That is the root. Gambling is a tax on alienation from God.

Should we be surprised? The book of Proverbs has been telling us all along that there is a kind of "tax" on sin. Proverbs begins with a contrast between the wisdom of communion with God and the folly of alienation from him:

The fear of the LORD is the beginning of knowledge;
    fools despise wisdom and instruction. (Prov. 1:7)

Folly leads to "taxes":

a babbling fool will come to *ruin*. (Prov. 10:8)

the fool *will be servant* to the wise of heart. (11:29)

By the mouth of a fool comes a *rod* for his back. (14:3)

The fool folds his hands and *eats his own flesh*. (Eccles. 4:5)

So the "tax" on gamblers is one form of the tax on fools, which in turn is one form of the tax on alienation from God. If you want to live your life well and fruitfully, the way to do so is to live your life as God in his wisdom intends it. This you will find if you come through Christ to have fellowship with God. "And this is eternal life, that they know you the only true God, and Jesus Christ whom you have sent" (John 17:3).

A PUZZLE IN PROBABILITY

We meet various puzzles in dealing with probability. Our untrained intuition about a situation does not always match what can be calculated from careful reasoning about probability. This lack of correspondence points to the fact that God's knowledge exceeds ours. God has ordained that normative, existential, and situational perspectives on probability will harmonize (chapter 18). But they harmonize only with the proviso that our initial existential intuition about probabilities is fallible, while God's knowledge is complete.

A WEEKLY QUIZ SHOW

Consider an example.[1] Betty is hostess for a television quiz show that airs once a week. Every week, at one point in the show, Betty shows the contestant three identically shaped boxes, labeled *A*, *B*, and *C*. Every week one of the boxes contains a prize, while the other two are empty. Every week, before the show starts, Betty selects one box at random, and the prize gets placed in the box. Although Betty knows which of the boxes contains the prize, the contestant does not. Betty then invites the contestant to pick one of the boxes. The contestant picks one. Then Betty proceeds to open one of the *other* two boxes, and shows that it is empty. (If the contestant has already picked the right box, Betty chooses at random the box that she will open; on the other hand, if the contestant has not chosen the right box,

---

[1] This puzzle is known as the Monty Hall Problem (Dimitri P. Bertsekas and John N. Tsitsiklis, *Introduction to Probability* [Belmont, MA: Athena Scientific, 2002], 27).

Betty deliberately chooses the one out of the two remaining boxes that does not contain the prize.) Finally, Betty asks the contestant whether, after he has seen the empty box, he wants to change his selection. The whole sequence of events takes place every week. One week, the contestant is Albert. Let us suppose that Albert has already seen some previous episodes of the show, so that he knows the procedure for the boxes. When Betty asks, he chooses box A. Betty then opens box B and it is empty. Should Albert stick with box A, which he has already chosen? Or should he switch to box C?

Confronted with this example, many people intuitively think that Albert's chances of winning are now half-and-half. They reason that there are two boxes left, A and C, and either of them might contain the prize. Which one Albert picks makes little or no difference. That is how it seems to their subjective intuition.

But if people were to perform repeated trials in this situation, they would find that their intuition is wrong. When Albert first picked box A, his chance of picking the box with a prize in it was 1/3, because he had no way of knowing which was the correct one. In 1/3 of the cases he will be right, and in 2/3 of the cases he will be wrong. Once the second box B is opened, he has further information: the prize is not in box B, so it must be either in A or in C. At this point, people's intuitions may tell them that the two options are equally likely. But they are not. The probability of Albert being right with his initial pick is still 1/3. It is not affected by Betty's opening box B, since every week she opens one out of the two remaining boxes. It follows that the probability of finding the prize in box C, *given that Betty has opened B*, is 2/3.

How can this be? Does the prize magically leap from box B to box C? Of course not. But if the prize had been in box B, Betty would have opened box C rather than box B, thereby directing Albert to box B. In 2/3 of the cases, namely, when the prize starts out in box B, and also when it starts out in box C, Betty's act of opening one box directs Albert to the other, correct box.

To some readers, this reasoning may still seem fishy. Let us try it another way. It is best for Albert to think about his options before he ever arrives at the studio for the quiz show. He will consider all possible strategies, and pick the strategy that is most likely to give him the prize.

If he picks box A to begin with, he has four possible strategies for continuation after Betty has opened one of the two other boxes:

(1) pick box *A* and stay with it no matter what.
(2) pick box *A* and then switch only if Betty opens box *B*.
(3) pick box *A* and then switch only if Betty opens box *C*.
(4) pick box *A* and then switch no matter which of the boxes *B* or *C* is opened.

We may also suppose that at the beginning the probability that the prize has been placed in box *A* is 1/3. Likewise for box *B* and box *C*.

Just as there are four possible strategies that begin with picking box *A*, there are four more strategies that begin with Albert picking box *B*, and then switching or not switching. But since at the beginning Albert has no idea which box contains the prize, and since the prize is equally likely to be in any one of the three, the strategies that begin with picking box *B* will lead to results on the average that are no better than beginning with box *A*. A similar argument holds for strategies that begin by picking box *C*. So for simplicity we can confine ourselves to the four strategies that begin by picking box *A*.

With strategy (1), Albert wins if the prize is in box *A*, and loses otherwise. His probability of winning is 1/3.

Consider strategy (2). If the prize happens to be in box *C*, which is 1/3 of the time, Betty will open box *B*. Albert will switch to box *C*, and he will get the prize. If the prize happens to be in box *B*, which is 1/3 of the time, Betty will open box *C*. Albert will stick with box *A*. Since box *A* is empty, he will get nothing. Finally, suppose that the prize happens to be in box *A*, which is 1/3 of the time. Betty knows that it is there. She could open either box *B* or box *C*. She chooses at random, and there is 1/2 chance that she will open box *B*, and 1/2 chance that she will open box *C*. Thus (1/3) × (1/2) of the time we will have the sequence in which the prize is in box *A and in addition* Betty opens box *C*. For this 1/6 of the time, Albert will not switch, and consequently he will win the prize in box *A*. But for another 1/6 of the time, the prize will be in box *A* and Betty will open box *B*. Then Albert switches to box *C*, and he loses. He wins the 1/3 of the time when the prize is in box *C*, and in addition 1/6 of the time when the prize is in box *A* and Betty happens to open box *C*. In total, he wins (1/3) + (1/6) = 1/2 of the time.

Similarly, strategy (3) leads to winning 1/2 of the time.

For strategy (4), if the prize happens to be in box *A*, which is 1/3 of the time, Albert loses, because he always switches away from box *A* to something else. On the other hand, if the prize is in box *B* or in box *C* to begin with, Albert wins, because he will switch away from box *A* to whichever box contains the prize (being guided by the fact that Betty opens the other box that does not contain the prize). He wins 2/3 of the time.

Table C.1 indicates the outcomes in each case.

Table C.1: Quiz Show Strategies

Albert's strategy	prize in A (1/3 time)	prize in B (1/3 time)	prize in C (1/3 time)	total chance of win
(1) pick *A* and stay	win	lose	lose	1/3
(2) pick *A* and switch only if *B* is opened next	win half of the time, depending on whether *B* or *C* is opened	lose	win	1/3 + (1/3) × (1/2) = 1/2
(3) pick *A* and switch only if *C* is opened next	win half of the time	win	lose	1/2
(4) pick *A* and switch whichever box is opened next	lose	win	win	2/3

This example about prizes in boxes shows that many people's initial intuitions about probabilities do not match the actual probabilities. It thereby illustrates the principle that God's wisdom is greater than man's. But we have also shown that we, like Albert, can reason the whole thing through and develop a better strategy than our original intuition. We can learn. We can think God's thoughts after him.

QUIZ SHOW WITH ALTERATIONS

The probabilities depend not only on the information that Albert receives from opening one box, but on other information about the quiz show set-up. We can illustrate by considering, not a weekly quiz show, but a one-time quiz show. Betty shows Albert three boxes, *A*, *B*, and *C*, as before. She says truthfully that one contains a prize and the other two are empty. She invites Albert to choose one. Albert chooses box *A*. Then Betty opens box *B* and shows that it is empty. She asks Albert whether he wants to switch. Should he?

This situation sounds almost exactly the same as the previous one, but it is not the same. In a one-time quiz show, there is no precedent—there are no previous quiz shows. Therefore, there is no regular pattern, according to which we already know that Betty is going to open one of the other boxes. Suppose that, secretly, Betty wants Albert to win. She could have a strategy of her own. If Albert picks the right box on his first try, Betty simply opens that very box right away and gives Albert the prize that it contains. If, on the other hand, Betty sees that Albert has chosen incorrectly, she "gives him a second chance," as it were, by opening one of the other boxes and inviting him to switch. If Albert knows that Betty is following this strategy, he should definitely switch, because he is certain to get the prize. By offering the second chance, Betty has already indirectly revealed that Albert's first choice was wrong.

But now suppose that Betty secretly wants Albert to *lose* rather than to win. If Albert picks box *A*, and Betty knows that the prize is not there, she simply opens the box *A* and says, "Sorry, you lose." If, on the other hand, the prize happens to be in box *A*, Betty, knowing that it is there, offers Albert a chance to reconsider by opening box *B*, and then asks Albert whether he wants to switch to box *C*. If Albert realizes that Betty is plotting against him, he should stick with box *A*. The very fact that Betty is offering him an alternative gives Albert information that implies that his initial pick was correct. If, on the other hand, Albert does not realize what Betty is doing, he may rely on the reasoning given earlier, which is appropriate for a regular, repeated quiz show. Albert switches to box *C*, and he loses.

We can picture still another scenario. We go back to a regular, weekly quiz show. Albert, let us say, has carefully studied the situation with the boxes, and has determined that on the average the prize appears to be placed in box *C* not 1/3 of the time, but 1/2 of the time, while it is in box *A* 1/3 of the time and in box *B* 1/6 of the time. His best strategy is to pick box *B* first, and then switch after the opening of one of the other boxes. He will thereby lose only when the prize has been placed in box *B*, which is 1/6 of the time. He wins 5/6 of the time. He wins for the 1/3 of the time when the prize is in box *A*, and for the 1/2 of the time when the prize is in box *C*, for a total of $1/3 + 1/2 = 5/6$.

These altered scenarios show that the interaction of human beings and what they know about the tendencies of other human beings have notable effects on probability estimates. Such factors also come into play in card games like bridge or poker. In these games, a player may reckon not only on the probabilities of getting certain winning situations, but on the tendencies of other players. Do some of the other players give away information by their mannerisms? Do some of them regularly make mistakes or regularly commit themselves to specific tactics that have low chances of winning?

RECKONING WITH PARTIAL KNOWLEDGE

The altered scenarios show the importance not only of reckoning with partial human knowledge, but also of reckoning with the multiple perspectives of multiple human beings participating in a situation. It may be valuable, for example, for Betty to think about Albert's intentions, and for Albert to think about Betty's intentions. They may develop better strategies by taking into account what the other person is likely to do. These multiple perspectives, as usual, are ordained by God. God reflects his archetypal unity and diversity in the unity and diversity of created human thinkers.

The use of multiple perspectives also helps to show why people's initial intuitions about the quiz show may not be so bad after all. Suppose Betty does not always open a second box. Suppose that Albert, the contestant, does not know for sure what Betty's intentions are. Albert may guess that there is half a chance (probability of 1/2) that Betty is working in his favor and half a chance that she is working against him. Albert chooses box A; Betty then opens box B and shows that it is empty. Should Albert stick with box A or switch to box C? If Betty is working against him, he will certainly lose if he switches (the fact that Betty opens box B is a sure sign that she knows that the prize is in box A). If she is working for him, he will certainly lose if he sticks with box A (her opening box B is a sure sign that she is trying to coax him to switch to box C, where she knows the prize is). There is half a chance that the prize is in box A (namely, if Betty is working against him), and half a chance that the prize is in box C (namely, if Betty is working for him). The prize is equally likely to be in either box, and Albert gains no advantage by choosing one rather than the other.

Consider still another situation. Suppose that Betty herself does not know the location of the prize. Every week, after the contestant chooses one of the three boxes, Betty opens one of the other two boxes *at random*. If the prize is in the box that Betty opens, the contest rules specify that the contestant loses his chance for the prize. On the other hand, if the box is empty, the contestant gets to decide whether to stick with his first choice or switch to the remaining box that has not been opened.

Suppose that Albert begins by choosing box A. We can plot out how Albert will fare for each of the possibilities (Table C.2).

Table C.2: Albert's Chances

Albert's strategy	prize in A (1/3 time)	prize in B; B opened (1/6 time)	prize in B; C opened (1/6 time)	prize in C; B opened (1/6 time)	prize in C; C opened (1/6 time)	total chance of win
(1) pick A and stay	win	lose	lose	lose	lose	1/3
(2) pick A and switch	lose	lose	win	win	lose	1/3

Albert does not change his chances, no matter what strategy he adopts. Why? In the earlier scenarios, which box Betty opens depends on her private information about the location of the prize. So the extra information given by opening the box can be used by Albert to improve his chances. But if Betty opens a box at random, it either makes Albert lose or provides no further information about which of the remaining boxes contains the prize. We can express the same principle by asking what are Albert's chances of winning, once Betty has opened one of the other boxes and it turns out to be empty. The information that it is empty eliminates some of the possibilities, but the remaining possibilities have the same proportions as before.

P(prize in A | B opened and empty) = P(prize in A & B opened)/P(B opened and empty) = P(prize in A) × P(B opened)/[P(B opened and empty | B opened) × P(B opened)] = (1/3) × (1/2)/[(2/3) × (1/2)] = 1/2.

This situation of equal probabilities matches the naive intuition of people who think that the chances are equal that the prize will be in box A or box C.

It is possible, then, that naive reasoning has confused the initial quiz show situation that we described with the situation of a random opening, which would provide Albert with no extra information relevant to his choice. It is also possible that people are influenced by uncertainty over background information, including uncertainty over Betty's role. In such a situation, their intuition may be to "default" to equal probabilities.

COMPLEXITY IN CONDITIONAL PROBABILITY

The quiz show puzzle also shows some of the complexities that can arise with respect to conditional probability. Simple reasoning about conditional probability assumes that, when extra information narrows the field of possibilities, the narrowing process takes place in a kind of equally proportioned way. For example, suppose Jill rolls a die and it comes up 5. If Jill tells Karen that it has come up odd, Karen assumes that this information does not affect the ratios between the likelihoods of 1, 3, and 5. Each is equally probable. So for Karen, P(5 | odd) is 1 out of 3 or 1/3. But this simple reasoning clearly does not work for Albert's situation in the quiz show. Before Betty opens box B, the chances for finding the prize in each of the boxes is 1/3. Opening box B eliminates 1 out of the 3 possibilities, so that one might naively think the other two retain the same ratio as before. But if Betty is influenced by her knowledge of the prize location, that need not be the case.

Consider again the situation with Jill rolling a die. It comes up 5. Jill tells Karen that the result is odd. Karen knows that it could be 1, 3, or 5. Before Jill provided her information, each of these results had a probability of 1/6. After the information is given, each of the probabilities for 1, 3, and 5 is divided by the same ratio, 1/2. Each now has a conditional probability of 1/3.

But is the assumption of constant ratios valid? It is not always valid. Suppose that Jill has agreed beforehand that, if 3 comes up, she will announce the result, but if 1 or 5 comes up, she will announce only that the result is odd. Then the fact that Jill says "odd" eliminates 3, and leaves only 1 and 5, with equal probabilities of 1/2. Or suppose that Jill has agreed that she will announce only "odd" or "even." Karen nevertheless knows that 3 is Jill's favorite number. Karen estimates that there is a 1/3 chance that, if 3 comes up, Jill will reveal by a smile on her face that it is a 3. What actually happens is that Jill says "odd" with a straight face. What is the probability that the result is a 5? We cannot rightly say that the probability of 5 is 1/3, because the probability of a 3 is somewhat less than 1/3, and presumably the probability of 1 or 5 is somewhat more than 1/3. How much?

Before Jill provides her information, the underlying probabilities are 1/2 for an even result (1/6 + 1/6 + 1/6 for 2, 4, and 6), 1/6 for 1, 1/6 for 5, (1/6) ×

(1/3) = 1/18 for 3 with a smile, and (1/6) × (2/3) = 1/9 for 3 with a straight face. (We are assuming that a smile would be a sure sign that 3 has come up, not a smile that might be completely unrelated to the outcome.) When Jill gives her information (minus the smile), it eliminates all the even outcomes and the outcome with probability 1/18 that the die has 3 up and Jill smiles. This elimination leaves 1/6 for 1, 1/6 for 5, and 1/9 for 3. If we assume that these probabilities retain their ratios to one another, the conditional probability of 5, given Jill's revelation, is (1/6)/[(1/6) + (1/6) + (1/9)] = (1/6)/(8/18) = 3/8 = 0.375. This probability is slightly higher than 1/3 = 0.333, the appropriate probability for the situation where Jill has no tendency to give away the presence of a 3. The appropriate probabilities depend not merely on the actual information that Jill provides, but on influences that alternative information might have on Karen's estimates of the ratios of the probabilities between remaining live outcomes. In other words, in real life it can be complicated, because people are complicated.

God has so constructed the world that we do confront situations in which probabilities can be calculated in a straightforward way. But he has also created a world with complexity. Not every situation is as simple as the ones usually used as examples.

APPENDIX D

INTERACTING WITH SECULAR PHILOSOPHICAL VIEWS OF PROBABILITY

In chapter 18 we considered briefly three major concepts of probability: a quasi-logical concept, a subjective concept, and an objective concept.[1] When these concepts occur within a secular environment, which ignores God, they are all inadequate.[2] Within a Christian view, they are complementary or perspectivally related. How would we interact with the secular approaches to probability?

The twentieth and twenty-first centuries have seen much complex discussion of the different views of probability, and variations within each view. We cannot undertake a full discussion.[3] We must content ourselves with a beginning.

We may keep in mind several principles for interaction:

1. All people know God and rely on God in their intellectual reflections. By the principle of common grace, they may achieve insights that are valuable. We should respect other people's work, and not dismiss it just because we are suspicious of its religious roots and motivations.

---

[1] Alan Hájek, "Interpretations of Probability," *The Stanford Encyclopedia of Philosophy (Winter 2011 Edition)*, ed. Edward N. Zalta, http://plato.stanford.edu/archives/win2011/entries/probability-interpret/, §3, accessed January 18, 2012.

[2] For a similar critical interaction with views of statistical inference, see Andrew M. Hartley, *Christian and Humanistic Foundations for Statistical Inference: Religious Control of Statistical Paradigms* (Eugene, OR: Resource Publications, 2008).

[3] See Maria Carla Galavotti, *Philosophical Introduction to Probability* (Stanford, CA: Center for the Study of Language and Information, 2005); D. H. Mellor, *Probability: A Philosophical Introduction* (London/New York: Routledge, 2005); and the bibliography in Hájek, "Interpretations of Probability," §4.

2. If people do not acknowledge God, they end up employing substitutes for him. In no arena of intellectual endeavor do we simply reason and conduct our affairs in independence of God. We either serve him or rebel, and that affects how we think, since as human beings we think God's thoughts after him. So in thinking about probability, as in any other area, we need to watch for substitutes for God that people may employ. In particular, how do they account for the predictabilities and the unpredictabilities regarding probability?

3. Often, a substitute for God takes the form of some creaturely reality, or one aspect of reality. This aspect is viewed as the source for the rest. For example, objective probability (probability in the world) can be treated as the ultimate nature of probability, which must then explain the other two concepts (probability as a logical norm, or subjective probability). But such explanations end up exhibiting tensions and deficiencies, because nothing except God has the character suitable for ultimate explanation.

4. In the area of probability, the very concept of probability depends on the relationship of God's faithfulness to his creativity. It also depends on the relation of God's infinite knowledge—including knowledge of the future—to our finite knowledge. There is no uncertainty with God. So a concept of probability can get off the ground only by appealing to God's creativity and to the distinction between human and divine knowledge, or by using a substitute. Chance with a capital C is the usual substitute for God's creativity. And, instead of acknowledging God, a person may treat the limitations of human knowledge as ultimate.

QUASI-LOGICAL PROBABILITY

Now let us consider some examples. What do we say from a Christian point of view about the secular view that starts with a quasi-logical interpretation of probability? This view is closely related to the use of evidence in supporting a hypothesis or a conclusion. The support of evidence for a conclusion rests on God's wisdom. God has ordained the relations between evidence and conclusions. Human beings made in the image of God can think God's thoughts after him in this area. So quasi-logical relations with respect to evidence, which are the focus of the normative perspective, cohere with subjective human intuitions about evidence, where the human intuitions belong to the existential perspective. And of course the evidence comes from the world—from situations that are the focus of the situational perspective. Weighing evidence involves coherence of these perspectives (see chapter 18).

Bayes's theorem, which is the focus of appendix G, provides a simple mathematical model for evidential inference in many controlled situations of probabilistic inference. But as usual there are limitations (see chapter 27). Juries weighing evidence for a crime have to make complicated inferences about the credibility of witnesses and the likelihood of alternative explanations as they may be sketched by a defense attorney. Their deliberations take into account a lot of background human knowledge. We cannot automate such knowledge, and a mathematical model for inference involves simplification.

In addition, a limitation is evident when we ask how we establish what initial probabilities we use before the evidence comes in. Using conditional probabilities to move from evidence to conclusions depends on having initial probabilities associated with individual propositions and conditional probabilities for the relation between various propositions. The difficulty is analogous to a difficulty with deductive logic. Deductive logic verifies valid reasoning based on premises, but does not establish the truth of the premises. Likewise, evidential reasoning based on probabilities does not establish the initial probabilities on which it rests. Initial probabilities will then have to derive either from earlier conditional probabilities, in an endless regress, or from subjective or objective estimates of probability. Using either of the latter raises the question of the coherence between different interpretations of probability, and shows the insufficiency of the quasi-logical approach, when used by itself.

SUBJECTIVE VIEWS OF PROBABILITY

Let us next consider subjective views of probability. Subjective views try to define probability in terms of degrees of belief. Degrees of belief belong to persons, and persons may differ in their beliefs. So we find ourselves talking about particular personal agents. Let us choose one, let us say, Alice. What is Alice's degree of belief with regard to some event? How do we measure degrees of belief quantitatively? One attractive route is to ask, given some uncertain event E, how much Alice is willing to surrender in return for the prospect of receiving a fixed payoff (say $1) if the event E takes place?[4]

---

[4] Ibid., §3.3.2.

If she is willing to surrender 50 cents, her subjective probability for E is taken to be $0.50/$1 or 0.5.

But different people may display a different willingness to bet, even when they have the same information. So the theorists have tried to improve the subjective approach by talking about degrees of belief for a *rational* agent. Alice must not be just anyone, but someone who thinks and acts rationally. This new definition appears to be an improvement, but it puts a big burden on deciding what is rational. And reflections on rationality may easily lead to returning to a quasi-logical definition: a rational agent uses quasi-logical argumentation to establish a probability. Or they may lead to returning to an objective approach: a rational agent follows the information given by previous outcomes of comparable events (previous trials). These moves indicate that part of the challenge with understanding probability is the interlocking between logical, subjective, and objective aspects, all of which belong together.

SUBJECTIVE FALLACIES

We also confront a tension in the realm of subjective probabilities because the ideal of a purely "rational" decision is not always attained in practice. On the one hand, we have to bring into our account real human agents, because the information they already have affects what they think probable. On the other hand, their actual intuitions about probability do not always match probability defined in other ways. Appendix C illustrates the difference between subjective intuition and objective probability with a puzzle from a quiz show.

The puzzle from the quiz show indicates that many people's initial intuitions about probabilities do not match the probabilities that can be calculated from evidential reasoning. So a *purely* subjective approach to defining probability is not satisfactory. On the other hand, new information, such as the opening of a box that does not have a prize, can legitimately result in a shift in probabilities. So we cannot simply *ignore* human subjectivity.

From our Christian point of view, this result makes sense. God, not man, is the standard for all probability calculations. So human intuitions can go astray at times, without threatening to make the whole field of probability a mess. On the other hand, human beings are made in the image of God, so we can correct our sense of probabilities as we reason through situations like the quiz show.

By contrast, in a secular approach it is difficult to bring together the need on the one hand for taking into account previous information that an agent like Alice may have, and the need on the other hand for distinguishing between Alice's subjective intuition and an ideal rationality.

SUPERIOR HUMAN JUDGMENT?

Further reflection on the quiz show puzzle and on other situations involving subjective judgments can suggest that people may be influenced by a lot of background knowledge. In the quiz show, the contestant Albert may be influenced by whether he thinks the host, Betty, is plotting against him or in his favor. The bridge player or poker player is influenced by his knowledge of the habits of the other players. Such information cannot always be easily integrated into a simple, one-dimensional probabilistic model of the objective situation.[5] In such situations, people's subjective judgments may sometimes be better than rigorous mathematical calculations of probability, because the people intuitively include a more robust understanding of the total situation and go beyond the simplifications in a probabilistic mathematical model (see chapter 27). If the principle of human capability applies to bridge and poker, it surely applies to many social situations that are far more complex than a card game.

In addition, when we look at variations in the quiz show setup and variations in the intentions of the quiz show host, the resultant probabilities vary. Simple approaches based on calculations with conditional probabilities may not always work, if these approaches assume that probability ratios remain the same after the arrival of new information. When we try to reckon with complex influences on probabilities, we end up bringing in reflections that depend on the situational and normative perspectives, not simply a narrow version of the existential perspective.

OBJECTIVE PROBABILITY: THE PROPENSITY APPROACH

Consider now the objective view of probability, which says that probability is a property in the world. In chapter 18 we already discussed the approach to probability using frequency. A second approach seeks to define probability as an objective *propensity*. According to this view, probability is the *propensity*

---

[5] Mathematical game theory constructs probabilistic mathematical models for cases of human interaction and competition. But it must make simplifications about the human beings involved.

of a coin or a die or another object (or a whole situation) to produce an outcome (such as coming up heads). Some analysts prefer to think in terms of "single-case" propensity. On one selected roll, a die has a propensity to turn up with four on top with a probability of 1/6. Other analysts deal with *long-run* propensities. The die has a long-run propensity to turn up with four on top 1/6 of the time during a sufficiently long run of trials.

One major challenge for the propensity interpretation, and for the frequency interpretation as well, lies in the fact that propensity needs to be understood in the context of a range of possible cases—cases of coin tosses, or die rolls, or whatever the situation may suggest. Human beings must already have a sense of which other cases are analogous, and in what way they are analogous. A single-case approach to propensity has to judge that we are talking about a coin toss, and that it belongs to a larger class of coin tosses, similar to the one on which we focus. A long-run approach to propensity has to specify the long run of cases about which it is speaking, which presupposes that it has identified relevant similarities between the cases.

Judgments about analogy may look easy when we deal with typical chance events like coin tosses. But they become more challenging in the context of scientific experiments. A scientist must try to figure out whether some unanticipated factor, such as vibration or change in temperature or humidity, is interfering with the course of his experiment. The extra factor, if it exists, affects the outcome, and therefore implies that two experiments that superficially look the same may have vastly different outcomes, depending on the presence or absence of the unnoticed factor. The possibility of an unnoticed factor means that, despite appearances, two experiments may not be *analogous* in the right way. If they are not analogous, the probability of an outcome from the one experiment does not provide decisive information about the probability of an outcome in the second experiment.

There is no simple recipe for determining beforehand what might be a source of interference, a factor that affects the outcome. What the factors might be depends on the nature of the world—not simply individual objects, like coins or dice, but interactions between objects. For example, oily fingers might make a die slippery on some edges. Or an electromagnet might affect a coin that has iron embedded in it.

The challenge becomes even more difficult when we deal, not with a carefully controlled scientific experiment, but with the hurly-burly of social life. What is the chance that a stock market index will fall 100 points tomorrow? To answer the question we have to consider whether the situation today is analogous to situations on previous days. Is it analogous to other situations of bull markets or bear markets? The situation never exactly repeats itself, so no one can weigh with perfect confidence the analogies and dissimilarities. Moreover, in this process of weighing, the influence of subjectivity and the influence of quasi-logical relations between events makes its presence felt. As usual, the objective view of probability is not isolated from the other two perspectives on probability.

A second major difficulty with the propensity interpretation is that it is not so clear what exactly a propensity is, in spite of the attempts to define it. Is the word *propensity* simply another way of labeling the facts or perhaps our subjective intuitions about the facts? What good does it do us to use this label? We can suggest an analogy in the field of medical conditions. Do we explain a cold by saying that the human body has a propensity to have colds, and the body's propensity includes a propensity for the colds to last so many days? Do we explain the positions of the sun by saying that the sun has a propensity to take successive positions in the sky over the period of daylight? Does using the word *propensity* really illumine these situations, or is it little more than a cover for our ignorance?

Perhaps the advocate of propensity might admit that the word covers our ignorance, but that it still points to an explanation that we could have if we knew enough. For example, the propensity for the moon to move in orbit around the earth is explained by Newton's law of gravitation. Likewise, a person's propensity to get a cold is explained by the existence of cold viruses and by the capabilities of his immune system. So the propensity for a coin to come up heads might potentially be explained by various complex scientific analyses of the coin.

This explanation of propensity makes a good deal of sense when we understand its limits. But we should still ask what kind of assumptions people are making about the nature of the world. In the estimation of many people, science provides the most basic information about the nature of the world. But does it? It is easy to confuse the pragmatic and technical triumphs of science with a modernist worldview that claims to be built on scientific progress but in fact imports ungrounded assumptions.[6]

---

[6] See Vern S. Poythress, *Redeeming Science: A God-Centered Approach* (Wheaton, IL: Crossway, 2006), chapter 1.

Various sciences explain various phenomena, in one sense of the word *explain*. But sciences do not explain themselves. The laws that scientists discover, including probabilistic regularities, are ordained by God and testify to God. In contrast to the Christian view of the world, modern materialistic philosophy tends to suppress the personal character of law and to suppose that coin flips take place in an impersonal, essentially mechanical world (or the indeterministic world of quantum mechanics, conceived impersonalistically). When people use the word *propensity*, do they presuppose an essentially mechanical worldview? In this worldview, they might admit that they have not yet figured out all the mechanisms, but they already assume that mechanisms must exist because the world is mechanical. The word *propensity* then labels the mechanism that is there but is not yet known.

Is the word *propensity* simply a synonym for *property*? Perhaps. Why use the word *propensity*, then? To my ear, the word *propensity* in ordinary use differs somewhat from the word *property* by suggesting a subjective inclination. I have a desire, let us say, to eat, and that inclines me to engage in acts in which I actually eat. My propensity to eat leads to eating. There is a cause-effect relation.

But if we use this analogy to explain coins and dice, we are in danger of personifying coins and dice, by pretending that they have desires. This quasi-personification has as its background the difficulties of replacing God, who is the real author of predictabilities and unpredictabilities. God's personal, rational, language-like word specifies the behavior of coins and dice. Coins and dice behave as they do because of God's desires or "propensities." God expresses his propensities, including his creativity, in his words of command. If we try to replace his personal word with a substitute, it is easy, by using words analogically, to smuggle in the quasi-personal background that we still instinctively feel that we need.

In addition, the impersonalist substitute, because it no longer has rational origin, threatens to become opaque to human understanding. Why is it that coins or dice have the propensities that they do rather than other propensities? Because they *want* to behave in these ways? The word *want* personifies the coins and dice, and pretends that they have desires. If propensity is not a kind of personal desire, what is it? So let us consider the word *tendency*, which can be used as a synonym for propensity. Someone might say that coins have a tendency to come up heads with a probability of 1/2. But what is a *tendency*?

The word *tendency*, to my ear at least, does not always suggest semipersonal associations. Yes, we can use the word to describe personal inclinations: one person has a tendency to order steak at a restaurant. But we can also use the word with respect to inanimate objects: "A ball has a tendency to fall to the ground." What we mean is that it actually will fall to the ground unless something else intervenes. But that kind of picture does not really help us forward with probabilities, because it is still a picture suggesting physical determinism. The failure of a "tendency" to produce its usual result leads us to look for what sorts of causes have intervened to thwart the otherwise consistent results of the tendency. Real indeterminism, if it exists, has not been explained.

If we adopt an impersonalist worldview, a property or propensity or tendency just *is*. We remain in the dark about its origin and its rationale, because impersonalism fails to postulate any deeper origin or rationale. Propensity threatens to become irrational, and the possibility looms that we can make no confident inferences at all, not even about long-run frequencies.

We can see a hint of substitution for God in the background, because propensities are supposed to reside *in* a creaturely object (in a die or a coin) or else *in* a situation or an experimental setup as a whole. How a propensity can be in a whole situation without being in the parts is somewhat mysterious. But even leaving that difficulty aside, we confront a mystery about both properties and propensities if we try to regard them as self-sufficient. If we say that the properties are just *in* the objects, as finite objects, without any origin, we are substituting the creature (the objects) for the Creator. It is God who specifies order and unpredictabilities, who gives to the objects all their behavior through all time. Moreover, if we do not invoke God, who rules over both object and human observer, our human relation to these objects and to quasi-logical principles becomes darkened. Why and how do propensities, if they can irrationally be anything at all within an impersonalist worldview, relate to what is "in our heads"?

RELATIONSHIPS TO BROADER PHILOSOPHICAL ISSUES

The major philosophical approaches to probability also have ties with broader philosophical commitments. Modern views of probability are influenced by views of what there is (metaphysics) and how we know (epistemology)—which are broader philosophical debates. Historically, the quasi-logical view of probability has ties with logicism and rationalism, which see logic (and more broadly reason) as a main key to knowledge. The subjective view of probability has ties with subjectivist and pragmatist philosophies, which try to explain the world starting with the human subject. The objective view of probability, as a property of the world, has ties with empiricism, which starts with the world as it is, or with the world as perceived, and tries to explain how human knowledge can build itself up from sense experience.

Any of the three views of probability can also be held by philosophers who belong to other traditions, but the influence of a broader philosophical commitment can still make itself felt. The broader commitments to rationalism, subjectivism, and empiricism have the same tensions that we observed earlier (chapter 18) using John Frame's three perspectives on ethics. God has ordained rationality (the source for rationalism), created human beings (the source for subjectivism), and made the world (the source for empiricism). God holds together the normative perspective (focusing on norms, including norms for logical inference), the existential perspective (focusing on subjective response from people), and the situational perspective (focusing on the world). Without God it is difficult to explain how and why the perspectives fit together.

The secular views on probability then suffer from any limitations or tendencies toward reductionism that reside in the broader philosophical movements that influence them.

PERMUTATIONS AND COMBINATIONS

If we flip a coin 8 times in a row, what is the probability that it will come up heads 6 times out of the total of 8? How do we find the probability?

CALCULATING TOTAL NUMBER OF OUTCOMES

Let us first ask how many possible outcomes there are in all for 8 successive flips of a coin. The first coin flip can come up either heads or tails, for a total of 2 possible outcomes. Let us say that the outcome is heads. The second flip of the coin then has two possible outcomes. So we have these outcomes:

HH (heads followed by heads)
HT (heads followed by tails)

Likewise, there are also two possible outcomes if the first flip is tails:

TH
TT

So the total number of outcomes for two successive flips is 2 + 2 = 4.

With a third flip, we divide each of the four initial outcomes in two, so that there are now 8 possible outcomes in all:

HHH
HHT
HTH
HTT

THH
THT
TTH
TTT

Similarly, for four flips, the number of outcomes will be $8 + 8 = 8 \times 2 = 16$. 16 is 2 to the fourth power, that is, 2 multiplied by itself for a total of four occurrences: $2 \times 2 \times 2 \times 2$. It is abbreviated by writing the four as a super-script: 2^4. We can see the pattern. For 8 flips, the total number of outcomes will be 2 multiplied by itself repeatedly, for a total of 8 occurrences of 2, or 2 to the 8th power, or $2^8 = 256$.

We are using a general principle, which is sometimes called the *counting principle*. If there are m possible outcomes for a first stage, and n possible outcomes for a second stage, the total number of possible outcomes for the sequence of two stages is $m \times n$. In the case of two flips of a coin, there are 2 possible outcomes for the first flip, and 2 for the second flip, so there are $2 \times 2 = 4$ possible outcomes for the sequence. For a sequence consisting of one coin flip followed by one roll of a cubical die, there are 2 possible outcomes for the coin flip and 6 for the die, for a total of $2 \times 6 = 12$ possibilities for the sequence of two events.

For sequences of more than two events, we just keep multiplying. If stage one has n_1 possible outcomes, stage two has n_2 outcomes, and stage k has n_k outcomes, the total number of outcomes for a sequence of k stages is

$$n_1 \times n_2 \times n_3 \times \ldots \times n_k.$$

So for a sequence of 8 stages, each of which involves a coin flip with 2 outcomes, the total number is

$$2 \times 2 \times 2 \times 2 \times 2 \times 2 \times 2 \times 2 = 2^8 = 256.$$

FINDING A SHORTCUT FOR COUNTING FAVORABLE OUTCOMES

There are a large number of possible outcomes for 8 coin flips. Out of all of these, how many contain exactly 6 heads? We could laboriously go through all 256 possibilities, but that would be time-consuming. And we might possibly make a mistake in counting, and not come up with the right number in the end. Is there an easier way?

Mathematicians have found an easier way. There are two key concepts, namely *permutations* and *combinations*. In ordinary English, the words *permutation* and *combination* are similar in meaning. But in their use in mathematics, each word has a precise meaning, and the two are carefully distinguished from one another.

PERMUTATIONS

To understand what a *permutation* is, consider a situation where Barbara takes a pack of 52 playing cards and separates out all the kings and queens. There are four kings and four queens, for a total of eight cards. She shuffles these eight cards, and then draws two in succession, placing them on the table. What is the probability that she will draw two kings?

How many ways are there of drawing two kings from the eight cards? Barbara could draw any one of four kings on the first draw (king of spades K♠, king of hearts K♥, king of diamonds K♦, and king of clubs K♣). After that king has been drawn, there are only three kings left among the remaining cards. Hence, there are only three possible favorable outcomes for the second draw. The total number of favorable outcomes is 4 × 3. We can list them if we like:

Table E.1: Outcomes Drawing Two Kings

K♠, K♥	K♥, K♠	K♦, K♠	K♣, K♠
K♠, K♦	K♥, K♦	K♦, K♥	K♣. K♥
K♠, K♣	K♥, K♣	K♦, K♣	K♣, K♦

The number 12, the number of possible outcomes with two kings, is called the number of permutations of four objects taken two at a time. In this case, the four objects are the four kings. To get a single permutation, we choose two kings out of the total of four. That is, we take the kings "two at a time." Each particular possibility, such as K♠, K♥, is one example of a permutation of four objects taken two at a time. Mathematicians have invented a special abbreviation for the total number of such permutations: the symbol $_4P_2$ designates the number of permutations of 4 objects taken 2 at a time. Within this symbol, the letter P stands of *permutations*. We calculated above that $_4P_2 = 12$.

The 12 permutations with two kings are the favorable outcomes. But

Barbara could draw various permutations involving queens as well as kings. What is the total number of possible outcomes when she draws two cards from the eight original cards? The first draw could be any out of eight possibilities. After this one card is drawn, there are seven cards left, so there are seven possibilities for the second draw. By the counting principle, the total number of possibilities is 8×7. This number, 56, is the number of permutations of eight objects taken two at a time. The abbreviation is

$$_8P_2 = 56$$

The eight objects are of course the four kings and the four queens, taken together.

We have established that, out of a total of 56 possible outcomes, $4 \times 3 = 12$ are favorable. Using the principle of symmetry, we can infer that, for a well shuffled deck of cards, each of the 56 outcomes is equally likely. So the probability of getting a favorable outcome is $12/56 = 3/14$.

This particular example is not too hard, because there are a relatively small number of possible outcomes. But we can consider more difficult cases.

Suppose that Barbara draws five playing cards in succession from a deck of 52 cards. She displays the cards from left to right on the table. How many possible distinct sequences of cards could she produce? (Two sequences are considered distinct even if they have the very same cards, but in two distinct orders.)

The first card she draws can be any one of the 52 cards. So there are 52 possible outcomes. The second card can be any one of the remaining 51 cards (obviously, she cannot possibly draw the first card again, because it is already lying on the table). According to the counting principle, the total number of outcomes is now 52×51.

Barbara can now draw any of 50 cards for her third draw. The total number of possible outcomes is now $52 \times 51 \times 50$. The reasoning goes on in the same way for the remaining cards that she will draw. When she has drawn five cards, the total number of outcomes is $52 \times 51 \times 50 \times 49 \times 48$. Each possible outcome is again called a *permutation*.

More precisely, if Barbara draws a total of five cards in succession, the total number of possibilities is described as the number of permutations of 52 cards taken 5 at a time. The number of permutations of 52 objects taken 5 at a time, is $_{52}P_5 = 52 \times 51 \times 50 \times 49 \times 48$.

Suppose instead of stopping after five cards, Barbara continues until the whole deck of 52 cards has been laid out in a sequence on the table. How many ways are there of doing this? There must be $52 \times 51 \times 50 \times 49 \times 48 \times \ldots 3 \times 2 \times 1$ ways, which can also be written $_{52}P_{52}$. Mathematicians have invented a compact notation for this series of multiplications. They use the exclamation point as a special mathematical symbol. They write 52! as an abbreviation for $52 \times 51 \times 50 \times 49 \times 48 \times \ldots 3 \times 2 \times 1$. Using this same notation, $2! = 2 \times 1$. $3! = 3 \times 2 \times 1$. $4! = 4 \times 3 \times 2 \times 1$. In general, for a positive integer n,

$$n! = n \times (n-1) \times (n-2) \times \ldots \times 2 \times 1.$$

In oral English, 3! is called "3 factorial," and $n!$ is "n factorial." The number of possible sequences of 52 playing cards is 52!, or "52 factorial." By convention, $1! = 1$ and $0! = 1$.[1]

Consider now

$$_{52}P_5 = 52 \times 51 \times 50 \times 49 \times 48$$

the number of permutations of 52 cards taken 5 at a time. We can multiply and divide it by $47 \times 46 \times \ldots \times 2 \times 1$ to obtain

$$_{52}P_5 = \frac{52 \times 51 \times 50 \times 49 \times 48 \times 47 \times 46 \times \ldots \times 2 \times 1}{47 \times 46 \times \ldots \times 2 \times 1}$$

Using the notation for factorials, this becomes

$$_{52}P_5 = \frac{52!}{47!}$$

In general, for nonnegative integers n and k,

$$_nP_k = \frac{n!}{(n-k)!}$$

---

[1] The specification that $0! = 1$ may seem strange to some people; it might seem more logical to make $0! = 0$. But there is a good reason for making $0! = 1$. With this definition, most of the formulations involving factorials, permutations, and combinations will still hold for cases involving a value of 0. To see the logic in having $0! = 1$, note first that for any integer n greater than 2, $n! = n \times (n-1)!$

$n!$ is composed of all the factors $n \times (n-1) \times \ldots \times 1$, and it is always the case that it has just one more factor n besides the factors $(n-1) \times (n-2) \times \ldots \times 1 = (n-1)!$. So $n! = n$ [one extra factor] $\times (n-1)!$ [including all the other factors]. Now let $n = 2$. The equation $n! = n \times (n-1)!$ becomes $2! = 2 \times (2-1)!$ Since $1! = 1$, this equation checks out. For $n = 1$, the equation $n! = n \times (n-1)!$ becomes $1! = 1 \times (1-1)! = 1 \times 0!$. If we want to have the equation hold for this value of n, only the definition $0! = 1$ will work.

Or we can write it out:

$$_nP_k = n \times (n - 1) \times (n - 2) \times \dots \times (n - k + 1)$$

Using permutations, we can solve some probability problems. What is the probability that Barbara will draw from the deck a royal flush, in such a way that the cards are in descending order of rank: ace, then king, queen, jack, and ten, all of one suit, and in that order? Since there are four suits (spades, hearts, diamonds, and clubs), there are only four possible outcomes that match that description. The total number of outcomes, as we have observed, is $52 \times 51 \times 50 \times 49 \times 48$. We assume, using the symmetry principle, that each outcome is equally likely. So the probability of producing a royal flush in the proper order is the number of ways of producing a favorable outcome (the royal flush in order), divided by the total number of outcomes. It is $4/(52 \times 51 \times 50 \times 49 \times 48)$, or 0.000000013, or 13 in a billion.

Consider another problem. Suppose we have 15 billiard balls labeled with the numbers 1–15. Suppose we draw them one at a time out of a bag, and lay them in order from left to right on a table. What is the probability that we will draw the balls 1, 2, and 3 in succession?

There is only one outcome that draws the balls 1, 2, and 3 in that order. The total number of possible outcomes is $15 \times 14 \times 13$ ($= {}_{15}P_3$). Using the symmetry principle, we infer that each of the possible outcomes is equally likely. So the probability of drawing balls 1, 2, and 3 in order is $1/(15 \times 14 \times 13) = 0.00037$.

What is the probability that we will draw three odd balls in succession? Out of 15 balls, there are 8 odd balls in all: 1, 3, 5, 7, 9, 11, 13, and 15. So there are 8 favorable possibilities for the first draw. There are only 7 favorable possibilities for the second draw, since the first draw has eliminated one odd ball by placing it on the table. And there are 6 favorable possibilities for the third draw. The total number of favorable outcomes is $8 \times 7 \times 6$ ($_8P_3$). The number of all possible outcomes (including the even balls) is $15 \times 14 \times 13$ (which is $_{15}P_3$). The probability of a favorable outcome is $_8P_3/_{15}P_3 = (8 \times 7 \times 6)/(15 \times 14 \times 13) = 0.123$.

COMBINATIONS

Now let us return to Barbara's situation, where she draws five cards in succession from a deck of 52 cards. Suppose that we no longer insist on having a particular order for the cards that she lays on the table. What is the probability that she will draw a royal flush, with the cards in any order (not just the order ace-king-queen-jack-ten)?

In Barbara's situation, how many different orders can there be for five cards? If we have specified which five cards are in the hand, the first card can be any of the five. The second card must then be any of the remaining four, for a total of 5×4 possible outcomes. The third card can be any of the remaining three, for a total of $5 \times 4 \times 3$ outcomes. The fourth card can be any of the remaining two, while the final card is forced, once the other cards have been chosen. The total number of outcomes is $5 \times 4 \times 3 \times 2 \times 1$, or $5!$ or $_5P_5$.

There are four ways of making a royal flush, one for each suit. For each suit, there are $5!$ arrangements of the sequence of cards. So the total number of favorable outcomes is $4 \times 5!$. These favorable outcomes occur within a total of $_{52}P_5$ possible permutations of the cards. So the probability of drawing a royal flush is $4 \times 5!/_{52}P_5 = (4 \times 5!)/(52 \times 51 \times 50 \times 49 \times 48)$.

Rather than asking how many distinct sequences there are ($_{52}P_5$), we can ask how many distinct *hands* there are, each composed of five cards, without regard to sequence. For each hand of five cards, there are $5!$ distinct sequences. So the number of hands will be the number of 5-card sequences ($_{52}P_5$), divided by $5!$:

hands of five cards each $= _{52}P_5/5!$

This value is called the number of *combinations* of 52 objects taken 5 at a time. The notation for combinations is $_{52}C_5$. In effect, a *combination* is a permutation where we no longer distinguish the order of the draw. $5!$ distinct sequences of cards are all counted as *one* hand of cards, once we no longer pay attention to the order in which the cards are drawn.

How do we calculate the number of hands? As we have just seen, the number of hands is the number $_{52}P_5$ of sequences, *divided by* the number $5!$, which is the number of distinct sequences that correspond to a single *hand*. We write

$_{52}C_5 = _{52}P_5/5! = 52!/[(52\text{-}5)!5!]$

In general, the number of combinations of n items taken k at a time is

$_nC_k = _nP_k/k! = n!/[(n - k)!k!]$

The number of five-card hands is $_{52}C_5$. The number of hands that are royal flushes is 4. The probability of a royal flush is the number of favorable outcomes divided by the total number of outcomes, or $4/_{52}C_5$.

Suppose we have a stripped deck of cards that contains only face cards (kings, queens, and jacks). There are twelve cards in all, four kings, four queens, and four jacks. How many distinct hands of five cards can we make up from such a deck?

As before, a "hand" of cards is considered the same no matter what the order of the five cards within the hand. So this case deals with combinations rather than permutations. The number of hands is the number of combinations of 12 objects taken 5 at a time: $_{12}C_5 = 12!/(7!5!) = (12 \times 11 \times 10 \times 9 \times 8)/(5 \times 4 \times 3 \times 2 \times 1) = 11 \times 9 \times 8 = 792$.

THE COIN TOSSING PROBLEM

Now we are ready to return to our earlier question about coin tossing. In a sequence of 8 tosses, how likely is it that heads will come up exactly 6 times? We have to look at this question from the right angle, if we are going to make the solution easy to obtain. Let us treat the result of each distinct coin toss as if it were a possible ball or card that we might pick. If we have 8 coin tosses in all, we get out 8 balls. We label the balls with numbers, 1 to 8, one ball for each distinct coin toss. Out of a total of 8 distinct balls, we now determine to select exactly 6 for special treatment. Those 6 will correspond to coin tosses that come up heads, while the other, unpicked balls will correspond to the coin tosses that come up tails. (See tables E.2a and E.2b, where we pick balls 1, 2, 4, 6, 7, and 8 in the first trial, and where we pick balls 1, 3, 4, 5, 6, and 7 in the second trial.)

Table E.2a: Balls 1, 2, 4, 6, 7, and 8 Picked in First Trial

coin tosses:	H	H	T	H	T	H	H	H
balls picked:	1	2		4		6	7	8

Table E.2b: Balls 1, 3, 4, 5, 6, and 7 Picked in Second Trial

coin tosses:	H	T	H	H	H	H	H	T
balls picked:	1		3	4	5	6	7	

If we reflect carefully on this situation, we can see that the correspondence is exact—it represents one more harmony in the world that God has made. For each selection of balls, there is exactly one pattern of 6 heads and 2 tails—and vice versa. So the total number of ways of coming up with exactly 6 heads is the same as the total number of combinations for picking 6 balls, out of a total of 8. That is, we need the number of combinations of 8 items taken 6 at a time, $_8C_6 = 8!/(6!2!) = (8 \times 7)/2 = 28$. The total number of distinct outcomes for all possible combinations of heads and tails is $2^8 = 256$. By the principle of symmetry, we assume that each of the outcomes is equally likely. So the probability of coming up with exactly 6 heads out of 8 tosses is 28 outcomes out of 256, or a probability of $28/256 = 0.11$.

What is the probability of coming up with exact 15 heads out of 20 tosses? The total number of outcomes is now $2^{20} = 1,048,576$. The number of combinations with 15 heads is $_{20}C_{15} = 20!/(5!15!) = (20 \times 19 \times 18 \times 17 \times 16)/(5 \times 4 \times 3 \times 2 \times 1) = 15,504$. The probability of achieving 15 heads is $15,504/1,048,576 = 0.015$.

The number of ways of coming up with exactly 10 heads out of 20 tosses is $20!/(10!10!) = (20 \times 19 \times 18 \times 17 \times 16 \times 15 \times 14 \times 13 \times 12 \times 11)/(10 \times 9 \times 8 \times 7 \times 6 \times 5 \times 4 \times 3 \times 2 \times 1) = 184,756$. The probability of one of these favorable outcomes, among the total of $1,048,576$ possible outcomes, is $184,756/1,048,576 = 0.176$.

We can see that when the total number of tosses is large, counting the combinations one by one would be exceedingly laborious. Once we understand the nature of the concepts of permutations and combinations, the calculations are simpler.

In all these cases, we must be careful to distinguish between the two concepts, permutations and combinations, and apply the right one in each circumstance. A hand of cards does not depend on the order of the cards within the hand, and so the appropriate concept is the concept of combinations. A "combination" is the *same* combination regardless of the order of the items within it. For a sequence of cards, where we care about the order of the sequence, the concept of permutation is the appropriate concept. For counting how many outcomes consisting in 20 tosses come out with 15 heads, the concept of combinations is appropriate. Why? When we translate the problem with coin tosses into the problem with picking numbered balls, we do not care which ball is picked first. The numbered labels on the balls are what lead to an exact correspondence with the coin tosses.

Now let us try another problem. If we roll a die 5 times, what is the probability that it will come up with four on top exactly twice?

First, what are the total number of outcomes? Each roll can result in any of six outcomes. As we add on an extra roll, it multiplies the total number of outcomes by six. For five die rolls, the total number of outcomes is therefore $6 \times 6 \times 6 \times 6 \times 6 = 6^5 = 7{,}776$. What is the number of outcomes with four on top on the first two tries, but not on the last three? There is only one choice for the first two tries. But for each of the last three tries, any one out of five choices will do (1, 2, 3, 5, or 6; only 4 is excluded). The total number of ways of having two fours and then three more tries with no four is $1 \times 1 \times 5 \times 5 \times 5 = 125$. But the situation where the first two outcomes have four on top is one of several combinations. There are a total of $_5C_2$ arrangements where the two fours will occur somewhere among the five rolls. So altogether there are $_5C_2 \times 125$ favorable outcomes. $_5C_2 = 5!/(3!2!) = 10$. So we have 1,250 favorable outcomes out of a total of 7,776. By symmetry, we infer that each outcome is equally probable. So the total probability of getting exactly two fours is $1{,}250/7{,}776 = 0.16$.

In all these cases we can observe a tight linkage between mathematics and the world. In the world we have coin flips, cards that we draw from a deck, and balls that we draw from a bag. We use mathematics to make calculations of the number of permutations, the number of combinations, and the probability of specific outcomes. God has ordained both the patterns of the world and the mathematics. The two match, because they go back to the original harmony in God's nature, and the derivative harmonies in his plan for the world. All these harmonies should stimulate our praise to God and admiration for his wisdom.

We can also appreciate harmonies within mathematics. There are many. Permutations and combinations are closely related to one another, according to the formula $_nC_k = {_nP_k}/k!$ Both are related to the fundamental properties of the factorial operation:

$$_nP_k = n!/(n-k)! = n \times (n-1) \times \ldots \times (n-k+1)$$

$$_nC_k = n!/[(n-k)!k!]$$

Praise God for harmony!

For another illustration, see the next appendix.

SAMPLE PROBLEMS

1. If you flip a coin four times in succession, what is the probability that exactly two of the flips will come up heads?

2. A high school basketball team has ten eligible players who come out for the game. Only five of these are active on the team at any one time. How many distinct teams can the coach make from his ten players? Now suppose that one player gets injured, and a second one cannot play because he has come down with the flu. How many possible teams can the coach make using the remaining eight players? (In this problem, we are ignoring the issue of whether different players are assigned to different positions on the team.)

3. Suppose Barbara uses a stripped-down deck of cards composed only of face cards (four kings, four queens, and four jacks). If she draws three cards, what is the probability that she will draw a hand of three queens?

APPENDIX F

THE BIRTHDAY PROBLEM

Many people have heard of the birthday problem: if 20 people are gathered together in one room, what is the chance that two of them will have the same birthday? Even if people have heard that the chance is about 1 in 2, they can hardly believe it. To untrained intuition, it seems as if the chance would be very low, maybe 1 in 10 or 1 in 30. We can treat this problem as another instance where naive intuition differs from the actual probability (compare appendix C). We can also see here a puzzle, where the challenge is partly to calculate the actual probability, and partly to explain why naive intuition does not match the calculated probability.

UNDERSTANDING THE PROBLEM

Let us first understand the problem in detail. We must include some assumptions about the situation. We assume that in the gathering of 20 people, there is no pair of twins. A pair of twins would radically change the probability. We also assume that there are 365 possible birthdays in all. We ignore the problem of leap years; we assume that no one out of the 20 was born on February 29. In addition, we assume that if we pick a person at random from the human population, each of the 365 days of the year is equally likely to be his birthday. This assumption is an idealization. It is not quite true, because more babies are conceived at certain times of the year than at others. For our purposes, slight variations of this kind can be ignored.

If we look carefully at the situation with 20 people, we can see that there are several possibilities: (1) no two people have the same birthday; (2) only one pair have the same birthday; (3) three people or more all have the very same birthday; (4) one pair share one birthday, and a second pair share a second birthday; (5) three pairs have three different shared birthdays; and so on. The number of different possibilities of this kind makes the situation complex. The original question about shared birthdays is usually intended to ask, "What is the chance that we would turn up *at least* one case where two people share the same birthday?" If we turn up more, or if we turn up a case where three or four people all have the very same birthday, the result is even more striking. But for our purposes we lump all these variations together, and ask for at least one case. By doing so, we are asking for the chance that any one of the options (2) through (5) and beyond would occur. This is equivalent to asking what is the chance that option (1) does *not* occur.

CALCULATING THE PROBABILITY

Our calculation will be far easier if we concentrate on option (1), where no two people have the same birthday. If the probability for no pairing is p, the probability of at least one pairing is $1 - p$, because of the principle for probabilities of complementary events. Either option (1) will hold, with probability p, or option (1) will not hold, with probability $1 - p$.

What then is the probability p that we will find no two people with a birthday in common? It is simpler if we go at the problem by stages. Suppose we have, not 20 people, but only one. There can be no pairing. If there are two people, a pairing exists only if the second person has a birthday on exactly one out of the 365 possible days, namely, the day already fixed by the inclusion of the first person. So the probability of a pairing is 1 out of 365, or 1/365. The probability that there will be no pairing is $1 - 1/365 = 364/365$.

Suppose, then, that we have no pairing after including the second person. When we include a third person, we will get a pairing of birthdays if the third person's birthday matches either the first person's or the second person's. Thus, the probability of a pairing is 2 out of 365, or 2/365. The probability of no pairing is $1 - 2/365 = 363/365$. Now the inclusion of the second person already took us down to a probability of 364/365. Out of all the cases of this kind, only 363/365 of them will have no pairing due to the third person. So the probability that we will have no pairing after including both the second person and the third is

$$(364/365) \times (363/365).$$

When we include a fourth person, there will be a pairing if the fourth person's birthday matches any of the three birthdays of the first three people. These three birthdays are distinct from one another, since we are now thinking only of the cases where we still have no pairing among the initial group of three. That is, we are thinking of $(364/365) \times (363/365)$ out of all the cases. For these cases, the fourth person's birthday will pair with one of the three in 3 cases out of 365 in all, for a probability of 3/365. The probability of no pairing is $1 - 3/365$ or 362/365. So the total probability for no pairing for a group of four people is

$$(364/365) \times (363/365) \times (362/365)$$

By now, we can see a pattern. The addition of a fifth person brings in an extra factor of (361/365), and the sixth person brings in a factor of (360/365). For 20 people, the probability of having no pairing at all is

$$(364/365) \times (363/365) \times (362/365) \times \ldots \times (347/365) \times (346/365)$$

A calculator shows that this is 0.589. The probability of having at least one matching pair is $1 - 0.58856 = 0.411$, which is below 1/2, but still close to 1/2. The tipping point comes if we increase the group to 23 people. The probability of having a match is then 0.507, a little more than 1/2. With 25 people, the probability of having a match goes up to 0.569. With 30 people, the probability of having a match is 0.706, or over 70% of the time. With 40 people, the probability of having a match is 0.891, or almost 9 out of 10!

A SECOND CALCULATION

We can use an alternate route to arrive at the same result. For a gathering of 20 people, how many possible alternatives are there for the selection of all of their birthdays? The first person may have a birthday on any of 365 days, for a total of 365 possible alternatives. For *each* of these alternatives, the second person may have a birthday on any of the 365 days. By the counting principle (appendix E), there are now 365×365 alternatives for the two people taken together. For three people, there are $365 \times 365 \times 365 = 365^3$ alternatives. For 20 people, there will be 365^{20} alternatives.

Out of all these alternatives, how many cases will there be where there are no matching pairs among the 20 people? For each of the 20 people, we must pick one birthday out of 365. But now there will be a total of 20 distinct birthdays that we must assign to the 20 people. The number of alternatives of this kind is the number of permutations of 365 objects taken 20 at a time. (Permutations are understood to take 20 *distinct* objects, with no repetitions.) The number is $_{365}P_{20} = 365!/(365 - 20)!$ The probability of getting one of these alternatives with no matching pair, out of 365^{20} total alternatives, is then

$$_{365}P_{20}/365^{20},$$

or

$$(365 \times 364 \times 363 \times \dots \times 346)/(365 \times 365 \times 365 \times \dots \times 365)$$

If we cancel out the first factor of 365 in both the numerator and denominator, and then pair the subsequent factors in the numerator with those in the denominator, we get

$$(364/365) \times (363/365) \times (362/365) \times \dots \times (346/365),$$

which is exactly the same series of fractions that we had earlier.

As usual, the harmony between these two approaches to obtaining the probability is a harmony ordained by the God of harmony.

WHY IS INTUITION WRONG?

We can also ask, "Why is the ordinary intuition of most people at odds with the calculated probability?" We cannot be sure of all the reasons. But one influence may be a false analogy with previous experiences with birthdays. A single individual, say, Carol, finds that if she meets 19 different people, the probability that at least one of them will have the same birthday as Carol is small. The probability that the first one will not have the same birthday is 364/365. The probability that the first two will both not have the same birthday as Carol is $(364/365)^2$. The probability that all 19 will not have the same birthday is $(364/365)^{19} = 0.949$. So the probability of at least one having the same birthday is the probability of the region complementary to 0.949, which is $1 - 0.949$ or 0.051—quite small. Even if Carol tries 50 people, the probability will still be small—0.128. It is easy to carry this kind of experience over into the setting of a different type, where we are interested not only in whether we can pair up Carol's birthday, but in whether we might be able to pair up any other two people within the group of 20.

As we have said, the probability for Carol finding a match with one out of 19 others is only 0.051. But the inclusion of many other possible pairings has the effect of steadily increasing this initially small probability. There are $_{20}C_2$ distinct possible pairings of 20 people, where $_{20}C_2 = (20 \times 19)/2 = 190$. That is, there are 190 possible pairs that might prove to share a birthday. Moreover, if we meet a case where the first 19 people have no matched pairs, there are already 19 distinct birthdays among the 19 people. The 20th person must have a birthday distinct from all 19 of the previous ones. So the number of available birthdays steadily diminishes as we continue to add more people to the group. The joint effect of these group interactions brings the probability down to 1/2 by the time we reach a group size of 23 people.

God's consistency is the foundation for why we can apply the reasoning of permutations and combinations to the birthday problem.

DISEASES AND OTHER CAUSES

We can use conditional probabilities to help us in dealing with cases where we want to infer a cause from its effect.

A MEDICAL TEST

Consider an example. Roberta takes a blood test to determine whether she has cancer of the liver. The lab knows that the test is 99% accurate in detecting cancer. That is, if a patient has cancer of the liver, the test will be positive in 99% of the cases, but will give a false negative in 1% of these cases. In addition, if a patient does *not* have liver cancer, the test will give a false positive in 2% of the cases. (In these cases, the test will correctly indicate 98% of the time that the patient does not have liver cancer.) The test comes back positive in Roberta's case, so she is worried.

Roberta asks more questions. Her doctor tells her that for people like her in the general population, the probability of having liver cancer is only 1 out of 100,000, or 0.00001. Given these facts, how likely is it that Roberta has liver cancer? How likely is it that the test is a false positive?

Many people might naively think that Roberta has a 99% chance of having liver cancer. After all, the test is right 99% of the time in positively detecting cancer when it is there. But this reasoning is fallacious. To see why, we have to consider the possibility that the test has given a false positive. The test gives a false positive result in only 2% of the cases where people do not have liver cancer. But if the test is applied to thousands of people in the general population, there will be quite a few false positives—about 20 out of every 1,000 people. All in all, there will be more false positives than true positives, because true positives will come up only in the unusual case where the person being tested does happen to have cancer of the liver.

This case with Roberta is one example where we want to reason backwards from an effect to a possible cause. The effect in this case is the positive test result. One of the possible causes is that Roberta has cancer. But there is another possible cause, namely, that the test is an instance of a false positive. Which cause is the right one? What are the probabilities?

CALCULATING THE PROBABILITY OF A CAUSE

So how do we calculate the probability for Roberta? We have to deal with conditional probability. The relevant probability, the one that matters for Roberta, is the probability that she has liver cancer, given the fact that the test has come up positive. Let C be the event that Roberta has liver cancer. Let T be the event that the test comes up positive. Roberta wants to know $P(C \mid T)$.

We do not yet know the value of $P(C \mid T)$. But we do know some other probabilities. For example, $P(C) = 0.00001$. That is, before any test is done, the probability that a person such as Roberta has liver cancer is 0.00001. We also know that $P(T \mid C) = 0.99$. The test will come up positive (T) in 0.99 of the cases when, as a condition, we already know that there is liver cancer (C). If "not-T" is the event where the test comes up negative, $P(\text{not-}T \mid C) = 0.01$. This value takes care of the false negatives. $P(T \mid \text{not-}C) = 0.02$, which expresses the chance of having a false positive result from the test.

By the general equation defining conditional probability (see chapter 19),

$$P(C \mid T) = P(C \text{ and } T)/P(T).$$

Can we calculate both $P(C \text{ and } T)$ and $P(T)$?

Let us begin with $P(C \text{ and } T)$. $P(C \text{ and } T)$ is the probability that Roberta has cancer and that the test comes out positive. This is the same as the probability that Roberta has liver cancer as a part of the general population $(P(C))$ multiplied by the probability that the test comes out positive, given that she has cancer. That is,

$$P(C \text{ and } T) = P(T \mid C) \times P(C),$$

according to the equation defining conditional probability $P(T \mid C)$. We know that $P(T \mid C) = 0.99$, and $P(C) = 0.00001$. So $P(C \text{ and } T) = 0.0000099$.

Now we need to calculate $P(T)$, the probability that the test comes out positive. Consider a population of 100,000 people, one of whom has liver cancer. In the one case with liver cancer, the test will come out positive 0.99 of the time. In the other 99,999 cases the test will produce a false positive 0.02 of the time, for a total of $0.02 \times 99,999 = 1,999.98$ cases. The total number of positives is $0.99 + 1,999.98 = 2,000.97$. Since there are a total of 100,000 cases, the probability of a positive test is $2,000.97/100,000$ or about $2/100$. This is the value of $P(T)$.

Finally, $P(C \mid T) = P(C \text{ and } T)/P(T) = 0.0000099/(2/100) = 0.0005$. Despite the bad news, Roberta still has only 0.05% chance of actually having liver cancer.

A GENERAL RELATIONSHIP

We can generalize, based on the example with Roberta. Note that in general $P(A \mid B)$ is not the same as $P(B \mid A)$. $P(A \mid B)$ is the probability that A will occur, once we know that B has occurred. $P(B \mid A)$ is the probability that B will occur, once we know that A has occurred. We can illustrate the difference using a situation with a red and a white die. If A is the probability of the white die coming up 2 and B is the probability that the sum of the white and red die is 5, $P(A \mid B)$ is 1/4, as calculated in chapter 19. $P(B \mid A)$ is the probability that the sum will be 5, once we know that the white die has come up 2. There are six possible outcomes from rolling the red die, and only one, namely when the red die comes up 3, leads to a sum of 5. So that probability $P(\text{sum-of-5} \mid \text{white-2}) = 1/6$.

Though the two probabilities $P(A \mid B)$ and $P(B \mid A)$ are in general different, there is a relationship between them. The fundamental property $P(A \& B) = P(A \mid B) \times P(B)$ enables us to obtain an additional equation. $P(A \& B) = P(A \mid B) \times P(B)$ and also $P(A \& B) = P(B \mid A) \times P(A)$ (by interchanging the roles of A and B). Equating the two,

$$P(A \mid B) \times P(B) = P(B \mid A) \times P(A).$$

If $P(B)$ is not 0,

$$P(A \mid B) = P(B \mid A) \times P(A)/P(B).$$

RETHINKING THE CASE WITH ROBERTA

If we substitute C for A and T for B, we are back with the problem with Roberta that we just considered:

$$P(C \mid T) = P(T \mid C) \times P(C)/P(T).$$

$P(C \mid T)$ is the probability in which Roberta is interested. $P(T \mid C)$ corresponds to the 99% reliability of the test in positive detection of cancer. $P(C)$ is the probability of liver cancer in the general population. The only probability that is more difficult to obtain is $P(T)$, the total probability of a positive result, which might arise either from a true positive or a false positive.

We can divide the problem of obtaining $P(T)$ by calculating separately the probability of a true positive and the probability of a false positive. The true positive is represented by

$$P(T \text{ and } C) = P(T \mid C) \times P(C),$$

which is the probability $P(C)$ of cancer in the general population times the probability of the test producing the true positive from a cancerous sample $(P(T \mid C))$.

The false positive is represented by

$$P(T \text{ and not-}C) = P(T \mid \text{not-}C) \times P(\text{not-}C),$$

which is the probability $P(\text{not-}C)$ of not having cancer in the general population, multiplied by the probability of getting a false positive from a noncancerous sample. The total probability $P(T)$ is simply the sum of the mutually exclusive alternatives of a true positive and a false positive:

$$P(T) = P(T \text{ and } C) + P(T \text{ and not-}C) = P(T \mid C) \times P(C) + P(T \mid \text{not-}C) \times P(\text{not-}C).$$

This results in a calculation almost identical to what we already did:

$$P(T) = 0.99 \times 0.00001 + 0.02 \times 0.99999$$
$$= 0.0000099 + 0.0199998 = 0.02 \text{ (when rounded)}$$

$$P(C \mid T) = P(T \mid C) \times P(C)/P(T) = 0.99 \times 0.00001/0.02 = 0.0005.$$

FINDING A CAUSE IN THE GENERAL CASE

In the general case, with conditional probabilities A and B,

$$P(A \mid B) = P(B \mid A) \times P(A)/P(B).$$

If we are reasoning back from an effect B to a possible cause A, we will be able to obtain a value $P(B \mid A)$ based on how frequently the cause A produces effect B. We will be able to obtain $P(A)$ by knowing the general frequency of the cause A. $P(B)$ will be more difficult, because of the problem with false positives and false negatives. We divide it up into two cases, where B accompanies A and where B accompanies not-A.

$$P(B) = P((B \text{ and } A) \text{ or } (B \text{ and not-}A)) = P(B \text{ and } A) + P(B \text{ and not-}A)$$
$$= P(B \mid A) \times P(A) + P(B \mid \text{not-}A) \times P(\text{not-}A).$$

Putting everything together,

$$P(A \mid B) = P(B \mid A) \times P(A)/P(B)$$
$$= P(B \mid A) \times P(A)/[P(B \mid A) \times P(A) + P(B \mid \text{not-}A) \times P(\text{not-}A)].$$

This formula enables us easily to find the probability of a cause A when we know only an effect B.

We can generalize another step if we consider more than one possible cause for the effect B. Suppose we have possible causes A_1, A_2, A_3, ... , and A_n. We assume that these causes are mutually exclusive: for $i \neq j$, $P(A_i$ and $A_j) = 0$. Together, they make up the entire set of probabilities:

$$P(A_1) + P(A_2) + \ldots + P(A_n) = 1.$$

When we have observed effect B, we want to know the probability that one particular cause, namely A_1, is the cause that has led to B. How do we do it?

The total probability $P(B)$ of B is the sum of the mutually exclusive probabilities where B occurs together with each one of the A's:

$$P(B) = P((B \text{ and } A_1) \text{ or } (B \text{ and } A_2) \text{ or } \ldots \text{ or } (B \text{ and } A_n))$$
$$= P(B \text{ and } A_1) + P(B \text{ and } A_2) + \ldots + P(B \text{ and } A_n)$$
$$= P(B \mid A_1) \times P(A_1) + P(B \mid A_2) \times P(A_2) + \ldots + P(B \mid A_n) \times P(A_n)$$

So

$$P(A_1 \mid B) = P(B \mid A_1) \times P(A_1)/P(B)$$

$$= P(B \mid A_1) \times P(A_1)/[P(B \mid A_1) \times P(A_1) + P(B \mid A_2) \times P(A_2) + \ldots +$$
$$P(B \mid A_n) \times P(A_n)]$$

This formula (called *Bayes's theorem*) enables us to obtain a probability $P(A_1 \mid B)$, which represents reasoning backwards from an effect B to cause A_1. We obtain this probability using only (1) probabilities $P(A_i)$ having to do with causes and (2) probabilities $P(B \mid A_i)$ that move from cause (A_i) to effect (B). This formula is therefore valuable in many situations where we are trying to estimate the probability of a particular causal explanation.

AN INVESTIGATION OF A DEFECT

Consider another example. A company has four suppliers, Alpha, Beta, Gamma, and Delta, from which it can obtain a particular part that it uses in its manufacturing. Because of variations in the price of parts and the availability of parts from the four suppliers, the company uses all four suppliers from time to time. The probabilities of using the four suppliers for any one purchase are 0.1 (for supplier Alpha), 0.2 (for Beta), 0.3 (for Gamma), and 0.4 (for Delta). The probability of company Alpha supplying a defective part is 0.05. The probabilities for companies Beta, Gamma, and Delta are 0.01, 0.005, and 0.02, respectively. Given that a defective part has just arrived, what is the probability that it came from supplier Beta?

This problem is another case where we are reasoning from an effect (a defective part) back to a cause (which supplier is at fault?). The key event is the arrival of a defective part. We will label this event B. The probabilities concerning defects that we supplied in the preceding paragraph are conditional probabilities. The probability of B, given that the part came from supplier Alpha, is 0.05. That is, $P(B \mid A_a) = 0.05$, where A_a represents the event that the part came from supplier Alpha. Likewise, $P(B \mid A_b) = 0.01$ for supplier Beta, $P(B \mid A_g) = 0.005$ for supplier Gamma, and $P(B \mid A_d) = 0.02$ for supplier Delta. $P(A_a) = 0.1$ is the probability that the part came from supplier Alpha, before we know whether the part is defective or not.

We use the formula that we have already developed in order to obtain the probability $P(A_b \mid B)$ that the part came from supplier Beta:

$$P(A_b \mid B) = P(B \mid A_b) \times P(A_b)/P(B)$$
$$= P(B \mid A_b) \times P(A_b)/[P(B \mid A_a) \times P(A_a) + P(B \mid A_b) \times P(A_b) + P(B \mid A_g) \times P(A_g) + P(B \mid A_d) \times P(A_d)]$$

$$= 0.01 \times 0.2/[0.05 \times 0.1 + 0.01 \times 0.2 + 0.005 \times 0.3 + 0.02 \times 0.4]$$
$$= 0.002/0.0165 = 0.12.$$

Likewise, the probability that the part came from Alpha is

$$P(B \mid A_a) \times P(A_a)/P(B) = 0.05 \times 0.1/0.0165 = 0.30.$$

The probabilities for the part coming from Gamma and Delta are

$$P(B \mid A_g) \times P(A_g)/P(B) = 0.005 \times 0.3/0.0165 = 0.09 \text{ and}$$
$$P(B \mid A_d) \times P(A_d)/P(B) = 0.02 \times 0.4/0.0165 = 0.48.$$

The laws for conditional probabilities allow an exact calculation. As usual, the calculation relies on regularities established by God in the realm of chance events and probability. We also rely on these regularities in more informal ways, whenever we try to determine the probable cause for an event. Criminal investigations, scientific investigations, medical tests, and repair work (for autos, computers, washing machines, etc.) frequently rely on these regularities that God has ordained in his wisdom.

PROOFS FOR PROBABILITY

In chapter 25 we described the three postulates that are normally used for the mathematical theory of probability. Here we provide proofs for three of the theorems.

CALCULATING THE PROBABILITY OF A COMPLEMENT

The following theorem provides a way for calculating the probability of the complement of an event A.

Theorem 1: $P(A^c) = 1 - P(A)$ and $P(A) = 1 - P(A^c)$.

Proof: The complement A^c can be defined as the unique set such that (1) it is disjoint from A (nonoverlapping with A; $A^c \cap A = \emptyset$) and (2) its union with A is the entire sample space S: $A^c \cup A = S$. Since S is the entire space, $P(S) = 1$ (postulate 3). Since $A^c \cup A = S$, $P(A^c \cup A) = 1$. Since $A^c \cap A = \emptyset$, we can apply the postulate of additivity, and $P(A^c \cup A) = P(A^c) + P(A)$. Since we saw that $P(A^c \cup A) = 1$, $1 = P(A^c) + P(A)$. Subtracting $P(A)$ from both sides,

$P(A^c) = 1 - P(A)$.

Similarly, if we subtract $P(A^c)$ from both sides of the equation $P(A^c) + P(A) = 1$, we obtain

$P(A) = 1 - P(A^c)$.

PROBABILITIES FOR LARGER SETS

A second theorem shows that if we increase the size of a set, the probability does not decrease.

Theorem 2: If A is a subset of B, $P(A) \leq P(B)$.

Proof: The set B is composed of A plus that part of B that is not in A, that is $B \cap A^c$. We can check this using a spatial diagram (see fig. H.1).

Fig. H.1: B and A and Complement of A

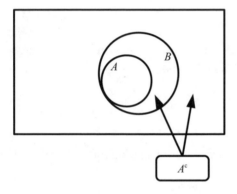

So $B = A \cup (B \cap A^c)$. The two regions A and $B \cap A^c$ are disjoint, so the probabilities add:

$P(B) = P(A) + P(B \cap A^c)$.

By postulate 1, $P(B \cap A^c) \geq 0$. Adding $P(A)$ to both sides of the inequality,

$P(A) + P(B \cap A^c) \geq P(A)$.

Since $P(B) = P(A) + P(B \cap A^c)$, it follows that $P(B) \geq P(A)$, which was to be proved.

Theorem 3: For any two subsets A and B of S,

$$P(A \cup B) = P(A) + P(B) - P(A \cap B).$$

Proof: The set $A \cup B$ is composed of three distinct disjoint sets, $A \cap B^c$, $A \cap B$, and $A^c \cap B$ (see fig. H.2).

Fig. H.2: A Union B Divided into Three

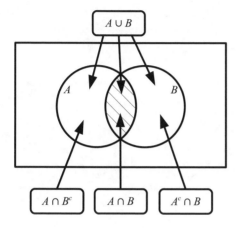

By additivity (postulate 2),

$$P(A \cup B) = P(A \cap B^c) + P(A \cap B) + P(A^c \cap B).$$

Since the two areas $A \cap B^c$ and $A \cap B$ are disjoint and together make up the region A,

$$P(A \cap B^c) + P(A \cap B) = P((A \cap B^c) \cup (A \cap B)) = P(A)$$

Plugging this into the previous equality, we get

$$P(A \cup B) = P(A) + P(A^c \cap B).$$

The two areas $A \cap B$ and $A^c \cap B$ together make up the region B.

$$P(A \cap B) + P(A^c \cap B) = P((A \cap B) \cup (A^c \cap B)) = P(B).$$

Subtracting $P(A \cap B)$ from both sides,

$$P(A^c \cap B) = P(B) - P(A \cap B).$$

When we plug this in to

$$P(A \cup B) = P(A) + P(A^c \cap B)$$

we get

$$P(A \cup B) = P(A) + P(B) - P(A \cap B),$$

which proves the theorem.

APPENDIX I

STATISTICS

Statistics depend on ideas related to probability and randomness. We cannot enter into the details here, but we will illustrate the relevance of probability to understanding two basic ideas in statistics, the idea of a *mean* and the idea of variation from the mean.

THE MEAN

Suppose that we want to find out about the annual income of U.S. residents. There is too much information to digest easily. So we can talk about the *average* income. The word *mean* is used as a more precise expression for the idea of an average. The *mean* annual income of U.S. residents is the sum of all their incomes, divided by the number of residents. Rather than getting information from every person, we can take a random sample of people. If the sample is reasonably large and unbiased, we can sum all the incomes from people in the sample, and then divide by the total number of people in the sample to obtain the mean.

Similarly, if we inquire about the age of people in the sample, the *mean* age or average age is the sum of the ages of all the individuals, divided by the number of individuals.

Questions about mean or average values crop up frequently when people want a general picture of a population or a large sample. That is why we have reports about average age, average income, average working hours, average taxes, average body weight, and so on.

VARIANCE AND STANDARD DEVIATION

More complex analyses also use the concept of *variance*. If the mean age of people in a population is m, the *variance* is defined to be the mean or average of $(A - m)^2$ where A represents the age of any one individual. For example, if the average age is 30 and a particular individual is 35, the contribution of that individual to the variance is $(35 - 30)^2 = 5^2 = 25$.

Now the values for age cluster around the mean value m, with m being a kind of "center." So any individual age A will sometimes take values greater than m, and sometimes values less than m. Therefore, the quantity $A - m$, which represents the difference in age A from the mean m, may be either positive or negative, depending on the value that A takes in a particular case. However, whether $A - m$ is positive or negative, $(A - m)^2$ is always positive (multiplying a negative number by itself always results in a positive number: $-3 \times -3 = 9$). So every instance where A deviates at all from the mean value m will be counted positively in calculating the variance.

The variance is therefore a measure of the dispersion of the values of age around the mean. How widely dispersed from the mean are these values, on the average? Statisticians also use the concept of *standard deviation*, defined as the square root of the variance.

The meaning of the standard deviation is easier to interpret than the meaning of variance, because it has the same units of measurement as does the original quantity being measured. For example, if we are measuring the income of a sample person in the United States, measured in dollars, the mean income is also measured in dollars, let us say $20,000 per year. The variance will be in units of dollars-squared, which is awkward; but the standard deviation will be in dollars. If the standard deviation were $3, it would mean that almost everyone had an income very close to $20,000. If the standard deviation were $10,000, it would mean that quite a few of the people had incomes ranging much more widely, from $10,000 or less to $30,000 or more.

Since some of the people in the United States are children, a better indicator might be household income. The standard deviation from the mean household income may be an indication of how much of a gap there is (again, on the average) between poorer and richer households.

STATISTICS AND SAMPLES

Whenever statistics are compiled from samples rather than from a complete analysis of everyone in a population, they rely on probability. The sample is supposed to be a *random* sample, and the probability of picking one person to be part of the sample is supposed to be the same as the probability for any other person.

Once the statistics are compiled, more probabilities can be estimated using them. If we have statistics for the age of a population, we can talk about the probability that a randomly chosen person is older than 50 years. Using statistics for income, we can talk about the probability of a sample household having an income less than $15,000. In many practical cases, statistics and probabilities are closely related.

GOD'S PROVISION

The use of statistics frequently involves averages such as what we have seen. It therefore depends on the wisdom of God and the sustaining power of God. It is God who also enables us as human beings made in his image to do calculations that give us information about large populations, without overwhelming us with the details for each person or each household or each biological cell or each molecule or each flip of a coin. Praise the Lord for this provision, among all the others.

> For he [God] makes his sun rise on the evil and on the good, and sends rain on the just and on the unjust. (Matt. 5:45)

THE LAW OF LARGE NUMBERS VERSUS GAMBLERS

The law of large numbers is a statement about what happens with a large number of trials of the same random experiment, like flipping a coin. Roughly speaking, it says that, as the number of trials increases, the proportion of outcomes that come up in one particular way becomes, on the average, closer to the theoretical probability. For coin tossing, assuming a fair (unbiased) coin, the proportion of heads approaches 1/2, as does the proportion of tails. Similarly, for an unbiased die, the proportion of outcomes with four coming up approaches 1/6. For example, if we flip a coin 10,000 times, and it comes up heads 5,033 times, the proportion of heads is 5,033/10,000 = 0.5033, which is close to 0.5 or 1/2, the expected proportion of heads.

Establishing the law of large numbers requires some mathematical reasoning. Readers who do not care to pursue it may rest content with the knowledge that the conclusions about the results of repeated trials are mathematically sound.

TWO FORMS OF THE LAW OF LARGE NUMBERS

The law of large numbers takes two forms, called *the weak law of large numbers* and *the strong law of large numbers*. Let us explain them. Suppose that we pick a small real number or fraction d—let us say 0.01 or 1/100. This number will represent the margin of deviation that we will allow, between the expected proportion of heads (namely 1/2) and the actual result of conducting many trials. We want to know if the outcome of many trials will give us a resulting proportion of heads that is within the margin d of the expected value of $1/2 = 0.5$. We are then asking whether the actual outcome of the trials results in a proportion of heads somewhere between $0.5 - 0.01$ (= 0.49) and $0.5 + 0.01$ (= 0.51). For example, if the actual result of the trials is a proportion of heads that is 0.5033, is the difference between 0.5033 and 1/2 less than d? The difference is $0.5033 - 0.5 = 0.0033$, which is less than $d = 0.01$.

The *weak* law of large numbers says that, no matter how small a number d we pick to begin with, we can always find a sufficiently large number n, whether it be 10,000 or 100,000 or even larger, such that the result of conducting n trials is very likely to be a value within the margin d of deviation from the expected proportion of 1/2. The *strong* law of large numbers says that we can pick a number n large enough so that, not only from a series of n trials, but from a series that extends beyond n, it is very likely that the series will never, beyond the point n, develop an average result more than the margin d of allowable deviation.[1] Proofs of these laws can be found in textbooks on probability.

THE LAW OF LARGE NUMBERS VERSUS THE GAMBLER'S FALLACY

How can the law of large numbers be consistent with the gambler's fallacy, discussed in appendix A? After a run of six or seven cases of odd numbers on the roulette wheel, or six or seven successive coin flips coming up heads, many gamblers are prone to think that surely the opposite outcome is more likely to come up on the next spin of the wheel or the next flip of the coin. But, as discussed in appendix A, they are wrong. The probability of an odd number coming up on a roulette wheel is still 18/37 (if we count in the existence of a 37th pocket, the zero pocket), and the probability of heads is still 1/2. The next spin of the roulette wheel or the next flip of the coin is probabilistically independent of the previous spins or flips.

How can this situation be consistent with the law of large numbers? The law of large numbers says that the average frequency of heads will

---

[1] For a more precise formulation of the strong law, see, for example, Eric Weisstein, "Strong Law of Large Numbers," mathworld.wolfram.com/StrongLawofLargeNumbers.html, accessed January 19, 2012.

get closer to 0.5 with more trials, and the average frequency of odd on a roulette wheel will get closer to 18/37. The gambler's fallacy reads this law as if the roulette wheel had a "memory" of previous outcomes, and that the wheel actively "tried" to balance out the frequency. But it does not. The roulette wheel remembers nothing. Suppose it has come up odd seven times in a row. The frequency of odd, averaged over those seven times, is 1. But there remain 10,000 spins in the future. In principle, we can contemplate 1,000,000 spins. On each of those spins, the probability of odd is 18/37. The contribution to the average made by all the other outcomes eventually "drowns out" the contribution to an average made by the first seven spins. It is the huge number of future spins, not an active tendency to "balance out" past deviations, that eventually results in an average close to 18/37.

Let us consider an example with coin flips. The first seven flips come up heads, let us say. If we calculate the frequency on the basis of these seven trials, the frequency of heads is now exactly 7/7 = 1. But the expected frequency is 0.5. There is a very noticeable "bias," if that is what we want to call it.

Suppose the next 93 flips come up 47 heads and 46 tails. The total number of heads is now 7 (from the first 7 flips) plus 47 (from the next 93 flips), for a total of 54 heads. The frequency of heads is 54/100 = 0.54, which is already getting comfortably close to the theoretical expected value of 0.5.

Suppose the next 9,900 flips come up 4,962 heads and 4,938 tails. For the first 10,000 trials, we now have 7 + 47 + 4,962 = 5,016 heads and 4,984 tails. The average frequency from 10,000 trials is 5016/10,000 = 0.5016. The average frequency is obviously getting close to the expected frequency of 0.5. But there is no need for a memory or an active "interference" with the new flips, in order to force the process to even out. A close approach to the expected frequency comes about, not from an innate tendency to "balance out" the past, but from the fact that a sufficient number of future trials will overwhelm by their numbers any temporary "bias" at the beginning.

"But," says an objector, "how do we know that the same biased pattern of 7 successive heads will not occur later on?" Well, it could. In fact, if we undertake to have a sufficient number of flips, the same pattern will almost certainly occur again at some point. The chance of 7 successive heads is 1/128. So in the course of one million flips, it will reoccur not once but about 1,000,000/128 = 7,812.5 times. But the same is true for the occurrence of 7 successive tails. To keep a bias in place, the pattern of 7 successive heads would have to recur at a higher frequency than normal, and it would have to maintain that deviant frequency all the way through the million flips. The probability of maintaining such a higher frequency of average occurrence goes down as the number of flips increases.

The law of large numbers is rightly termed the law of *large* numbers, with emphasis on the word *large*. The law talks about what will happen, not with the next few flips, but with a sufficiently large sample, which may run into the millions or billions or billions of billions, depending on how close an approach to the expected frequency we desire to obtain. And even with billions of billions of coin flips, there is no absolute guarantee that the actual frequency of heads will be near 0.5. All we can say is that a small deviation d from the expected frequency has a high probability. How high is the probability depends, as usual, on the number d and the number of trials n over which we average.

WONDER

The law of large numbers is a wonderful result. The randomness in the outcome of any one event does not disappear when we consider a large number of identically structured events (such as a long sequence of coin flips). In a sense, the randomness increases, because the number of distinct possibilities for the outcomes from all the events taken together increases exponentially with the number of events. For example, if a single event can have two possible outcomes, the number of possible sequences of outcomes for n events of the same type is 2^n.

At the same time, the *average* for many events settles down as the number n of events increases. Not only does it settle down, but with large enough n the probability of significant deviation from the expected average can be made as small as we like. It is a marvelous regularity arising out of a random base.

COHERENCE FROM GOD

In all this reasoning we depend on the thorough coherence between mathematical reasoning on one side and physical realities on the other. Coin flips, dice rolls, and numbers expressing probabilities go together. Reasoning with numbers leads to conclusions that hold true for coin flips and dice rolls. God has specified this wide-ranging coherence. He specifies the inner coherence in the mathematics, the coherence in repeated coin flips, and the coherence linking the two areas. He specifies harmonies in the world in imitation of the harmony that originates in him. His character is harmonious, and the persons of the Trinity are in harmony with one another. The numerical aspect of this world has its original in the one God in three persons in the Trinity. The physical behavior of coins and dice has its origin in the providential word of God governing chance events. The two cohere in God.

BIBLIOGRAPHY

Ash, Robert B. *Basic Probability Theory*. Mineola, NY: Dover, 2008.

Bertsekas, Dimitri P., and John N. Tsitsiklis. *Introduction to Probability*. Belmont, MA: Athena Scientific, 2002.

Blanchard, John. *Right with God: A Straightforward Book to Help Those Searching for Personal Faith in God*. Edinburgh/Carlisle, PA: Banner of Truth, 1985.

Collins, C. John. *Genesis 1–4: A Linguistic, Literary, and Theological Commentary*. Phillipsburg, NJ: Presbyterian & Reformed, 2006.

———. *Science & Faith: Friends or Foes?* Wheaton, IL: Crossway, 2003.

Eagle, Antony. *Philosophy of Probability: Contemporary Readings*. London: Routledge, 2010.

Ellis, George F. R. "Does the Multiverse Really Exist?" *Scientific American* 305/2 (August 2011): 38–43.

Frame, John M. *The Doctrine of the Christian Life*. Phillipsburg, NJ: Presbyterian & Reformed, 2008.

———. *The Doctrine of God*. Phillipsburg, NJ: Presbyterian & Reformed, 2002.

———. *The Doctrine of the Knowledge of God*. Phillipsburg, NJ: Presbyterian & Reformed, 1987.

———. *The Doctrine of the Word of God*. Phillipsburg, NJ: Presbyterian & Reformed, 2010.

———. *Perspectives on the Word of God: An Introduction to Christian Ethics*. Eugene, OR: Wipf & Stock, 1999.

Galavotti, Maria Carla. *Philosophical Introduction to Probability*. Stanford, CA: Center for the Study of Language and Information, 2005.

Hájek, Alan. "Interpretations of Probability." In *The Stanford Encyclopedia of Philosophy (Winter 2011 Edition)*. Edited by Edward N. Zalta. http://plato

.stanford.edu/archives/win2011/entries/probability-interpret/. Accessed January 18, 2012.

Hartley, Andrew M. *Christian and Humanist Foundations for Statistical Inference: Religious Control of Statistical Paradigms*. Eugene, OR: Resource Publications, 2008.

Hilgevoord, Jan, and Jos Uffink. "The Uncertainty Principle." In *The Stanford Encyclopedia of Philosophy (Spring 2011 Edition)*. Edited by Edward N. Zalta. http://plato.stanford.edu/archives/spr2011/entries/qt-uncertainty/. Accessed January 5, 2012.

Hodge, Archibald A., and Benjamin B. Warfield. *Inspiration*. Grand Rapids, MI: Baker, 1979.

Huff, Darrell. *How to Take a Chance*. Illustrated by Irving Geis. New York: W. W. Norton, 1959.

Keller, Timothy. *The Reason for God: Belief in an Age of Skepticism*. New York: Dutton, 2008.

Mellor, D. H. *Probability: A Philosophical Introduction*. London: Routledge, 2005.

Oliphint, K. Scott. *Reasons (for Faith): Philosophy in the Service of Theology*. Phillipsburg, NJ: Presbyterian & Reformed, 2006.

Packer, J. I. *A Grief Sanctified: Through Sorrow to Eternal Hope*. Wheaton, IL: Crossway, 2002.

———. *Knowing God*. Downers Grove, IL: InterVarsity Press, 1993.

Plantinga, Alvin. *Where the Conflict Really Lies: Science, Religion, and Naturalism*. Oxford: Oxford University Press, 2011.

Poythress, Vern S. *In the Beginning Was the Word: Language—A God-Centered Approach*. Wheaton, IL: Crossway, 2006.

———. *Logic: A God-Centered Approach to the Foundation of Western Thought*. Wheaton, IL: Crossway, 2013.

———. *Redeeming Science: A God-Centered Approach*. Wheaton, IL: Crossway, 2006.

———. *Redeeming Sociology: A God-Centered Approach*. Wheaton, IL: Crossway, 2009.

———. *Symphonic Theology: The Validity of Multiple Perspectives in Theology*. Grand Rapids, MI: Zondervan, 1987. Reprint. Phillipsburg, NJ: Presbyterian & Reformed, 2001.

Rumsey, Deborah. *Probability for Dummies*. Hoboken, NJ: Wiley, 2006.

Schrödinger, Erwin. "The Present Situation in Quantum Mechanics: A Translation of Schrödinger's 'Cat Paradox Paper,'" trans. John D. Trimmer, http://www.tu-harburg.de/rzt/rzt/it/QM/cat.html. Accessed July 19, 2011. Originally published in *Proceedings of the American Philosophical Society* 124 (1980): 323–338.

Sproul, R. C. *Not a Chance: The Myth of Chance in Modern Science and Cosmology*. Grand Rapids, MI: Baker, 1994.

———. *When Worlds Collide: Where Is God?* Wheaton, IL: Crossway, 2002.

Spurgeon, Charles H. *Morning and Evening: Daily Readings*. McLean, VA: MacDonald, n.d.

Stevens, Michael. "Probability and Chance." In *Encyclopedia of Philosophy*. 2nd ed. Edited by Donald M. Borchert. Detroit/New York/San Francisco/San Diego/ . . . : Thomson Gale, 2006. 8:24–40.

Stonehouse, Ned. B., and Paul Woolley, eds. *The Infallible Word: A Symposium by Members of the Faculty of Westminster Theological Seminary*. 3rd rev. printing. Philadelphia: Presbyterian & Reformed, 1967.

Talbott, William. "Bayesian Epistemology." In *The Stanford Encyclopedia of Philosophy (Summer 2011 Edition)*. Edited by Edward N. Zalta. http://plato.stanford.edu/archives/sum2011/entries/epistemology-bayesian/. Accessed May 1, 2012.

Warfield, Benjamin B. *The Inspiration and Authority of the Bible*. Ed. Samuel G. Craig. Philadelphia: Presbyterian & Reformed, 1967.

Weisstein, Eric. "Strong Law of Large Numbers." mathworld.wolfram.com/StrongLawofLargeNumbers.html. Accessed January 19, 2012.

Westminster Confession of Faith. 1646.

GENERAL INDEX

Joash, 36
Job, 41–45, 115
Job, book of, disasters described in,
    41–45, 53
Jonah, 37, 66, 67
Joseph (Old Testament), 35, 51, 52,
    53–54, 54–55, 87
Joshua, 35, 66
Josiah, 37
Judaism, 94n6
Judas Iscariot, 66

knowledge of God, suppression of,
    164–165

language, 88n6, 95, 104, 120, 164, 252;
    language concerning possibility and
    probability, 145, 213, 264
law, of God, 163; power of, 163
law of large numbers, 337; and the
    gambler's fallacy, 338–340; two forms
    of (the weak law and the strong law),
    337–338
limitations, of human thinking concern-
    ing probability, 249; analogy in events,
    251; context of events, 252; form and
    meaning of events, 252; implications
    of limitations, 255; involvement of
    persons in events, 252–254; proposi-
    tions in logic, 249–251; religious
    commitments in relation to events,
    254–255; stability of meaning, 251;
    unity and diversity in events, 251
logic: logical conjunction, 236; logical
    disjunction, 236; propositions in logic,
    249–251
logicism, 302
loop quantum gravity, 214
love, 113n4, 172–173, 217. *See also* God,
    love of
luck, 19, 92, 96, 133, 138, 139–140,
    141–142, 280

magic, 137–138
materialism, 123, 133; philosophical
    materialism, 125, 258
Matthias, 66

Micaiah, 33
micromanagement, 87
Monte Carlo fallacy, 266
moral judgment, 254
Mordecai, 37
Moses, 35
M-theory, 214

natural laws, 117, 129
natural science, 133–134
naturalism, 123; methodological natural-
    ism, 129–131, 130n5. *See also* evolu-
    tionary naturalism
Newton's law of gravitation, 103, 108
Noah, 102, 111

objective propensity, 297–301; challenges
    for propensity interpretation, 298–299;
    and propensity as a synonym for
    property, 300
odds, 152–153
Old Testament, divine authority of, 20

Packer, J. I., 52
Pascal, Blaise, 146
Paul, 37
Peter, 37
Plantinga, Alvin, 130n4
polytheists, 94
Pontius Pilate, 205
postulates. *See* probability, and math-
    ematical postulates
power, and probability, 162–163
prayer, 94n3, 140
preternatural, the, 129, 130
probability, 145–146, 257–258; *a pos-
    teriori* probability, 156, 159, 214; *a
    priori* probability, 156, 159, 207, 214;
    benefits of *a posteriori* probability,
    156–158; calculation of conditional
    probability, 183–187; calculation of
    the probability of a complement,
    328; conditional probability, 181–183,
    198, 199, 290–291; conducting trials
    concerning probability, 148–150; dif-
    ferent concepts of, 169–170, 170n4,
    175–177; difficulties concerning differ-

ent approaches to probability, 171–172; existential perspective concerning, 175; frequency interpretations of, 170; and God's knowledge, 180–181; interaction with secular views of probability, 293–294; logic of, 236; mathematical proofs for, 329–332; multiple perspectives concerning, 235–237; normative perspective concerning, 175; numerical probability, 146–148; objective concept of (objective propensity), 175–176, 297–301; origin of, 177; probability estimates, 148, 170–171; probability law, 232; probability measure, 232; propensity interpretations of, 170; quasilogical concept of, 170, 171, 174–175, 294–295; relationship of probability to broader philosophical issues, 301–302; situational perspective concerning, 175; spatial representation of, 221–227; subjective concept of (including subjective fallacies), 170, 171–172, 295–296; and subjectivity, 179–180; theory of, 146. *See also* limitations, of human thinking concerning probability; probability, and complex influences; probability, and mathematical postulates; probability, theistic foundations for

probability, and complex influences, 189–190; and the benefits of independence, 194–195; and the independence of probabilities, 191–194; simple cases of, 190–191

probability, and mathematical postulates, 229–230; the advantage of utilizing postulates, 230–231; basic constituents of mathematical models, 231–233; basic deductions derived from postulates, 234–235; and the multiple perspectives on probability, 235–237; and the postulate of additivity, 233, 236; and the postulate of nonnegativity, 233; and the postulate of normalization, 233–234; and sample space, 232, 253

probability, theistic foundations for: and the addition of exclusive probabilities,

239–242; immateriality, 162; multiplicative harmony, 242–245; power, 162–163; regularities, 161–162, 162n1, 163–164; symmetries, 239; transcendence and immanence, 163; truth, 162

providence, and science, 27–28

quantum mechanics, 14, 81, 84n5, 209; experiments concerning the predictions of, 83; and practical effects, 84; and quantum effects, 80–81; quantum indeterminacy, 85, 130n4

quiz show puzzle (the "Monty Hall Problem"), 283–286, 296, 297; the quiz show puzzle with alterations, 286–288; and reckoning with partial knowledge, 289–290

Rachel, 34–35, 53, 91–92
Rahab, 35
random events/randomness, 42, 79, 257, 340; example of a classic random event, 65–67; generation of random sequences, 207–209; and the practical importance of God's control over events, 69, 209–210; pseudo-randomness, 207–208; random sequences, 206–207; reliance on randomness, 210–211; suppression of truth concerning chance events, 117–120
rationalism, 125, 302
"reasonable doubt," 145–146
Rebekah, 34, 53, 91
redemption, 258–259
regularities, 161, 202, 216, 257; as personal, 163–164; in time and space, 161–162
rituals, 139–140
Ruth, 35–36, 53

salvation, 20, 45, 52, 55–56, 72, 121, 259
Satan, 42–43, 44, 86
Saul, 66, 181
Schrödinger, Erwin, 84, 84n5
Schrödinger's cat, 84, 84n4
science, 124, 131; and chance, 14–15; implications of evolutionary naturalism

SCRIPTURE INDEX

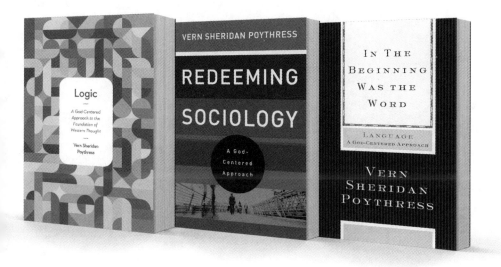

Also Available from
VERN POYTHRESS

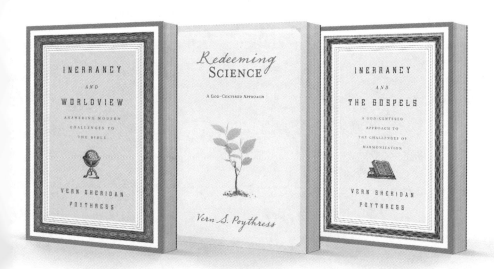